Talking About Therapy

Talking About Therapy

Talking About Therapy

Donna D. Comarow and Martha W. Chescheir

Foreword by Rita J. Simon

BERGIN & GARVEY
Westport, Connecticut • London

Library of Congress Cataloging-in-Publication Data

Comarow, Donna D., 1944–
   Talking about therapy / Donna D. Comarow and Martha W.
Chescheir ; foreword by Rita J. Simon.
     p. cm.
   Includes bibliographical references and index.
   ISBN 0–89789–537–1 (alk. paper)
   1. Psychotherapy patients—Interviews. 2. Psychotherapist and
patient—Miscellanea. 3. Psychotherapy—Anecdotes.
4. Psychotherapy—History—Chronology. I. Chescheir, Martha W.,
1929– .
   II. Title.
   RC464.A1C66   1999
   616.89'14—dc21   98–20127

British Library Cataloguing in Publication Data is available.

Library of Congress Catalog Card Number: 98–20127
ISBN: 0–89789–537–1

First published in 1999

Bergin & Garvey, 88 Post Road West, Westport, CT 06881
An imprint of Greenwood Publishing Group, Inc.

Printed in the United States of America

The paper used in this book complies with the
Permanent Paper Standard issued by the National
Information Standards Organization (Z39.48–1984).

10 9 8 7 6 5 4 3 2 1

This book is dedicated to the people whose stories illuminate its pages.
We thank you for your courage, candor, and desire to help others.

Contents

Foreword

Talking About Therapy provides a wonderful opportunity for individuals who have been in psychotherapy at some period in their lives to describe what it did and did not do for them, and how it helped or failed to help them. It also allows readers who have never undergone therapy as well as those who have been in treatment to experience the process vicariously or to compare their therapy experiences with those described in this book.

All told, the work contains fifty-two narratives covering a range of six decades from the 1940s through the 1990s. At the beginning of each chapter, the authors set the scene by briefly describing the significant social trends and characteristics of the decade. The major forms of therapy and noted theoreticians and practitioners are identified as the work proceeds along with the debates surrounding the efficacy and cost, among other things, of different treatment forms. Thus for each decade, the reader receives an account of the intellectual ferment that prevailed in the mental health world, the leading figures involved, and the often bitter controversies about which approach was best. For example, was it five-days-a-week for five or more years on the couch in the classical Freudian analytical mode, or one-day-a-week for a couple of years sitting up and talking face to face?

As described in the Introduction, the authors culled these fifty-two respondents from more than 300 men and women who were willing to participate, but in no way do they suggest that they have a representative sample of individuals in treatment during each decade. They collected potential respondents by placing ads in *The New York Review of Books,* *Washingtonian,* *The New York Times Book Review,* and local papers. They also placed notices in bookstores and grocery stores. Nevertheless, the broad range of responses is worth noting: geographically from thirty-four states; an age range of fifty-one years—from forty to ninety-one; and an occupational distribution that includes professionals, executives, entrepreneurs, artists, journalists, technicians, and others. The different forms of therapy are well represented as are wide variations in the amounts charged per hour and the length of treatment.

The long expanse of time covered in this volume allows the reader to wonder about the kinds of problems and pain for which respondents sought treatment in different decades, and perhaps even to see some patterns emerge. To what extent did World War II and its aftermath influence the need for therapy? Did the Korean and Vietnam wars play similar roles? Did other major public crises send respondents to therapy? As the traditional Freudian type of analysis came under attack and less intense, less frequent, more interactive forms of talk therapy gained prominence, did different types of respondents seek help? With the "pharmaceutical revolution," which made the patient's ability to artic-ulate problems much less important, did individuals with different types of problems or with different social characteristics enter treatment?

As you become more and more immersed in the respondents' narra-tives you will, I believe, ask yourself: Did it work? Was the treatment successful? Did it really help? Did it change the person's life? Was it worth the time and money? You will ask these questions on a case-by-case basis, but you will also ask them after you have read a number of narratives that describe the same form of therapy. You will find yourself evaluating the effectiveness of different types of therapy and considering the likelihood that different forms of therapy are effective for different kinds of people—men and women, young and old, professionals and academics as compared to executives and entrepreneurs versus artists and technicians, and so forth. These are the patterns that you the reader are likely to draw for yourself. For those who have never been in ther-apy, you are very likely to ask where you would be most likely to fit and what might be, or will be, the best type of treatment for the problems you had or are currently confronting. For those of you who have gone through the experience, there are likely to be lots of, "Oh, yes! That sounds familiar!" or "There but for the grace of . . . go I" or "Why didn't I have that much insight?" or "That person made the same mistakes and got stuck in the same situation I found myself."

More than most, this book is not likely to be read passively; it invites a reader's active participation—and your active involvement will be well rewarded.

Rita J. Simon

Acknowledgments

We would like to thank the following people for their encouragement and support: Megan Schreiber Carter, Margaret Crockett, Frances Eyster, Justin Frank, Christopher L. Hoxie, Joyce S. Lowenstein, Warren Poland, Dorothy A. Starr, and Elizabeth Timberlake. We are grateful to *The New York Times Book Review* wherein the author's query ran in the summer of 1996. The response gave us a book. We thank Lynn Taylor, our editor at Greenwood Publishing Group, for her assistance and advice throughout this venture.

Rita J. Simon, scholar, author, wife, mother, and loyal friend, helped us when we needed it and never mentioned her own commitments. We are honored to dedicate a portion of the proceeds from the sale of this book to her Women's Freedom Network, an organization that rejects both extreme feminism and extreme anti-feminist traditionalism and defines women and men, not by gender, but as individuals.

Most of all, we thank our families and our husbands, Murray Comarow and John Boren.

Introduction

In April 1921, Sigmund Freud accepted Abram Kardiner, a thirty-year-old psychoanalyst from New York, for a personal analysis. Freud's letter was short, only four paragraphs, but he outlined the basics: "Six months are a good term to achieve something both theoretically and personally. ... My fees are $10.00 an hour or about $250 monthly to be paid in effective notes, not in checks which I could only change for crowns."[1]

Dr. Kardiner was elated. "This letter changed my fate and my world."[2] He says that while he might not have revealed his personal biography earlier in life, at eighty-five he felt free to write his own case history to describe Freud's technique: "At the time I was in Vienna, 1921–1922, he had nine patients and, so far as I can tell, he did not treat them all alike. Most of those who were there at the time complained that he never said anything. Some left disappointed and some felt they got nothing from the experience. I got a great deal from it."[3]

What do people get out of psychoanalysis and psychotherapy? Why do they go? How long does it take? How much does it cost? And when all is said and done, how does it affect the rest of their lives? These questions occurred to me when I studied with an interdisciplinary group at the Washington School of Psychiatry. While a case conference reveals a great deal about a patient's life and mental functioning and can stimulate heated debate among the disciplines, accounts of treatment stop where treatment ends. What came afterward? That's what this book is about. It is the other side of the story, a collection of case conferences from the former patient's point of view.

To find out if people would like to talk about therapy, I placed an author's query in publications such as *The New York Review of Books, Washingtonian, The New York Times Book Review*, local papers, and, for good measure, put 3 × 5 cards in grocery stores and bookstores. The query read: "For a book about the impact of analysis and psychotherapy on people's lives, I would like to confidentially interview individuals at least 40 years old who have been, but are not currently, in analysis or psychotherapy."

More than 300 people between forty and ninety-one years old, some of whom began treatment in the 1940s, volunteered to discuss their experiences. They are from thirty-four states: Alabama, California, Colorado, Connecticut, Florida, Georgia, Illinois, Kentucky, Maine, Maryland, Massachusetts, Michigan, Minnesota, Missouri, New Hampshire, New Jersey, New Mexico, New York, North Carolina, Ohio, Oklahoma, Oregon, Pennsylvania, Rhode Island, South Carolina, Tennessee, Texas, Utah, Vermont, Virginia, Washington, West Virginia, Wisconsin, and Wyoming; and the District of Columbia and Puerto Rico. Three people originally from Australia, England, and Singapore, who spend half the year in those countries, also replied.

Interviewees include writers, college professors, advertising executives, an "over-seventy" female marathon runner, nurses, fundraisers, prisoners, small business owners, foreign service officers, musicians, librarians, artists, teachers, politicians, historians, an environmentalist, computer programmers, a court interpreter, a technical illustrator, government executives, poets, journalists, an actress, a stockbroker, a former actor turned Ph.D. psychologist, attorneys, physicians, priests, economists, a self-described former "spook," a former male model, anthropologists, sociologists, a nanny, retired military officers, a female bar owner, a playwright, several business executives, housewives, filmmakers, and a state trooper.

I began interviews in January 1996. This was an informal survey, either in person or by phone, and rather than use a question and answer format, I used a general outline of what I wanted to know, asking participants to describe themselves and their therapy. During the interview, I took notes, and most of my questions were answered. When they were not, I asked. Besides participants' vital statistics, this is what I wanted to know:

- What was your reason for seeking analysis or psychotherapy?
- What type of therapist did you see (psychoanalyst, psychiatrist, psychologist, clinical social worker, psychiatric nurse, or pastoral counselor)?

- What was that person's theory base (Freudian, Kleinian, Cognitive-Behavioral, Object Relations, etc.)?
- How did you choose your therapist?
- What was it about your therapist that allowed you to work with him or her?
- How did you feel about your therapist and how do you think your therapist felt about you?
- How did the work proceed? What did you say to your therapist? What did your therapist say that helped or hurt you?
- Were dreams analyzed? If so, did you find that useful?
- How long were you in treatment?
- Did you tell other people (friends, colleagues, neighbors) that you were in treatment?
- What did your treatment cost, in financial and emotional terms?
- How much did you learn about your therapist?
- Did anything significant happen to you or your therapist during treatment (such as births, deaths, marriages, or divorces)? How did that affect the work?
- How has religion or spirituality influenced your life?
- How did treatment end? Who proposed it? Was the decision unilateral or by mutual agreement?
- What is your post-treatment relationship with your therapist?
- Was psychotherapy worth the time and money you put into it? How did it affect the rest of your life?

After each interview, I transcribed my notes, paraphrasing and condensing as necessary for readability but taking care to retain the respondent's "voice." One of the first people I talked to asked to see his interview. I thought that was an excellent idea, so I began to send everyone a copy of their interview, asking them to correct errors, add anything they'd forgotten, and delete anything they had second thoughts about. If they chose to, they could then sign the release I enclosed permitting me to use their material in the book. Not one person asked me to omit any material and many phoned with additional information or sent copies of dreams from journals they'd kept for years. I was pleased when they said I'd been a pretty good scribe.

Some respondents, wishing to pay tribute to their therapists, asked that their names and their therapists' names be used, but others preferred to maintain confidentiality. A uniform level of confidentiality has been maintained by disguising all names, locations, and other identifying details. Respondents were invited to create their own pseudonyms and clearly enjoyed doing so. Sports heroes were popular among men; four women wanted to be "Lucy." Any resemblance to anyone other than the respondent is entirely coincidental.

As time went by, it became apparent that this study was important not only to me, but to the participants. Many kept in touch, checking progress. They sent relevant articles from newspapers—"just in case you missed this!" One man sent a magazine on alternative therapies. A film-maker wanted to make the book into a documentary. Some sent pictures or T-shirts; many visited when they were in Washington and invited me to visit them. Everyone worked hard to explain their lives and their treatments. Why were they willing to put so much effort into the study? Many said, "If my story can help someone, I want to do it. I want people to see what psychotherapy offers." Or, "Therapy's being trashed all the time now but it helped me. Being in the study is repaying a debt of gratitude." Those who did not have positive experiences were less sanguine: "I offer mine as a cautionary tale so that others won't subject themselves to what I went through."

I wondered how my colleagues would feel about the study. Most said, "What a great idea! Why hasn't someone done this before?" A few wanted to know if any of their former patients had responded. Two practitioners scoffed, saying retrospective studies are anecdotal and invalid because patients tend to say what they think their former therapists want to hear. I make no claim of rigorous methodology in this informal survey. Volunteers are as self-selected as are all who enter analysis and psychotherapy, unless treatment is court ordered. This book tells the stories of their lives in treatment.

After completing several dozen interviews, I went to my respected graduate and post-graduate school professor, Martha W. Chescheir, who agreed to help organize the material, develop the framework, and co-author the book. We decided that 200 people, out of the total of 323, would be a good sample and I thought I could complete the interviews in one year. It took twenty-one months.

We chose the fifty-two stories for this book on the basis of diversity in age, sex, profession, location, reason for seeking psychotherapy, type of treatment, and therapeutic outcome. Each chapter represents a decade between 1940 and 1999, and each person's story is included in its entirety in the decade when treatment began even when treatment spans more than one decade. In choosing the stories, we tried to control for geographic area by screening out fifty replies from California, Florida, and New York—states that were disproportionately represented. We eliminated thirty-two mental health professionals who were practicing therapists at the time they were in treatment because therapists often go into therapy for educational as well as personal reasons, but we included five people who entered the mental health field after completing therapy. Four people withdrew from the survey for personal reasons.

Chapters begin with a snapshot of the decade's vital statistics, A Guide to the United States of the decade. To amplify the sociocultural context, respondents were asked to recall something that made the news while they were in treatment: What was life like in America, their state, their neighborhood? Without exception, 1960s respondents remembered what they were doing when President Kennedy was assassinated. This fits within the Eriksonian framework. Erik Erikson points out that personal development and social history converge. He defined identity as a sense of self developing over the course of people's lives that both connects people to and sets them apart from their social/cultural milieu. "The history of humanity," he wrote, "is a gigantic metabolism of individual life cycles."[4]

As we have looked into the private lives of those who shared their experiences with us, we have paid attention to the historical backdrop as well as the personal narrative each person created. In 1990, psychologist Jerome Bruner, who has played a major role in shaping the development of cognitive psychology for over forty years, observed that "The stories people tell about themselves are shaped by the prevailing culture because social/political ideologies determine one's self definition and the opportunities and direction one's life may take."[5]

We will look at how psychiatric treatment has changed over the past sixty years, noting theoretical developments, and the resulting trends in treatment. We include biographical sketches of seminal theoreticians as varied as Karen Horney, Carl Jung, and John Bowlby, and conclude with the contemporary views of relational theorists such as Jean Baker Miller and Stephen Mitchell. We define technical terms, such as "neo-Freudian," "resistance," and "transference" as we go along. We describe the six disciplines represented: psychoanalysis, psychiatry, psychology, clinical social work, psychiatric nursing, and pastoral counseling. For purposes of clarity, psychoanalysts are referred to as analysts; those in the other disciplines are referred to as therapists or clinicians.

This study is a retrospective look at some of the ways people have created meaning in their lives and shaped their ideas about themselves in a particular sociocultural climate. We are not looking for a predetermined outcome and have tried to set our biases aside, capturing and reporting the essence of what we heard and organizing this rich and fascinating material so that readers may understand a little better why people go into therapy and what they get from it. We hope that our work is a catalyst for further much-needed research into patients' post-treatment evaluations of their therapies.

Donna D. Comarow

1 The 1940s: The Heyday of Classical Freudian Analysis

[I]t is possible to foresee that at some time or other the conscience of society will awake and remind it that the poor man should have just as much right to assistance for his mind as he now has to the life-saving help offered by surgery. . . . We shall then be faced with the task of adapting our technique to the new conditions [and] the large-scale application of our therapy will compel us to alloy the pure gold of analysis freely with the copper of direct suggestion.

Sigmund Freud

A GUIDE TO THE UNITED STATES OF THE 1940s

Population: 132,164,569

Average salary: $1,315 per year

Coal miners: $1,235

Farm laborers: $463

Federal employees (civilian): $1,894

Medical/health services workers: $927

Public school teachers: $1,435

Inflation: 0.4 percent

Unemployment: 14.6 percent

Social welfare: $8.80 billion

Births/1,000: 19.4

Marriages/1,000: 12.1

Divorces/1,000: 2.0

Deaths/1,000: 12.1

Average household size: 3.16

Women in labor force: 25.2 percent

Cost of living: Clothing: Enna Jettick's women's shoes, $6.00; Thom McAn men's shoes, $4.20

Food: bread, 8 cents a loaf; coffee, 21 cents a pound; eggs, 33 cents a dozen; milk, 13 cents a quart; oranges, 21 cents a dozen; round steak, 36 cents a pound

Housing: Eight room townhouse, New York City, $2,600

Transportation: Nash Ambassador, $925

Fun: Nickel jukeboxes, the Lindy Hop, and the first McDonald's restaurant

Pulitzer Prizes: Biography: Ray Stannard Baker, *Woodrow Wilson, Life and Letters*

Drama: William Saroyan, *The Time of Your Life*

History: Carl Sandburg, *Abraham Lincoln, The War Years*

Sources: Robert Famighetti (ed.), *The World Almanac and Book of Facts, 1997* (Mahwah, NJ: World Almanac Books, 1997), pp. 324, 325, 381; Scott Derks (ed.), *The Value of a Dollar, 1860–1989* (Detroit, MI: Gale Research Inc., 1994), pp. 290, 291, 301; Lois Gordon and Alan Gordon, *The Columbia Chronicles of American Life, 1910–1992* (New York: Columbia University Press, 1995), pp. 288, 296; U.S. Bureau of the Census, *Historical Statistics of the United States, Colonial Times to 1970, Bicentennial Edition, Part I* (Washington, D.C., 1975), pp. 40, 41, 49, 59, 64, 132, 135, 213, 340.

As the century's fifth decade opened, the United States was coming out of a bitter depression with unemployment rates that reached 25 percent. We were about half our present population, 132,164,569 Americans overwhelmingly sympathetic to a Europe being ravaged by a cruel German onslaught, but mostly determined to stay out of the war.

By June of 1940, the German army had crushed Poland, rampaged through Belgium and Holland, and goose-stepped through Paris. President Franklin D. Roosevelt urged Congress to repeal the Neutrality Act so that America could furnish arms to the allied nations. On December 7, 1941, Japan bombed Pearl Harbor. The following day, the United States entered the war.

The need for more workers to fill defense orders, coupled with the drafting of 960,000 men a year, virtually eliminated unemployment. "Rosie the Riveter," wearing slacks, took her place alongside men on assembly lines making bombers and ships. By the war's end in 1945, 18 million women had held jobs, and by the end of the decade, one out of four married women worked outside the home.

But it was not all gravy. The poverty rate in 1940 was 33 percent. By

1949, it was 27 percent. Historian Ruth Cowan wrote that in 1940 "one out of three Americans was still carrying water in buckets, and two out of three Americans did not enjoy the comforts of central heating."[1] Only one-third of our farms had electricity.

Recruitment screening for the armed services revealed a previously underestimated condition: over 1,000,000 men were rejected because of psychological or neurological disorders, and 850,000 were hospitalized for mental problems during the war. In 1940, the Army had twenty-five psychiatrists. By the war's end, it had added 2,400 psychiatrists with the unplanned effect that psychiatry was promoted to a medical specialty.[2]

Over 800,000 refugees, mostly Jewish, began to flee Europe when Hitler came to power.[3] Between 1933 and 1943, the United States admitted 190,000 refugees, including scientists Albert Einstein and Enrico Fermi, and prominent European psychoanalysts such as Austrian-born Alfred Adler. Karen Horney had left Berlin for the Chicago Institute in 1932 and later taught at the New York Psychoanalytic Institute. The same year, Erich Fromm came from Germany and began teaching at New York's New School for Social Research. He married Frieda von Reichmann, who emigrated from Germany in 1935 and became renowned for her ability to treat the most disturbed schizophrenic patients.

Erik Erikson, whose ideas about identity, psychosocial theory, and the historic moment provide the primary framework for this study, sought a new life in this country. He started in Boston in 1933, the same year Freud's books were burned in Berlin, and a year after the Boston Psychoanalytic Society was founded. Erikson's connections opened doors for him at the Harvard Medical School and later at the Yale Institute of Human Relations. These were seminal times with much intellectual ferment. Analysts new to this country and notables from other disciplines, including William James, Margaret Mead, and Kurt Lewin, formed interdisciplinary study groups. The time was ripe for the flowering of Freud's exciting and controversial new "science."

We will now hear from seven people who sought the "pure gold" of analysis during this classical period. We begin with a college professor who entered a classical Freudian analysis because of problems with love and work.

In *classical Freudian psychoanalysis*, patients lie on a couch facing away from the analyst. They free associate (say whatever comes to their minds) four to five hours a week for perhaps several years. The analyst interprets the dreams, associations, and other thoughts and feelings patients bring to their sessions, keeping in mind the defenses the patient uses, the conflicts that surface, and the themes that are present. Freud believed that by making the unconscious conscious, people could resolve their neurotic conflicts. This intensive form of treatment depends on analytic interpretation of dreams and analysis of the transference (the patient's feelings, thoughts, and fantasies about the analyst) in an effort to effect a cure.

Matthew Allbright

Matthew Allbright is an eighty-year-old retired management consultant who lives in San Diego. "I worked designing fighter planes from 1943 to 1946. After the war, I didn't want to continue working on weapons of destruction but I couldn't seem to get a business career in motion."

I began a classical Freudian analysis in 1948 when I was twenty-nine. Some personal background is my father died when I was thirteen and I lived with my mother through college, graduate school, and for several years thereafter. In 1947, I met Eleanor and fell head over heels in love. When she went back home to New York, I decided to take my life savings—$500—and follow her. I found a job at a university quickly enough but it was hard to find an apartment I could afford. I ended up in an eight by twelve foot room with a view of a chimney and a shared down-the-hall bath.

Eleanor and some of my new friends talked about being in analysis. I knew nothing of Freud, neuroses, or the unconscious, but I knew I was having trouble with love and work. I decided to interview two psychoanalysts.

Most *psychoanalysts* are medical doctors and must be licensed by the states where they practice. They have additional training in the theory and practice of psychoanalysis, including didactic work—the study of relevant theory and technique—and experiential practice. The latter includes analyzing patients under the supervision of a training analyst. Psychoanalysts must undergo a personal analysis as part of their training.

The first one, I simply could not tolerate. He talked a lot about himself, used the lingo, and seemed to want to impress me with the books he'd written. But the second! Well, Louis Stein looked a little like my hero, Abraham Lincoln. He never talked about himself unless I asked, but then he usually would. He'd been in the German Army during World War I, barely escaped World War II's concentration camps, and arrived in the U.S. when he was in his late forties. He had to take the basic M.D. exam in English to be certified as a psychoanalyst in this country, and he passed the first time he took it—no small feat considering he'd studied medicine in German. Dr. Stein was accepted as an analyst with the New York Psychoanalytic Institute in 1947. I must have been one of his first patients in this country.

During the initial consultation, I told him, "I can't love and I can't work." [Laughs] Freud said those abilities define normality. One problem was that Eleanor, the woman I was chasing, didn't want me as her life's companion. Some of my more sophisticated acquaintances thought my mother must be the problem, but I assured him this was not the case. I remember he smiled a little. The other problem was that I was a college professor who wanted to be a businessman but simply could not get that career in motion. Dr. Stein said he thought analysis was indicated. He charged $15 a session and analysis required five sessions a week. I only earned $100 a week, but I told him that by very careful budgeting I thought I could manage $10 an hour—half my income! Dr. Stein agreed to reduce his fee with the understanding that I would pay more as my earnings rose. We began the analysis two days later and pursued it five days a week, forty-eight weeks a year, for four years and three months. Every month of the year except August.

At the first session, I found myself lying on his couch. He sat out of view behind my head. "We have only two rules," Dr. Stein told me, "Say whatever comes into your mind. No judgment is made here of good or bad, right or wrong."

We began with the problem of love. My relationship with Eleanor was fragile. Even as she would appear ready to commit to me, she'd turn cold, my short-lived happiness would dissolve, and I'd chase after her. It was a cycle we repeated over and over. Dr. Stein likened my submissive part in "the dance" to a dog anxiously trying to please its master. Free associating to my dreams brought back selected memories from childhood and adolescence: wondering at my mother's cleavage when, with my baby foot on her chest, she put on my socks; enemas she gave me in her exaggerated concern for regularity; her vigilance over my whereabouts when I was trysting with the girl across the street; protecting me from fights. "For God's sake, Claire," Dad would thunder, "let him learn to be a man!"

Perhaps a year into analysis, Dr. Stein suggested that if Eleanor finally gave herself to me, I'd probably reject her. I thought that was absurd, but when Eleanor and I began spending nights together, I suddenly decided I could save a lot of money by moving to Brooklyn. Eleanor lived in Manhattan, so that put quite a distance between us. She asked me to stay at her place, but I had an excuse. That apartment was really her mother's and her mother was one forbidding creature.

While I quickly came to an intellectual understanding that I fled intimacy by rejecting my partners, I could not for the life of me grasp the feelings underlying my behavior. Dr. Stein kept saying, "But you are not working! You come here and talk and talk but you just keep repeating the behavior."

"But I am trying," I would answer. "What do you want me to do?"

Usually he would be silent, but once he warned that I might have to leave Eleanor to proceed in analysis. He might as well have told me to jump off the Chrysler Building.

Some time during my dancing toward and away from intimacy, I had a dream. Actually, it was a nightmare. I was sliding and falling down the slope of a snow-covered mountain and I awoke with a pounding heart. When I reported the dream to Dr. Stein, he asked if I had heard of the Jungfrau, a mountain in Germany. I had not. He told me "jung-frau" means "young wife" in German. Suddenly, I grasped the meaning of the dream. The sliding and falling was connected to my fears of being engulfed by Mother. I was by then thirty, and it was the first time I'd lived away from her. She had shared my tiny bungalow while I was in graduate school and when I got my first job and wanted to live down at the beach like the other guys, where parties with girls lasted all week-end, Mother insisted on coming with me. I remember being repulsed when she would press against me in an embrace.

Gradually, I could see what I was doing and where it came from. I could get the feeling, fear of intimacy, tied to the behavior, rejecting my partner, thus making the unconscious conscious. I thus had in hand a solution to the problem. Everything I learned at home—morals, values—everything I learned at school—math, physics—all were tools. What I got from analysis was a tool I could use for the rest of my life.

The central obstacle to progress in my career was my difficulty dealing with male authority figures. In a university job I didn't really want, I was quite at ease with my director but my relationship with Dexter Bar-ton, president of the business where I consulted, was only cordial. When it was time to meet with him to discuss a pay increase, I got to the subway only to find myself becoming anxious, sweaty, and nauseous. I turned around and went home. This happened time and again.

Dr. Stein helped me probe the experience as if it had been a nightmare. To free associate, I put myself mentally and emotionally back on the subway platform. What emerged were memories of my father. I have good memories of him, just as I do of Mother, but the selectivity of the human memory amazes me. Every memory that surfaced carried hurt feelings and resentments. Dad was a businessman who traveled fre-quently. We almost never did anything together and I didn't know him very well. He died young, never having had the time or maturity to include me in his world. As a young man, I longed to break into the world of business, but I feared it was guarded by men who would ignore and reject me. There lay the roots of my anger, but this knowledge came later on. For now, let's go back to the memories.

When I was about eight, my older sister and I shared a room and sometimes we'd whisper to each other at night. One time, Dad called to us to stop talking and go right to sleep. I dutifully fell silent but Sis did not. Dad marched in, threw back my covers, and gave me a spank on the bottom. I deeply resented the injustice but I did not cry out, object, or state my case. I felt, but never expressed, anger and resentment.

Dr. Stein suggested that these two emotions might be operating in the debacle with Mr. Barton, and guided me toward recognizing the feelings that drove my behavior. I learned that I hid my hostility behind exaggerated politeness and my insincerity showed. I felt the hostility in others' responses, feared their anger, and feared being punished for my own. I came to see how my internal furor blinded me to people and situations as they really existed and crippled my effectiveness. At first, I could only be aware that a feeling was involved by recognizing the onset of automatic reactive behavior—the phony politeness. "Will I always have to grapple with this?" I asked Dr. Stein. "Well," he said, "You may always walk with a limp." Over the years, I learned to recognize my feelings and became able to intercept the behavior more quickly. Finally, only echoes of the old reactive behavior remained.

When I saw your author's query, I thought I ought to make an input. So many people have a low opinion of psychoanalysis today and I guess it's too labor intensive to work the way it did in my time, but when it works—well, I had a distinct improvement in my life and wanted to share my experience. I have had my share of friends whose analyses failed—they did not resolve their fundamental problems—and I have a theory as to why. They were very bright people who could not get off the intellectual level and free associate. And if they did, they would not pursue the associations, preferring debates with their analysts to discovering what was happening inside themselves. Intellectual debates kept them from getting to their feelings.

Maybe they should have gone to Dr. Stein. He was classically trained but also an experimentalist, who would use any available avenue to get the work done. I'd entered treatment so stiff that I could not turn my head without also turning my shoulders. It's what my children call "up tight." When a schedule conflict caused me to shift my sessions to evenings for a while, I arrived once having had a couple of drinks. I guess I was more loquacious than usual because Dr. Stein suggested I try that again. Ultimately, it didn't work out so well . . . and we dropped it. Then he sent me to a physical therapist and I began to get a grip on the mind/body connection.

Another example of Dr. Stein's willingness to experiment came when he learned that I liked to draw and paint. He encouraged me to draw pictures of my dreams and paint them like a free association. We made some real hay out of those dreams, and he wrote a paper on the use of analysands' paintings using mine as an example.

Going in, I didn't know anything about analysis and had no way of evaluating the analysts I interviewed. You would think your neuroses would keep you from choosing someone who could help you, but somewhere within me there must have been some part healthy enough to enable me to make the correct choice. I got the right analyst. I respected and admired Dr. Stein and I trusted him. I thought he was a superior human being, quiet spoken, thoughtful, evenhanded, and brave. He was definitely the male authority figure in the analysis, but he was never overbearing. I always thought he had a warm regard for the human being he was dealing with.

Toward the end of analysis, I met Giulia. We wanted to be married and I had lined up a job in business on the west coast, so I talked to Dr. Stein about ending the analysis. He thought I should stay another six months but I thought, "You are finished when you can leave."

Giulia and I were married on a snowy New Year's Eve in the rectory of a Lutheran Church on 54th Street. Upon arriving at the Plaza Hotel that night, we found flowers awaiting us: "With heartfelt wishes for your happiness, Kate and Louis Stein."

I never needed to return to analysis, but when I was in New York, I'd call Dr. Stein and see if I could drop by. The last time I saw him, his beard was completely white. He'd talk about analysis, and when psychotropic drugs first came out he said he thought they'd revolutionize psychiatry.

Dr. Stein died five—or can it be ten—years ago. Time gets away from me now. I felt sad. I cannot say he was a father. He was *stern*—kept my nose to the grindstone! But I am so grateful to Louis Stein.

Bright, articulate, and able to function in the world, Matthew Allbright was a good candidate for analysis because although he experienced considerable psychic conflict, he was not seriously mentally ill. Unlike other forms of therapy, classical psychoanalysis gives primary importance to the unconscious aspects of the mind. Freud developed the original techniques for gaining access to the unconscious: use of the couch, dream interpretation, analysis of transference/resistance, and free association. Analytic patients are encouraged to relax and relate everything they are thinking or feeling without censoring their thoughts. Free association is a difficult task for some. Matthew's friends preferred intellectual debates.

This suggests that transference, the patient's unconscious need to repeat old patterns of relating in current situations, was operating. When transference cannot be analyzed and understood, there can be serious resistance to the work itself. Transference works both ways. The analyst's reaction to the patient's transference is called countertransference. Resistance is the patient's unconscious effort to obstruct the aims and process of treatment. It must be worked through if the patient is to give up his symptoms, relax his defensiveness, and realistically understand how unconscious material affects conscious feelings, thoughts, and actions. Resistance is one reason treatment can be such a prolonged process. In short, it takes time to change.

Matthew was amazed by the selectivity of human memory. In our next case, Neisha Williams works with a lay analyst, trying to understand the connection between her memories and the problems that led her into analysis.

Lay analysts are not medical doctors but have fulfilled the requirements for the practice of psychoanalysis, including didactic training, the analysis of patients under the supervision of a training analyst, and a personal analysis.

Neisha Williams

Neisha Williams, a seventy-seven-year-old retired medical journalist, lives in Chicago. "I remember VE Day [Victory in Europe] and VJ Day [Victory in Japan]. Mother and I went out and sat on the stoop. It was just dawn but everyone was outside. Someone came over with a bottle of champagne. We were toasting each other and crying, 'The war is over! Thank God!'"

I was born in Paris in 1922. We moved to London when I was a year old and to Chicago when I was nineteen. I decided to enter analysis toward the end of the war, but I must give you some information on my early life that is relevant to that decision.

My parents were from the Near East. Father was considerably older than Mother and had been married before. I have several step-siblings as well as six natural brothers and sisters. My maternal grandmother and my mother's sister, Aunt Rose, lived with us. We were a big, loud, close-knit, loving family that clashed, culture-wise, with what was then a quite Victorian England.

Father died when I was three. Around that time, I remember walking back from the park with my sister and Nurse. I looked up to see Mother and Aunt Rose struggling on the balcony. Mother wanted to throw herself off. Soon after that, she went to a sanitarium. It was our first separation.

In 1926, my younger brother, Franc, got meningitis. We didn't have the antibiotics then that we have today, so Mother took him to Paris, where treatment was available. My siblings were away at boarding school and I was left for about a year with creepy Nurse watching my every move.

When I entered the University of Chicago, everyone was talking about psychoanalysis. Groups of students would sit on the grass discussing Freud. Analysis was what you did if you were an intellectual of the day. It was the Zeitgeist.

I married my first husband in 1943. I hardly knew Roger and I certainly didn't love him. When he went off for paratrooper training, one of my old beaus came to visit and we started necking. Since I was a married woman, I couldn't sleep with him but I gave him an orgasm. He tried to give me one but I was frigid with him, just as I had been with Roger. Something was terribly wrong.

I made an appointment with the same analyst two of my brothers were seeing. I told him I needed to get out of my marriage and I wanted to be a writer. He kept my brothers in treatment but referred me to Jack Emerson, a lay analyst becoming well known for his work with creative people. The first session, lying on the couch, I talked the whole hour. At the end, Jack leaned over so I could see him and asked, "By the way, what's your name?" [Neisha laughs.] He was charming!

Jack believed he could cure me by putting me in regression therapy. He told me that required several sessions a week if it was to be effective, so I started at four days a week, $5 an hour. I picked up some freelance work to pay for it, but eventually I dropped out of college, working to support the analysis. Through a friend of a friend, I got a chance to rewrite an analyst's paper that had been rejected by a psychoanalytic journal. After it was accepted, I got a lot more work like that. I learned a lot about analysis and a lot about writing.

Dream interpretation was an important part of the work with Jack. For many years, I'd had repetitive dreams. In one, I was about fifteen months old, happily sucking my bottle in my pram when someone reached in, ripped off my blanket, and began to hit me. Jack thought it was my mother but I never did.

Jack believed my other dream explained my frigidity. It originated in the real event of Aunt Rose's putting me and Franc in the bath together. I was old enough to hold him on my stomach. It was a dream of harmony and sweetness, but Jack believed it was an erotic dream stemming from molestation inflicted upon me by my older half-brother, Alex. I loved and idealized Alex, who was brilliant, insightful, and a major influence in my life. He died in the war. Jack was convinced that we'd had an incestuous relationship. He asked if Alex had ever threatened to kill me if I told. It was totally off the mark, but Jack was insistent. If I objected, I was in denial.

Jack was probably fifteen to twenty years older than I was and had an office in his apartment. There was no Freudian blankness at all. His wife was around sometimes and I met her at a writer's group I joined. Jack was trying to integrate the philosophies of Marx and Freud—that was popular at the time—and there was a bookcase full of Lenin's work in his office. We had some long, rambling discussions quite outside what we should have been working on.

After doing factory work like a good Commie, Jack decided to become an analyst. He took some courses and got to know the top Freudians.

They liked him, promoted his work, and sent him patients like me. Ultimately, he became rather famous, but I got worse in that analysis.

After eighteen years and something on the order of 3,000 hours on the couch, I quit. I'd turned forty and I'm sure that milestone influenced my decision. Also, the fee had gone to $20 an hour and I'd run myself into debt, owing him something like $750 in 1962. And Jack had been away. He'd had surgery—a hernia repair, I think he told me—and I learned that I could get by without him. When he came back, I told him of my decision. He said the work was not complete and connected my wish to leave with his having left me by going and having his operation. I told him how ridiculous that was. Looking back, I can see what a poor analyst he was. He'd had no training, really. But charming! When I left, he kissed me good-bye.

A few years later, Mother died and I inherited some money. I'd divorced Roger by then and married another disaster. I was still frigid and still beset by nightmares. I decided to find another analyst, and this time I wanted a woman.

Dr. Dore had an office at the Institute. She was about ten years younger than I, had just completed rigorous training, and had all the credentials one could wish. Like many bright, young Freudians, she employed techniques from other schools and did not use regression. I did not lie on the couch. I sat up and started to get better. And I went once a week, not day after day. It started off at $20 an hour, and I was paying $75 an hour nine years later when we ended by mutual agreement.

Within the first two months of treatment, I was able to make sense of my dreams. That is why I become so angry when I hear things about False Memory Syndrome. I'd had the dreams before analysis, but I didn't recover the associated memories until I worked with Dr. Dore. I couldn't understand the meaning of the dreams until I unearthed the memories and understood their connection.

We must return to my childhood for a moment. I remember I enjoyed being stimulated by my father when he squeezed me and "made bread" out of me. I don't remember that he fondled my genitals, but when I was seven or eight, I remember that an old woman visiting my mother squeezed my genitals tightly. I've watched my sister playfully tickle her young son's penis while she bathed him. My mother did the same with Franc. Such behavior did not seem aberrant.

These facts connect to the memory I recovered, which explains the pram dream. As a baby, I would put my hand down to play with myself. Nurse would jerk the blanket off and slap my hand. When I would persist, she would beat me. Nurse—not Mother—was a horrid, repressed creature who watched for any sign of life in me and squashed it. The key to the bath dream has to do with guilt. I had not liked being dislodged by Franc. When he got sick and nearly died—well, a child can take something like that and turn it into the belief that she is powerfully poisonous.

I have many thoughts about the analytic failure and why my subsequent therapy was successful. For one thing, Dr. Dore listened well. She was gentle, receptive, and I had a sense that she was in good shape psychologically. I regarded her as a woman of strength. I started my second therapy unable to hold a job and in precarious financial shape. I'd get a good job, run into a problem with a colleague—usually a man—and get myself fired. "We must insist upon your earning a living," Dr. Dore would say, and she began to coach me on how to handle routine disagreements. She worked constantly to strengthen my ego.

While I learned many things about Jack's personal life, I learned almost nothing of Dr. Dore's. I remember saying once that I would love to have a life similar to my sisters' with children and grandchildren. Dr. Dore indicated that she, too, wished for those things she did not have. I knew she could understand me.

In 1974, Dr. Dore and I were in agreement that we had achieved what was needed and I could end treatment. We shook hands good-bye. That's the way it should be done. Two equals. She made it clear that I could return if I needed to—the door was open—but I have not required further treatment.

I feel anguish over the years and the money I wasted in treatment with Jack. He was a charlatan and a mindscraper. So many horrid events in my life would not have happened if he'd known what he was doing. I would encourage others to know more about their analysts' training than I did when I went to him.

I live alone and sometimes I'm lonely, but when I finally got to Dr. Dore my fears vanished as did my nightmares and I achieved understanding. In my maturity, there is regret. I have come to accept it as part of the human condition.

Now I'm working on a mystery novel, using a manual typewriter. I have to buy a computer and learn to use it.

We asked Neisha why she stayed with Jack Emerson for eighteen years. She told us that even though she was not able to function well at work or sexually, she stayed because she felt safe in his presence and he charged a minimum fee she could afford. "He told me an M.D. psychiatrist would never take my measly $5 an hour. I had not yet learned to question authority figures, so I coughed up $20 a week and got nowhere except deeper into illness." Another reason might be that many women played subservient roles in relation to men in the 1940s.

Neisha continues, "I think that the transference, negative as well as positive, had a lot to do with it. He was the punishing, prohibitive nurse as well as the half-brother, Alex, who was brilliant and came across with insights that let you know he understood. Every so often, Jack would feel like my dead brother." But when Jack insisted that his interpretation of the material was the only correct one, even as Neisha strongly disagreed, the negative transference came to the fore and she would experience him as not being her ally, not understanding her, and incapable of appreciating her contributions to the work they were supposedly doing together.

Neisha's analyst committed a number of boundary violations. He allowed his patient to associate with his wife, shared his personal background with her, and kissed her when she ended treatment. While she looks back on Jack as "a charlatan and a mind-scraper," she never lost faith in the healing powers of psychoanalysis. The second time around, she got what she needed in a less-intensive format coupled with work in the here and now.

In the next case, classical Freudian analysis meets narcissism.

Narcissism is the term Freud used to describe excessive admiration of oneself. While some degree of narcissism contributes to an infant's overall level of self-esteem, too much narcissistic investment later in life can be pathological, impeding psychological growth and development, and interfering with the ability to form relationships with others.

Frederick Alexander

Frederick Alexander is a psychotherapist who practices in Greenwich Village. A former movie actor, he is seventy-nine. "I was politically active in the Forties. We young people thought we were the salvation of the world. Katharine Hepburn made a speech in 1948 supporting Henry Wallace for President and Truman almost lost! Complicated, energizing, interesting years. Just before McCarthyism."

In 1946, I was a twenty-three-year-old actor under contract with MGM in Hollywood. Boom time in the film industry. The reasons I went into analysis go back to my childhood. I was the younger, and unfavored, of two sons.

I promised my father I'd go to college, but after two years, Pearl Harbor was bombed and I enlisted. Then, after the war, my movie career took off and I stayed with it. Things slowed down during the war, but the possibilities of the postwar period seemed limitless. I was in several major motion pictures and with the advent of television, I entered every home in America on shows like *Playhouse 90*.

Because I was in the arts and almost everyone I knew was, too, it was not freakish to be in analysis. The rest of the world might have been contemptuous, but here it was de rigueur. I shopped around for an analyst, talked to four or five. One, a Dr. Cantor, had studied with Freud and was famous, even somewhat infamous, for his work with movie stars. I liked him.

"I am successful," I told him, "but I'm not happy and I want to go into treatment." He didn't seem to think I needed analysis. "I understand you would like to be happy," he said. "Wouldn't we all?" But I persisted, so he suggested I have a psychological evaluation and a battery of tests, including the Rorschach. You know, the inkblots. When Dr. Cantor read the results, he agreed to take me on. We began the following Monday.

My analysis lasted six years. It was classical Freudian, on the couch five days a week until the last two years when the frequency tapered off.[4] Dr. Cantor charged the going rate in 1946, about $20 an hour. He raised it to $25 later on. I've never added up the total, but it must have been $25,000. That was a lot of money in the Forties. It was worth every cent.

One of my problems was not well understood at the time. Many actors have trouble with narcissism, which was then considered untreatable. This was before Kohut and the self-psychologists. For me, narcissism is an unhappy little boy with a Superman cape. The little boy knows he is not so powerful as his father. He feels unimportant and unloved, but he can put on his Superman cape and fly! Great training for an actor! He can puff himself up and feel good. But it's artificial. Somewhere inside, he knows he's just a little boy with a rayon cape from the five-and-dime. His worth as a human being is not acknowledged and he's angry. He withdraws behind a facade as perfect, beautiful, and thick as he can make it.

When I began analysis, I had no sense of humor, especially about myself. Fortunately, Dr. Cantor had a great sense of humor. I remember once going on and on about some trivial event, like the wardrobe mistress bringing me a green tie with a blue suit. I raised Cain! Dr. Cantor said, "You sound like an outraged prince." Ka-pow! And he was right! [Frederick laughs.] But in real life, outraged princes drive others away and they are lonely. Hard work for an analyst. How do you work with someone who is pained when you breach the facade?

You do it by establishing trust. That's the basic thing that made treatment work. I knew Dr. Cantor took me seriously and cared about my well-being. That allowed me to trust and because of that, we developed a curative relationship. I can't stress enough that it is the relationship that cures.

After about a year of treatment, I told Dr. Cantor something I'd done the day before that I thought was not self-serving. I denied doing it to obtain virtuous, God-like, self-righteous feelings. On and on I went. Isn't there such a thing as disinterested altruism? "I doubt that," Dr. Cantor said. Because of our relationship and the trust I had in him, I could hear and reflect on his words. I didn't think he was trying to shoot me down.

Psychoanalysis fundamentally and permanently altered my life on a number of levels. I got a sense of my own worth and a sense of humor about myself. I took myself too seriously as a young man. In analysis, I came to see how ridiculous that was and the ridiculousness of the whole world, along with the tragedy. I did not become much of an existentialist, but absurdity is an ongoing important and liberating idea for me. I learned to think of myself without so much shame and, I hope, with some courage.

Dr. Cantor's approach to ending treatment was simple: "When the time and the money ain't worth the time and the money, it's time to level off and stop." And that's what we did. I never needed to re-enter analysis, but I did go back to see Dr. Cantor every year or so—sort of a 50,000 mile check-up. Or if there was a crisis in my life.

Psychoanalysis has acquired a bad reputation. People talk about the excessive cost, hours and hours on the couch, charlatans in the field, and other therapies that are just as good, take less time, and cost half as much. While I do not believe my own analysis could have been improved upon, I don't feel analysis is the only way to go.

Several years after my analysis, Dr. Cantor died while giving a lecture in Germany. He was an elegant and funny Viennese Jew. I'm not sure I ever told him what he meant to me, but I've never been secretive with my emotions. I am convinced that he knew.

When I decided to change careers, having finally awakened to my dislike of show biz, I didn't know what my options were. I decided to go into group therapy. This was in the early 1970s.

Group psychotherapy was used as early as 1905 by an internist named Joseph Pratt who began a group for his tubercular patients. He provided support and encouragement as well as educational lectures about the illness, and patients who had benefited from treatment shared their stories with the group. In 1925, Trigant Burrow, a psychiatrist and a founder of the American Psychoanalytic Association, developed the term *group psychoanalysis*. He believed there should be no stigma attached to emotional illness and that patients could benefit from observing and being observed by others. The practice of group psychotherapy grew after World War II because so many soldiers developed psychological problems (then called "war neuroses"). Because initially there were only twenty-five psychiatrists in the Army, necessity dictated that these soldiers be treated in groups.[5]

I still hadn't finished college and I didn't think of myself as bright. My middle-class Presbyterian upbringing did not permit feelings of specialness. Interestingly enough, I joined Mensa while I was in group. Group helps because you can get a very jaundiced, or at least limited, view of yourself in one-on-one treatment. I want to stress, though, that had I not been analyzed first, I could not have benefited from group. Group gives you an idea of your effect on others—how you function socially. That can give you a jolt. The group finally told me that they were tired of my complaining about show business. "Change things or don't," was the message, "but enough, already!"

After that, I returned to college and completed my doctorate in psychology. I thank my wife for supporting us both for the six years that required. In my own practice over the last twenty years, I've moved from ego psychology to Kohut's self-psychology and on into object relations. I am convinced that a lot of the things Freud said were wrong. Later theorists have added a great deal to his original ideas, but none of that matters as far as I'm concerned. Transference and countertransference don't exactly cover it, either. It's the *relationship* that cures.

In the next case, a young feminist develops relationships with three analysts, all followers of Karen Horney. American girls today find it difficult to believe that women were not guaranteed the right to vote in this country until 1920.

Karen Horney (1885–1952) was a medical doctor who took her training in Berlin with Freud's close associate, Karl Abraham. Horney agreed with Freud that neurotic conflicts began in early childhood, but did not agree that conflicts were solely rooted in sexual or aggressive drives. She argued that an infant's sense of helplessness and isolation were their primary causes.

A prominent neo-Freudian, Horney theorized that behavior patterns are established by the ways in which a child learns to cope with anxiety. Unlike Freudians, Horney took into account a patient's current fears and impulses in his or her social and environmental context.

Horney criticized Freud's view of female psychology, especially his penis envy theory, as an offshoot of male psychology. She asserted that people were able to grow and change at any age. A prolific writer, Horney's work won broad popular acceptance, especially with feminists and analysts interested in issues of self-esteem.[6]

Rachel Perlman

Rachel Perlman, one of the founders of a national women's political organization, is a seventy-one-year-old retired business executive who lives in Boston. "At our college graduation, those of us who were engaged [to be married] received a corsage. Those who were not received a lemon."

It was 1948, after the war, the beginning of the feminine mystique era. I had just finished college and I decided to go into analysis. I was twenty.

As a child, I was a quiet bookworm without many friends. When my mother and I fought, I thought it was all my fault. At the age of ten, I decided not to be obnoxious anymore. It became my self-imposed responsibility to get along with my mother, whatever, and keep things on an even keel at home. I became the quintessential parentified child.

This eagerness to please carried over into my social life where I'd never been confident. Naturally, I made a lot more friends, but something in me changed. I became what Horney calls "the compliant personality." Horney writes of three types: aggressive, compliant, and detached. Now I see that along with most other members of the human race, I have all three of these personality aspects in varying proportions.

The need that drove me into analysis was the people-pleasing. I did not go to "get a grip." I had that. A firm grip. I knew I had brains and ability. I'd been a newspaper reporter at age seventeen, and I graduated from college summa cum laude. There were very few women in my field when I started out, and at one of the companies where I interviewed in 1950, I was told, "Sorry, we don't take women writers." Ultimately, I became executive vice president of that company and was named Woman of the Year by a national magazine. I can see now it was a good thing my analysts were all from the Horney school. I would never have lasted in a Freudian analysis. Karen Horney was the first person to challenge Freud on his sexism.

When I entered analysis, I would not allow myself to make any mistakes. What I needed was to be less controlled and less poised. To allow some self-indulgence and be kinder to myself. I had to learn to love the hostile little girl I'd been and understand that she had been neglected. I needed to accept the part of me that is an aggressive woman and come to terms with the detached part of myself, the part that moves away from others.

I went to a lecture given by a Horneyite, a Dr. Morse, and made an appointment to see him. After two visits, he told me he was referring me to another Horneyite, Dr. Belcher. I asked why, and he said something to the effect that he found me too attractive. [Laughs.] So I read a few of Karen Horney's books and went to Dr. Belcher for about a year. Then he moved and referred me to Dr. Jacobs, also a Horneyite.

Dr. Jacobs was different from the other two analysts I'd seen, and even from other Horneyites if you expect all Horneyites to conform to textbook definition. He was not brilliant, whereas Dr. Morse probably was. But Dr. Jacobs was the right analyst for me in many ways.

He must have been in his early forties when I saw him, but I never regarded him as a father figure. I thought of him as a caring friend. I can see how his parenting his own child affected me. He would talk about bringing up his little boy in an atmosphere that was not tense with stress and worry. He sounded indulgent. That made me feel, "That's how you should be to yourself, Rachel."

Dr. Jacobs was very genuine and well-adjusted about himself. He'd talk about mistakes he made—without shame! [Laughs.] That made me see it's not so terrible! I was with him three days a week for seven years and sessions were $40 each. In the late 1940s and early 1950s, $120 a week was a lot of money, but I don't remember that it was a strain. I did well and was promoted right away. Dr. Jacobs raised the fee to $50 later—he might have been trying to get me to react. I was not a person who cried or emoted a lot. I think he felt I was too calm and unemotional about the analysis.

My friends and I knew about each other's being in analysis, but I kept it quiet at the office. My sessions were in the Village before work, and when I ran into a colleague one morning—he knew I didn't live in the Village—I indicated I'd stayed with friends overnight.

At the end of analysis, I got married and was very happy. I was becoming bored with the analysis and Dr. Jacobs and I decided to end with the understanding that I could always return, but I never needed to. My life was changed by analysis in ways both large and small. The small ways might not be important to everyone, but they are to me. Primarily, I learned to indulge myself. To enjoy good food. Good clothing. Life. But the major reason I think my analysis was successful is that I married the right person and we have been sublimely happy. Had I married another of the men I was dating, I could have become quite a shrew. I want to emphasize that my husband and I owe our happy marriage to psychoanalysis. Robert and I don't always agree, but we never fight.

Robert had two classical Freudian analyses before we met. Before analysis, he and I suffered from interpersonal relationship problems, hypersensitivity, and feelings of vulnerability. Problems like these might have destroyed our growing closeness during the courtship period. Analysis helped us see that we were strong enough to overcome disagreements and setbacks in life; that these were not the end of the world.

I recommend analysis highly. That's one reason I'm participating in the study. I want others to see the benefits.

Robert, Rachel's husband, responds: I am a retired physician over eighty years young. In 1942, I was twenty-nine years old and consulted a rather well-known psychoanalyst. Classical Freudian. After about a year and a half, he indicated that we weren't getting anywhere, which I knew, and he referred me to another analyst whom I saw for five years, four to five days a week on the couch. I paid $25,000 for my analyses at a 25 percent professional discount—I gave my physician patients the same reduction.

The reason I'd gone into analysis in the first place is that I was unhappy in my marriage. When my first wife and I parted company, my problems suddenly cleared up. The very next day a woman I knew invited me to a party. That's where I met Rachel.

Analysis benefited me in two particularly important respects: I learned more about the mind/body connection and could understand my patients' problems better because I could see how depression, for example, exacerbates a physical illness. More importantly, I learned to deal with my problems with intimacy. I doubt our marriage would be as happy as it has been if we had not been analyzed. Rachel and I don't always agree, but we never fight. We have children and grandchildren, we travel extensively, and we love good food, but we're not fat. Well, maybe a little.

Rachel Perlman is correct that Karen Horney was the first analyst to openly challenge Freud's attitude toward women. Horney pointed out that women are not inferior beings, that not all women suffer "penis envy," and, in a famous phrase, "Anatomy is not destiny." Horney's theory centered on the study of anxiety and self-hatred, which she attributed to social conditions and interpersonal relationships as well as unconscious processes.

Horney agreed with Freud on the importance of the unconscious and admired Freud's powers of observation and his pioneering work exploring the uncharted territories of the mind, but she felt that Freud did not pay sufficient attention to the power of the cultural conditions that mold human character. Nevertheless, Freudian analysts and analysts of the Horney tradition use similar therapeutic methods, such as the couch and frequency of sessions.

Rachel and Robert Perlman attribute their happy marriage to psychoanalysis. Our next interviewee went into analysis because she needed a divorce.

Brenda Shelton

Brenda Shelton is a practicing psychotherapist from New Canaan, Connecticut. She is seventy-three. "Terrific political battles raged in the United States when I was in my teens. Young and idealistic, I was attracted to the Communist Party. As an adult, I remained a leftist and wanted an analyst who could understand my political viewpoint."

I went into analysis in 1947 when I was twenty-one. There were two reasons. I'd dropped out of college and I wanted to finish my education, and secondly, I knew my marriage wasn't going to last. Bill fell asleep all the time. While he was eating. While we were making love. He probably had narcolepsy, but we didn't know anything about that in the Forties.

At the time, it was thought that analysis could cure anything, so Bill went to an analyst and I decided I would, too. I asked around and decided to interview a friend's analyst. Dr. Frank was an analytically trained psychologist.

Clinical psychologists are licensed or certified by the states where they practice and have a doctoral degree in psychology or an allied degree (such as a Ph.D. in education). Psychologists study mental and emotional processes and human behavior and may work with individuals and groups in the private practice of psychotherapy. They may specialize in learning theory, conduct psychological testing, and research mental health problems and the effectiveness of treatment. By "analytically trained," Brenda means her analyst had additional training in psychoanalytic theory and technique.

I didn't want to see a Freudian. You know, go a hundred years and the analyst says, "Uh-huh, uh-huh." No feedback. But probably the most important criterion was that Dr. Frank was also a Marxist.

I went three days a week and he charged $7.50 a session. My parents helped me pay for it. I was on the couch but Dr. Frank talked. He was supportive, solid, and real, and he understood that I needed to learn who I was. The way he validated me helped me gain a firmer sense of myself, but we were just getting started when he suddenly died. He was young—only about fifty—and I grieved that loss.

Within a couple of years, I returned to analysis and saw the psychologist who took Dr. Frank's practice. His name was David Larkin, he was about my age, and—just like Dr. Frank—he was supportive, solid, and real. I went twice a week, did not use the couch, and it cost a little more this time. In the early 1950s I think it was $12 a session, not the most expensive therapy around, but a lot of money for me. It was worth every cent.

I developed a firm connection to all my analysts, but especially David. He stressed that I was intelligent and pushed me to complete my education. I finished my undergraduate degree while I was with him. Then he developed cancer. He told me the truth and allowed me to come and visit him while he was dying. He was a brave man. A dear, dear friend and I loved him. When he died, I mourned for him.

By the 1960s, I'd divorced, completed my doctorate, and was in private practice. Work was good, but I was a single mother and I needed help with that as well as the unfinished work with David. I went to a friend of his, Dr. Wittenberg, another analytically trained psychologist, but more Sullivanian.

A Sullivanian is a follower of *Harry Stack Sullivan* (1892–1949), an American psychiatrist. A neo-Freudian, he believed that human nature

is modifiable, even in cases of severe mental illness, that social and
cultural forces are notable causes of psychopathology, and that people
need to be considered in an interpersonal context. The truism "We are
all more human than otherwise" is attributed to him. Sullivan helped
found the William Alanson White Psychiatric Foundation (1933) and
The Washington School of Psychiatry (1936), and directed both institutions until the mid-1940s.[7]

Dr. Wittenberg was just as real and down to earth as my first two
therapists. I went to him once a week, sat up, and it was $40 an hour. I
didn't have insurance then. I don't think many people did—for psychotherapy.

All my therapists were good for me because they gave direct guidance
and shared their opinions. When they talked to me, it sounded real—
not like something you'd read in a textbook. I felt a firm sense of connection to each one. I remember talking about how hard it was to lay
down rules with my rambunctious sons after the divorce. Dr. Wittenberg
said, "Kids that age can be such a pain in the ass!" Right on! That let
me know he really understood.

Beyond practical problems, I wrestled with philosophical issues. I had
always been disturbed by inequality. My mother always said, "Whoever
comes in need, you must help." While that was my philosophy, I never
thought of myself as a religious person. Dr. Wittenberg told me I was
deeply religious.

My analysts helped me the way I try to help my patients. Psychotherapy is an educational process. I ask questions. I encourage people to
explore and explain; examine their motivations, consider their options.
A good therapist should be able to help people stop tripping over their
own feet. A good therapist does not lay judgments. Above all, a therapist
is a guide and as such has to be real—not a blank slate. Blankness is
confusing to a patient. Hiding behind blankness can be harmful.

My own study began with Freud. I went on into ego psychology, self-
psychology, and object relations. While I draw on this background in
my work, I now include spiritual issues. People need to see that they
have a purpose in this world and know what it is. We are all connected
as a body of humanity. We need to raise individual consciousness and
live the best way we can within ourselves and in the world. I want to
share my life experience with others to help people know what therapy
is about and how growth and change occur.

Brenda Shelton is the only respondent in this chapter who was treated
by psychologists. Even though her first two therapists died while she
was in treatment, she was able to hold onto the goodness of the experiences rather than view the losses as insurmountable tragedies. People

vary in their ability to hold onto goodness. That ability—in therapist as well as patient—can make the difference between therapeutic success and catastrophe.

Our final case is that of a young mother whose husband chose her analyst.

Ann Blake

Ann Blake is a retired obstetrician who lives in Palm Beach. She is seventy-nine. "I entered analysis in 1949. Ben and I worked hard and things were good. We had a house. A car. A television. [Laughs.] The American Dream!"

My parents were divorced when I was a child and I had loyalty conflicts being caught between them. Ben, my husband, thought I could benefit from analysis—Ben was an analyst—and he selected one for me. She was Freudian, a medical doctor. I think all analysts were doctors then. After our third child was born—that was the winter of 1948—I began analysis with Dr. Young. I'd never met her, but she agreed to take me on. I was twenty-nine.

I realize now it would have been better if Ben had given me several names so I could have chosen the best analyst for me, but he was a traditional husband of the day. [Chuckles.] He chose my doctor and he paid for my analysis. I have no idea what it cost.

It was a classical Freudian analysis, on the couch, and it lasted from 1949 to 1951. The schedule was planned in advance without any input from me. The first year was three days a week; the second, two; and the third was once a week. Then termination.

I always had reservations about Dr. Young. She was about fifty, and because she'd never married I felt I knew more about having a husband and raising children than she did. I was never curious about her and I didn't develop much of a transference, but there were things about her I didn't like. When I couldn't get a sitter, I'd have to bring my youngest along and when she got bored, she'd lie on the floor in the room right over the treatment room and drum her heels on the floor. [Laughs.] Dr. Young didn't like that. And she thought the head of the psychiatry department at the hospital was God. I knew better.

I must have gotten something out of treatment, though. The year after it ended, I went to medical school. There were only two other women in my class. I felt more pressure in medical school than I had in college, probably because of having children. I was very involved in being a mother. I wasn't religious myself, having had a socialist father who was an athiest and would not permit any form of religious training—and my mother did nothing about it, either. But I thought our children should have religious instruction, so I took them back and forth from religious school and did all the marketing and cooking, too. Ben never had a problem with my working as long as I did everything else, too.

Around the time I took the state boards, I was feeling anxious so I went to another analyst. This time I chose my own. I suppose I should have gone to a man, but I chose another woman, Dr. Goldberg. She had never married, but I found her warm and it was easy to talk to her. I told her what was going on in my life and how I felt. This time I went once a week for about a year and I think it was $35 a session. I sat up in a chair—which I liked better—and I decided when it was time to end. I can't say I ever missed my analysts and I didn't keep in touch with them. I had a feeling I was using them for my own benefit, but that's what you're supposed to do in analysis.

The mental health field has changed. Back then there were very few analysts and they were a homogeneous, noncompetitive group. Ben would study and review cases with his colleagues. It was a much simpler and less stressful world. [Chuckles.] I guess we all look back with nostalgia. The internet and television have made the world Hillary Clinton's global village. It makes people nutsy! [Laughs.]

What did I get out of analysis? I've given that a lot of thought. Analysis helped me make peace with my mother, who, I thought, broke up the family and deprived me of a father when I needed one. I never saw much of him after the divorce, but he remarried after my analysis and I attended his wedding. And I went to his funeral. My two siblings, who were not analyzed, did not. I don't know if analysis would have changed them but it changed me. I learned to forgive others. And myself.

Of the 200 people interviewed for this book, eight men and twelve women were between twenty and twenty-nine years old when they entered therapy during the 1940s. This chapter includes seven of their stories. Except for children seen at child guidance clinics, psychoanalysis was the dominant treatment form, but even in this early period there were variations. Most of the practitioners were men. None were blank slates, but some disclosed more about themselves than others. Brenda Shelton, who could not tolerate Freudian blankness, found analytically trained psychologists who would talk to her. She and Rachel Perlman, a feminist who rebelled against sexism, were seen by neo-Freudians.

Neo-Freudians, American psychoanalysts, replaced Freud's biological emphasis with a concern for interpersonal relationships, ego functions, and the individual's social and cultural environment. Sometimes called the "Interpersonal School of Psychoanalysis," this group included Harry Stack Sullivan, Karen Horney, and Erich Fromm, who did not subscribe to what they saw as Freud's deterministic conclusions (the biological approach) and believed that human nature is modifiable throughout a person's life. Among other important influences, this group was inspired by Adler's concept of social interest and the pioneering work of anthropologists Margaret Mead and Ruth Benedict, who studied the widely different social patterns prevailing in other cultures.[8]

People speak of the sacrifices they made to be in analysis. While Blue Cross/Blue Shield began to offer insurance for hospital care during the Depression and was joined by other commercial insurance companies after the war, "the talking cure" was not a covered expense. People paid out of pocket for a treatment that could last for years.

No one reports a sense of feeling stigmatized by needing analysis. Two adults (Frederick Alexander and Brenda Shelton) became psychotherapists after treatment, and two respondents who were in treatment as children entered the mental health field later in life.

Several themes run through this first group. When asked what is the most important ingredient for a successful analysis, these respondents place primary importance on selecting analysts who are reliable and trustworthy, pay close attention, and are not inclined to show off their own knowledge or sit in judgment of what a patient is struggling to say. Most mention they rapidly developed a sense of connection to their analysts. Some seemed to enjoy "letting go" and free associating from the couch position; others did not. Most tolerated the usual frequency of sessions, four or five a week, but toward the end of the decade, we heard from some who preferred to come in once or twice a week and sit up to discuss themselves and their situations rather than free associate.

By 1947, World War II, which pulled us out of the Depression—Keynesian claims notwithstanding—was over and the Cold War began. Franklin Delano Roosevelt was dead and a former haberdasher from Missouri, Harry S Truman, was our president. The GI bill offered returning soldiers financial assistance for college educations and downpayments on houses, but there were unprecedented levels of labor unrest with long strikes in key industries such as steel and coal. As we enter the 1950s, the Soviet Union was testing atomic bombs and the United States was close to mastering the technology necessary for creation of the hydrogen bomb.

2   The 1950s: Variations on the Analytic Theme

Enthusiasm with the Freudian psychoanalytic method has resulted in the wholesale application of the technique to conditions for which it never was intended. The inevitable failures have caused many analysts to introduce modifications in the orthodox technique in the forms of greater activity and directiveness.

Lewis Wolberg

A GUIDE TO THE UNITED STATES OF THE 1950s

Population: 151,325,798

Average salary: $3,180 per year

            Coal miners: $3,245

            Farm laborers: $1,454

            Federal employees (civilian): $3,632

            Medical/health services workers: $2,067

            Public school teachers: $2,794

Inflation: 5.7 percent

Unemployment: 5.3 percent

Social welfare: $23.5 billion

Births/1,000: 24.1

Marriages/1,000: 11.1

Divorces/1,000: 2.6

Deaths/1,000: 9.6

Average household size: 3.37

Women in labor force: 28.8 percent

Cost of living: Clothing: Red Cross women's calfskin pumps, $12.95; Sears men's oxfords, shockless cushion insole, $8.98

Food: bread, 14 cents a loaf; coffee, 55 cents a pound; eggs, 72 cents a dozen; milk, 21 cents a quart; oranges, 52 cents a dozen; round steak, 94 cents a pound

Housing: Two-bedroom brick ranch house, Bayside Hills, N.Y., $12,900

Transportation: Ford Custom Victoria, $1,925

Fun: Square dancing, toy guns and Hopalong Cassidy clothes for children; 5,000,000 homes have television, 45,000,000 have radio

Pulitzer Prizes: Biography: Samuel Flag Bemis, *John Quincy Adams and the Foundations of American Foreign Policy*

Drama: Richard Rodgers, Oscar Hammerstein II, and Joshua Logan, *South Pacific*

History: O. W. Larkin, *Art and Life in America*

Sources: Robert Famighetti (ed.), *The World Almanac and Book of Facts, 1997* (Mahwah, NJ: World Almanac Books, 1997), pp. 324, 325, 381; Scott Derks (ed.), *The Value of a Dollar, 1860–1989* (Detroit, MI: Gale Research Inc., 1994), pp. 352, 360, 368; Lois Gordon and Alan Gordon, *The Columbia Chronicles of American Life, 1910–1992* (New York: Columbia University Press, 1995), pp. 382, 390; U.S. Bureau of the Census, *Historical Statistics of the United States, Colonial Times to 1970, Bicentennial Edition, Part I* (Washington, D.C., 1975), pp. 41, 49, 59, 64, 132, 135, 213, 340; Advertisement in *The New York Times*, January 2, 1955, p. A44.

The nuclear arms race continued. The United States tested the hydrogen bomb in November 1952, and the Soviets did the same nine months later. In June 1950, the North Korean army attacked South Korea, overrunning the corrupt and badly led South Korean forces. The United States, with modest help from a few other nations, counterattacked. This United Nations "police action"—Korea was never officially a war—resulted in the death of 33,629 American soldiers; 103,284 were wounded.[1]

The Red Scare escalated in intensity and would dominate domestic politics for the first half of the decade. March 1951 saw Julius and Ethel Rosenberg on trial as spies for the Soviet Union. Fear of being seen as "soft on Communism" was such that *The New York Post* and *The New Republic* refused to accept ads for the transcript of the trial.[2] The Rosenbergs were executed in 1953, the same year Stalin died and Charlie Chaplin was denied re-entry into the United States as a dangerous and unwholesome character.

The McCarthy phenomenon marred much of the early 1950s. In February 1950, Joseph McCarthy, seen by many as the worst Senator in Washington, announced to a women's club in Wheeling, West Virginia, that he possessed a list of 205 Communist spies working for the Department of State. Encouraged by the ensuing sensation, McCarthy enlarged upon his claims, citing different numbers at different times, and charged that Roosevelt and Truman Democrats had conspired to deliver America to the Reds. According to historian Samuel Eliot Morison, "not one of the hundreds of 'subversives' named by McCarthy in the State Department was found guilty after full investigation or trial,"[3] but hundreds of careers and reputations were ruined.

In 1955, there were only 4,700 fully certified psychiatrists in the United States, and only 500 new psychiatrists were being trained each year. The American Psychoanalytic Association had only 600 members in 1956. "In a decade of enthusiastic spending for medical research, mental health was shorted. . . . As a result, many mental institutions became little more than overcrowded warehouses where tormented people waited to die."[4] Perhaps 2 percent of patients were treated in small private hospitals, a few of which, such as Maryland's Chestnut Lodge, became renowned for the quality of care they offered, but it was expensive. Some private hospitals charged as much as $1,000 a month and treatment could last for years.

During the McCarthy years, anyone who decided to enter analysis or psychotherapy might well have kept it quiet. Potential analysands who had joined the Communist Party as teenagers or leaned toward the left as adults were faced with a special problem: Analysis requires honesty and trust. How do you find an analyst who won't turn you in? A word-of-mouth network arose through which one could find a Marxist analyst.

Ed Nathan

Ed Nathan is a seventy-one-year-old historian, author, and college professor who lives in Durham, North Carolina. "I went into treatment in 1953, but I'd never have done it without the recommendation of a woman who was my political comrade. Let me clarify that I was a Marxist and still am, but I was never a member of the Communist Party."

My presenting problem, if you want to call it that, was that my marriage was breaking up and I was losing my wife and children. I felt desperate. How would I survive? Emotionally, I mean. We'd married when we were nineteen.

I'd read psychology but owing to my political views, I was suspicious—especially of Freudians. I was wary that psychology would work at cross-purposes with my fundamental political beliefs; that it would make me less politically active and less comfortable with the commitment I had made to Marxism. I thought of myself at twenty-five as a fighter for peace against imperialism in a world characterized by struggle, conflict, and oppression.

I got a referral from someone I trusted politically. Having been in treatment with him herself, she recommended Dr. Arnold Siegel. I checked up on Arnold. He was a Columbia-trained psychiatrist who had also trained at New York's Postgrad.[5]

The reason I could work with Arnold has to do with the way he practiced his craft. At the time, I was subject to a lot of taboos. It was hard for me to recognize or talk about my feelings, but in the first couple of weeks, there were defining moments he set up—moments when I could say anything.

One such moment helped convince me that he could understand me as a person. He took a phone call while I was there and I overheard his part of the conversation. It was clear that he was handling the arrangements for his second marriage. I thought, "Here is a man who has been divorced." I asked him if that was the case and he said yes.

Eventually, I got around to talking about my parents' relationship. My father was a successful pharmacist but also a philanderer and my mother must have known. He brought his "proteges" to the house! There was an aura of sadness about my mother, which I recognized as early as age nine or ten. She represented to me all the oppressed and sinned against people in the world, and I developed an image of myself as a protector of women, especially the aggrieved, exploited, and downtrodden. Hence, I became a protector of all such people and I leaned to the side of the left. I did not want this self-philosophy cheapened or weakened in treatment, and I didn't want to be reduced to a textbook generalization: "He is a leftist because his mother was unhappy."

Arnold helped me see that understanding the genesis of my beliefs need not undermine them; that there was nothing wrong with leaning leftward with sympathy for my mother because of the way my father treated her. That was Arnold's greatest gift to me. It gave me a new lease on life and made me more politically effective.

I didn't always make it easy for Arnold to treat me. Early on, I would play intellectual games, provoking discussions of Freudianism and its validity. At first, he let me do this. Later, he would ask if it was useful to have philosophical dialogues or was I trying to avoid grappling with the problems I had come to get help with? He seemed to understand my fears of where self-knowledge might lead.

I remember Arnold as objective, but one time his mask fell off. I was very involved with my first wife and children even after our divorce. We managed to improvise a joint custody arrangement—before there was such a thing as joint custody—and we remained on fairly good terms. She would call me to do things for her, perhaps a carpentry project. Once when I was over there, we had sex. I went in and told Arnold,

"Serena and I slept together last night." He said, "You *what*?" It was such a dramatic reaction from him. He was not neutral about what he clearly considered my self-damaging behavior.

Another impact on Arnold's and my relationship came from the fact that I'm a very competitive person and would take any opportunity to outdo him physically. When he remarried, he moved to the West Side and his office was on the East Side. I would make a point of telling him how I, the macho athlete, biked or ran across town while he took a bus, or worse still, from my suspicious Marxist point of view, a taxi. That's the sort of stuff I would pull, and he would refer back to it: "Remember when you tweaked me for going across Central Park in a taxi? What were you really saying?" You could call that a confrontation, but it was always very gentle. Arnold was a gentle man. Sweet.

I got what I needed in that first round of treatment. It settled the question of politics and I got over the breakup of my marriage. I met another woman and married again, maybe following Arnold's example. After about three years of going three days a week—not on the couch—I was done. It cost about $40 an hour and insurance didn't cover it, but I could afford it. One of my books was a best seller.

A few years later, I had an argument with my second wife on the Boulevard St. Germain in Paris. It was the same street corner where I'd had an argument seven years earlier with my first wife. History was repeating itself. This time, I had an idea that my behavior was leading me to a second marital crisis.

As soon as I got home, I called Arnold. This was the early 1960s. Again, there was a moment right away when he let his mask fall. He asked, "What is it? A career crisis? Are you unhappy with the routine of your life?" I was shocked that he would say that. I thought maybe he was having the problems he asked me about.

This time in treatment, I didn't talk about who could run across Central Park faster or what was Freud's fatal mistake. I realized I was compulsively repeating my behavior and I wanted to stop it. I also wanted him to help me save my marriage, but I ended up getting his help dealing with the effects of ending it. I saw Arnold for about a year, going two or three weeks at a time, but not steadily. He was very accommodating about it although he had a crowded schedule. The only thing he said that struck terror into my heart was that if he didn't have a free hour, he might have to refer me to someone else. "How could I talk to someone else?" I thought. But it never happened. He always found the time.

It was during this second round of treatment that I received Arnold's second greatest gift to me: the ability to be aware of my feelings roughly when they were happening. "Within the same fiscal year," I would tell him. He liked that.

At termination, the door was always left open, but after I finished for the second time, Arnold went to have minor surgery and he died. I saw it in the paper. I was tremendously saddened. I dedicated a book to him. I called his wife. I thought of him frequently, dreamed about him. I still do.

I'm an amateur carpenter with quite a tool kit. I think of the work I did with Arnold as providing me a tremendously augmented psychological tool kit. For more than thirty years now I've applied what I won in therapy, and over that time I've discovered a third gift from Arnold: He rid me of my fear of the psychotherapeutic process. I began as an opponent of psychotherapy and was helped almost despite myself. When psychotherapy is successful, the patient can get through the rest of life—if not entirely on his own, then with a new set of strengths and the ability to call for help. I'd never been one to call for help. I'd been closed up and secretive. Therapy made me a much nicer guy, a better husband and father. I carry this with me, even though Arnold is no longer here.

Dr. Siegel's work with Ed was not psychoanalysis, but analytically-oriented psychotherapy, also known as insight-oriented psychotherapy, or analytic psychotherapy, which Robert Langs defines as "a relationship between two persons—a patient who is suffering with emotional problems and a therapist who has the professional skills to aid in their resolution."[6]

Langs writes that the goals of analytic psychotherapy include symptom resolution (the patient's life situation is addressed) and limited structural and personality changes, whereas the goal of psychoanalysis is revision of the total personality (the patient's life situation may not be addressed). The technique of interpretation is important in both forms of treatment but is used in greater depth in analysis. Confrontation may be used in analytic psychotherapy but is not part of an analysis. Free association is the analytic method. It is used to a lesser extent in other treatment forms.

In a classical Freudian analysis, the concentration is on the relationship between analyst and patient, which is more intense than it is in psychotherapy. Analysis is less "time bound" than analytic psychotherapy, which is face to face, one to three days a week, while analysis requires use of the couch with the analyst out of sight, four to five days a week in an open-ended format. Regression occurs to some extent in any interpersonal situation where dependence is involved, but is usually more limited in psychotherapy than in analysis, where it is encouraged.

There are boundaries in both forms of treatment, but they are more stringent in analysis, which always includes deprivation. For example, an analyst might not answer a patient's questions (grant wishes) whereas a psychotherapist might be more likely to do so. A patient in analysis might be encouraged to shift toward primary process thinking (the stuff of dreams and psychosis) while a patient in psychotherapy might not be. Finally, analysis is only for patients who have "the capacity to be analyzed"—have a personality that can tolerate the strictures of analysis with problems considered suitable to analysis; Psychotherapy is for a broad range of problems.

Ed Nathan actively sought a Marxist psychiatrist; our next socialist simply wanted an analyst.

James White

James White is a seventy-six-year-old former labor organizer who lives in Kansas City, Missouri. "I was very left-wing but anti-communist in the Fifties. My union was on the Attorney General's list. The night Stalin died, I dreamed about George Washington. When I told my analyst, he said, 'Stalin was the father of his country, too.' I was sort of shaken up. Communists were always threatening figures in my dreams. It was hard for me to equate Stalin and Washington."

In 1953, when I was about thirty, I was unhappy in a bad marriage and had to get some relief. I phoned a highly regarded analyst who'd been a patient of Freud's. He had no time available and referred me to Dr. Blute, an analyst about five years older than I. Sessions were $15, quite a bit for a factory worker like me, and Dr. Blute was even giving me a rate. We worked four-and-a-half years, four days a week, on the couch. I don't like the passive position and I didn't like the couch. That's just a way to avoid eye contact. After a while, it seemed somewhat convoluted.

I would start each session with a dream. I'd lie there and free associate and then discuss the associations. Dr. Blute didn't say much. At the end of the hour, he would usually imply what the dream was about. If I was in great distress, he might intervene more actively. For instance, when I was a young radical in conflict with the union leadership, I felt very threatened. Dr. Blute would ask, "Well, Mr. White, what's the worst thing that can happen?"

That made me realize my experience was not unique and not worth such anxiety. I was never beaten up and if I lost the election, so what? As it turned out, I never did lose an election, but if I had it would not have been the worst thing in the world. That was a very reassuring and positive aspect of analysis. The negative part was having to go in day after day and disembowel myself. I dreaded it, but I never missed a session.

I would frequently dream of being in the factory. In one dream, I represented the people in the boiler room and I needed to get there but I was lost in a maze of pipes wandering around in underground tunnels, searching, trying to find my way. The work I was doing then, trade union activity, was a very important part of my life but I wasn't sure I wanted to do it forever. I think the dream's message was, "Where am I going in life? How am I going to get there?" I remember talking to Dr. Blute once about a D. H. Lawrence novella I was reading. So he says, "Would you bring it in? I'd like to read it." I brought it in, he read it, and we discussed it. He was sensitive to how much this rough labor organizer wanted some sophistication.

I never idealized him. He was bright but I thought of myself, occasionally, as his intellectual superior. Still, he was so helpful with some little, niggling things. Once, I was inveighing against a colleague when he interrupted, "You feel competitive with him." I had never focused on that, but it was true. While that knowledge did not improve the relationship with my colleague, it remarkably reduced the intensity of our exchanges. It still stuns me that such a common-sensical remark could be so helpful. Another thing analysis did for me was give me a sense of realism. I was able to clarify my perspectives and see how self-defeating I was. It gave me a sense of my own motivations and those of others I'd brush up against.

My father's family was Irish and so was Dr. Blute's, so I felt a similarity to him, but we were never buddies. His office was in his home and sometimes I'd see his wife bringing in groceries or his kids playing out back, but we were never introduced. The analytic relationship is unbalanced that way. Dr. Blute and I had a professional relationship within which there was a significant rapport. I can't say I never reacted negatively to him, but overall I didn't have a furious, rageful analysis. That's surprising, considering I'd had a very angry relationship with my father. Churlish.

After four-and-a-half years, I was going on vacation and it seemed like a reasonable time to end. We talked about it and reviewed what we'd achieved. I'd divorced and remarried and begun graduate school. I didn't miss Dr. Blute after we ended, and I certainly didn't miss the sessions, but I appreciated analysis. It was worth the time, money, and emotional strain. It changed my life. Without it, I would have remained bitter and polemical.

You mentioned that other people you've talked to felt they needed left-wing or Marxist analysts. That never occurred to me. Socialism had to have a psychology but it did not have to be Pavlovian. There were some old Bolsheviks who could go along with Freud's ideas. Maybe the other people you talked to just wanted someone sympathetic to their political views. I suspect that analysts, much like Marxists, have quietly abandoned the enormous superstructure they inherited. If this is so, why couldn't a shaman or a clergyman or anyone be a successful analyst? Perhaps they could, but the fact is that every analyst goes through analysis. That torment alone creates a better understanding of the angst patients suffer. Sympathy is not enough. It must be informed by the analyst's personal experience of analysis and have a nonjudgmental, healing orientation.

James White describes what is known as "a corrective emotional experience." Joseph Weiss writes that in Freud's "1911–1915 theory, the patient's unconscious mind consists solely of impulses and defenses, not of beliefs that may be disproved by experience."[7] Here we have a patient seeking to disconfirm his pathogenic beliefs about himself—a "rough labor organizer" who engaged in self-defeating behavior and had an angry, churlish relationship with his father. James's analyst, Dr. Blute, was able to help his patient obtain the experiences he sought. "The therapist who attempts to pass the patient's tests by offering the patient the experiences he seeks need not fear that he will go far astray, for . . . he may check the pertinence of his behavior to the patient by the patient's reactions to him."[8]

Now we hear from a leftist who saw a lay analyst because of pain in his legs.

Caleb Keep

Caleb Keep is a sixty-five-year-old artist who lives in Burlington, Vermont. "The Fifties was a politically warlike period in American history. I had dear friends who were blacklisted and one whose husband lost his job for refusing to name names."

I was in my early twenties studying art and got a night job in a hospital so I'd be free to paint during the day. This was about 1955. I typed schedules and ran them off on an old-fashioned mimeograph machine you had to stand up to use and I developed excruciating pain in my legs. I had all sorts of tests—X-rays, blood work—but no one could find anything physically wrong.

While this was going on, my art professor, Abe Steinberg, invited me to join a drawing group that met at his house. One of the other students, Brad, worked part-time for a psychiatrist analyzing handwriting samples, and since Abe was interested in the connection between mental states and creativity, he asked us if we'd let Brad analyze our handwriting. All we had to do was copy a Hertz ad out of the newspaper, so I volunteered.

Two weeks later, I received a two-page analysis that read like an astrology report, but one sentence stopped me: "You believe you have something wrong with your legs." I asked Brad how that could show up in my handwriting and he explained that if there was something physically wrong—if I'd been crippled in an accident or had polio—it would not show up, but something psychosomatic would. Brad suggested I consult a lay analyst who specialized in treating artists, a Dr. Aronson. He was a Ph.D. who trained at one of the analytic institutes, not a medical doctor.

I made an appointment with Aronson and told him about my legs. He said I should see a medical doctor, so I told him what I'd already been through and that convinced him to take me on. I don't remember his fee, but it was based on my salary at the hospital. To give you a frame of reference, in a previous job, I got $37 a week working nights at a book bindery.

I felt an immediate connection to Aronson. I liked to do caricatures and we discussed humor and politics. I got the impression Aronson was leftist—it seemed to me we looked out the same window, politically speaking. I never learned a lot about his personal life, but I didn't want to. We were there to talk about me! And I never felt being in analysis was something I had to hide. In the Fifties, psychoanalysis was a fad. A wonderful opportunity to sit around and talk about yourself!

We began sitting face to face, once a week. Then I asked him why patients lay on the couch in cartoons and movies, and he explained about relaxing before going to sleep, letting thoughts of the day float up, reviewing those events. I went to the couch and soon asked for a second session each week, finding it helped to talk to an interested, objective stranger who was on my side. It was a unique experience.

We did a lot of dream analysis. When I got around to reading Freud, I learned that patients often have a dream before their first session. Freud declared this was a gift for the analyst and ought not to be interpreted. My dream went like this: I was in Abe Steinberg's living room. There was a model's stand in the center of the room. I didn't recognize any of the others present, but they were all crippled men. None were in wheelchairs and I don't remember canes. There was a swinging cripple who flailed about on crutches and took up much room navigating, and another guy who got my goat. Tall and skinny, he swung his leg up on the model's stand, raised his trouser, and adjusted a steel brace. I don't remember how I interpreted the dream but Aronson remained silent. I can see, now, that this dream was about a group of homosexuals. Abe had told me he was gay and my best friend at the time was gay, but I'd had no homosexual experiences and I had no designs on either one of them.

After less than a year of therapy, I had three dreams the night before a session. I find it terribly frustrating that I no longer remember the third dream, but in the first, I'm face to face with Marilyn, a girl I'd been dating. She's dressed as a goose girl and I'm a gray goose which, in black mythology, is invincible. [Laughs.] In no time, I change into a rooster, then a hen, and finally I'm a cooked chicken. I offer her one of my drumsticks.

In the second dream, I'm riding with my father on a bicycle built for two. He's in front and we're going along, but there's a problem. My left pedal is stuck up. When you get through snickering, I'll continue. Okay? Okay. My father's pedals are fine so he's doing all the work but he doesn't know the way and has to ask me for directions. The fact that at least I know the way to go saves what's left of my pride.

I related the dreams to Aronson and gave my interpretations. The cooked chicken—or goose—related to something that was going on in my life. I thought Marilyn and I were as good as engaged. She didn't, and our relationship fell apart. The bicycle dream goes back to when I was twelve years old. I'd had an undescended left testicle and needed an operation to place it into the scrotum. I was assured that this was routine surgery—nothing to be alarmed about—but I was given an experimental gas that exploded and punctured my lung. Since they were giving me oxygen at the time, air bubbles remained behind and caused me pain for days. The "routine" procedure thus became quite traumatic.

When I finished talking and Aronson made no comment, I jumped up, "standing on my own two feet"—one of my father's favorite expressions—and told Aronson this was it. I didn't need any more analysis and I wasn't coming back. I'd had the famous "Eureka!" experience, the sudden insight that the pain in my legs was connected to my insecurity about growing up, but it sort of hurt that Aronson didn't argue. He just accepted it! We went a few more sessions, shook hands good-bye, and that was that. I never saw him again.

I thought Aronson was a very good analyst. He never told me what to do. Abe's analyst was always telling him what to do. I wonder about analysts who direct their patients. Once I had a model who was excellent—would sit there, not moving, for hours. Well, her analyst told her to stop modeling for me. He said she was a masochist for exposing her body and I was a sadist for not reacting.

My case seems too neat and settled when I imagine other more complex problems, but I offer it for what it's worth. Intellectually, it may seem that my analysis cleared up nothing, but my leg problems disappeared. Forty years later and forty pounds heavier, I still prance about on pain-free legs.

Our next two respondents entered analysis in the time of *Ozzie and Harriet*, *Peyton Place*, and the McCarthy witchhunts in a culture that regarded homosexual practices as abhorrent, and even criminal. Alfred Kinsey's *Sexual Behavior in the Human Male* (1948) argued that social factors led to the development of exclusively homosexual histories. His 1953

Sexual Behavior in the Human Female revealed that about 50 percent of women were not virgins when they married, and that one in four had affairs by the time they were forty. The nation was shocked.

Jay Strickland

Jay Strickland is a seventy-one-year-old Atlanta banker. "In the Fifties, most analysts believed homosexuality was a developmental arrest that could be cured by psychoanalysis."

The background to this concerns how I flunked my army physical at the end of World War II. The evaluating psychologist asked me about my sexual orientation. I thought he was overly flirtatious, but I answered honestly, the Army rejected me, and I was sent to a psychiatrist who urged me to "get into analysis as fast as you can." Those two men made me feel I had some sort of raging insanity! The one thing they handled correctly was the referral. I was sent to Rosalind Burke, a distinguished psychiatrist who was a friend of Alfred Kinsey's and had studied with Theodor Reik.

> *Theodor Reik* (1888–1969) was one of Freud's first students. Their association lasted until 1938, when Reik immigrated to the United States. Naturalized in 1944, he helped found the National Psychological Association for Psychoanalysis, one of the few schools to offer analytic training to professionals who were not medical doctors. Criticized as disloyal to Freud for asserting that neither love nor neuroses had their roots in the sexual drive, Reik replied that some of Freud's concepts needed modification in light of later research. A sensitive, empathic therapist, Reik describes his authentic stance working with patients in *Listening with the Third Ear* (1948).

A little personal history: I was born in 1926 in Eden, Georgia. My mother died of tuberculosis when I was six months old. My father was able to keep my older sisters, but I had an allergic reaction to being put on cow's milk and nearly died. I was sent to my mother's brother and his wife, who were really too old to take an infant, but they wanted me. They doted on me and raised me like a little crown prince. My father came to visit often and I have priceless memories of him, but he died when I was six.

I didn't date during high school and my aunt put that down to shyness. The truth of the matter is that while I liked women, I was not sexually attracted to them. I had noticed men, though, and boys my own age. At N.Y.U. in the communal showers, I saw a profusion of naked male bodies for the first time in my life and I began to eye the other young men eyeing me. That's when I received my draft notice and was sent to Dr. B.

At our first meeting, we talked about my upbringing. Dr. B was also from a small town in Georgia and she understood my fumbling attempts to fit into the big city. At the end of the session, she asked me why I was coming to see her. "Why do you think?" I asked. She guessed, correctly, that other young men were making passes at me.

Dr. B was old enough to have been my mother. She had a soothing, lilting, feminine voice and a wonderful Southern accent. For all that she kept her hair cut short as a man's, she was quite womanly. [Jay goes to his desk and brings over a large framed photograph.] This is her picture. Doesn't she have a strong face?

When I began treatment, I did not advertise the fact that I was seeing a psychiatrist but I told my aunt and the next time she came to visit, Dr. B had us over for dinner. I told my uncle, too, but just in passing. I don't think he liked the idea. In some quarters, psychiatry was viewed with suspicion. Come to think of it, that's still the case.

Dr. B was still in analytic training when I began, so I saw her in weekly psychotherapy—$5 a session—until she qualified as an analyst in 1951 and raised her rates to the princely sum of $15 an hour. That would buy a good quality dress shirt those days. My "analysis proper" involved three sessions a week, on the couch, and much worry about how I could afford it. Dr. B told me she knew I'd pay when I could. That meant a lot to me. I felt it was quite a vote of confidence in her belief of my worth.

In a paper she wrote that year, Dr. B expressed the analytic opinion of the time: homosexuality was a medical, psychiatric problem—arrested development—and psychoanalysis could help an adult develop into heterosexuality. That was her goal for me. Mine, too.

I told Dr. B I had played with dolls in preference to trucks when I was a child. She believed I did this to be more like my sisters so my father would take me home with him. Her analytic supposition was that, for me, there was considerable attractiveness to a man who always went away. As an adult, I was still trying to find him.

After eighteen months, I received a fellowship to the London School of Economics. I had started dating women and while I was not yet sexually involved, it was progress. Dr. B agreed that we could stop, but I now recall she never said I had graduated. Still, when I left, I felt that the whole world lay before me.

Upon returning to New York, I joined a Wall Street firm and resumed analysis, working on the pressure for marriage I felt personally and professionally. Dr. B prescribed hormone shots I hated and vitamins I swallowed by the handful, but even as I worked with her, I began a serious relationship with a younger man. I told Dr. B about Paul, but we never got into it at a deep level. At times, I dreaded sessions, probably because of the effort I put into blocking what I didn't want to say. I think Dr. B was similarly hampered. She didn't want to risk the analytic relationship.

Paul and I had an on-again, off-again relationship. During one of our break-ups, I met a WAC [Women's Army Corps] quite a bit older than I was. Cathy and I went out a few times and we became engaged just before she was posted overseas. Dr. B asked if we'd had sexual relations. I said that we had not and she did not pursue the answer. She probably should have dug deeper.

The fifteen months we were married was a lacerating ordeal. Cathy's previous sexual experience caused her to disdain me as a novice—which I was—and, to my horror, I became an abused husband. I trained myself not to strike back because I knew it would complicate a divorce. As the situation deteriorated, we went to see Dr. B together and I was surprised when she took a strong dislike to my wife. I think she blamed Cathy for wrecking a marriage in which she had invested much professional time. I was a guinea pig that went wrong and I think my experiences were evaluated in her analytic circles. In our private sessions, Dr. B described Cathy as a "taker." She advised me, "No more sex!"—the supreme irony—saying that if we had a child, I'd be trapped. She referred me to the same attorney who had handled her divorce.

After I abandoned my sentimentality about marriage, I became all the more attracted to men, resumed my relationship with Paul, and began playing the field with a vengeance. There is a great deal of promiscuity among male homosexuals. AIDS is the only thing that has slowed it down.

Clearly, analysis did not change my sexual orientation. In 1951, Dr. B theorized that some homosexuals can never become heterosexual because their personality resources are too limited, or they've had psychologically castrating experiences that were too damaging, or their life situations present insurmountable obstacles. Well, that was forty-eight years ago. I think most analysts now realize that sexuality is a matter of nature and nurture, but mostly nature. It may be possible for a person with a homosexual predisposition to learn to function as a heterosexual, but I could not. Nor could I be bisexual. For me, it was all or nothing.

I do not consider my analysis a failure, though. Dr. B and I worked on a number of important issues, one of which was a damaging behavioral pattern that caused me to try to turn authority figures into parents. Then I'd become as demanding with them as I'd been with my aunt and uncle and sooner or later I'd be rejected. I did this time and again. Dr. B helped me connect my behavior to having been deserted as an infant. To a child, death is an abandonment. On the heels of this, I was taken by an old-fashioned couple who spoiled me to the point that I was completely unprepared for the give and take of life. Analysis taught me to understand the whys. I learned to catch myself in the act, so to speak, think about what I was doing, and stop it. Most of the time.

Dr. B was thoroughly accommodating. If I needed to patch up a relationship with someone she knew, she'd telephone that person; if I needed a place to work, she'd let me use a room in her house. She was a person who became thoroughly integrated into her patients' lives, sending Christmas cards every year and remembering names, relationships, and incidents mentioned years ago.

When I was depressed, I would heap guilt and harsh accusations upon myself. Once, I was indulging in a whole series of self-blame and she cried out, "Get a whip!" When I had trouble sleeping, she prescribed Seconal. For a different problem, she prescribed Dexadrine and I got hooked, but only for a while. Later, she prescribed one of the first antidepressants, Elavil, which I've used to good effect for years.

I was Dr. B's patient over a period of thirty-nine years. Two years before she died, we met for the last time and reviewed the years we'd been together. She told me she considered me her "professional son" and asked if I forgave her for permitting the marriage. She surprised me by saying she thought all along it would be tragic—that by the time I went to London, she knew she was up against a wall.

My love life has not fared so well, but I've had a successful business career, probably due to gaining an understanding of myself and an awareness of others I would not have except for Dr. B. When the chips are down, I find I do better when I consciously put her in mind and try to handle a situation as she would. The good analyst thus becomes a lifetime companion. What has saved me now that she is gone is my renewed religious faith.

Thirty-nine years is a long time, and Jay and Dr. B certainly had more than a professional relationship. Over-involvement in a patient's life is a therapeutic boundary violation. Patients who value a one-sided, protective relationship expressly because of its difference from ordinary friendship would be threatened by such a dual-role relationship, but Jay was not. Neither was our next patient, who found a neo-Freudian analyst who did not try to change his sexual orientation. His analyst was analyzed by Erich Fromm.

Erich Fromm (1900–1980) was born in Frankfurt and received his doctorate in sociology from the University of Heidelberg when he was twenty-two. Trained as a psychoanalyst by Theodor Reik, among others, Fromm was a neo-Freudian who used social science as a corrective to Freud's orthodox framework, asserting that humans are the products of their cultures. He immigrated to the United States in 1932 and by 1935 was writing that the patient-analyst relationship is the *sine qua non* of analysis. Fromm departed from strict Freudian boundaries, having social and professional relationships with some of his analysands. He abandoned free association and use of the couch and encouraged patient autonomy (freedom), whereupon his membership in the International Psychoanalytic Association was not renewed. A widely read, popular author in the 1950s and 1960s, Fromm wrote more than twenty books, including *The Forgotten Language*, a book on dream interpretation.

Steve Semmes

Steve Semmes is a sixty-nine-year-old scientist and writer who lives in Baton Rouge, Louisiana. "During the Fifties, most gays were still in the closet. If I had married, I know I would have suicided."

In my senior year at M.I.T., I had a severe depression related to coming out as a gay man and was advised to go into analysis. My father was a rather severe Christian type who didn't want me in psychological treatment, so I put it off until 1957 when my relationship with my lover fell apart. My supervisor, who was a close friend, suggested I see his former psychoanalyst, Melissa Eberhardt. Melissa's mother was a famous analyst who, she told me later in treatment, treated her more like a patient than a child.

I was twenty-seven and Melissa was old enough to have been my mother. Her office was in her home where I went three days a week, lay on the couch, and paid $10 an hour because I was on fellowship earning only $3,000 a year. My treatment had just begun when my parents arrived for a visit. They saw that I was living with a man and threatened to call the police. If they had, I'm sure I would have killed them. Melissa met with them once without me, and the situation was defused.

When I entered analysis, I was a totally fake person. A chameleon. A facade. The trick was to become real. When you ask how Melissa helped me to do that, I don't know what to say. There is a subtle mystery to these things. As well as I can explain it, she listened, she didn't espouse a lot of ideas or opinions, and she almost never gave advice. She certainly never tried to change my sexual orientation. Over time, I went from a chameleon to a Judas and then became myself. That's what my therapy was about.

Melissa had a wonderful tolerance for my incipient suicide. She never tried to medicate me or lock me up when I left her office feeling I wouldn't make it through the night. It takes real balls for a therapist to handle that. [Laughs.] Perhaps this little episode will help explain how Melissa was. She asked me a question once and I promptly wheeled out a glossy intellectual answer. She let it run a bit and then asked, "Must you always be so glib?" It almost knocked me off the couch. I have quite literally never been the same.

Dreams were a fairly important part of the analysis and were seen as both symbolic and direct expressions. Once, I related a dream of my older brother and I, who both wore glasses as children. In the dream, I dropped my glasses. Melissa did not see the eyes as testicles, but as eyes. The conflict in the dream was of sibling rivalry and sight itself. Did I really want insight? To see into oneself may be the occasion for terror.

Some analysts will not attend a dinner party if one of their patients will be there, but Melissa did not draw a rigid line between social and professional relationships. She came to a party at my place while I was in treatment. It meant a lot to me.

After three years, I thought I'd gotten what I needed and I told Melissa I didn't want to spend my life lying on the couch. She accepted my decision and we decreased the frequency to once a week for the final six months. After treatment, we attended an opera together and we keep in touch through friends.

I look back on myself some forty years ago and think I must have been a difficult patient—a pain in the ass—but Melissa did not complain. She was a good person, always kind and gentle. My idea of a superb therapist.

During the 1950s, the question of whether homosexuality was a matter of nature or nurture was much debated. Jay Strickland's therapist believed, at least when his treatment began, that environmental circumstances were at the root of the condition, whereas Steve Semmes' therapist accepted his homosexuality as a biological given. Current research seems to lean toward a biological explanation, but the nature/nurture controversy has yet to be resolved.

Steve gives high marks to his neo-Freudian analyst who did not strictly enforce therapeutic boundaries and recognized the importance of interpersonal relationships. Going back to what Rachel Perlman (Chapter 1) said about expecting therapists to conform to textbook definition, we see that therapists are individuals. Steve appreciated Melissa, but another patient of hers told us Melissa was not impartial and, in general, was not a credit to the profession. She said that Melissa screamed at her. Two views of the same person.

The post-war era was a time of conformity, especially in relation to sex roles. Women were admonished to content themselves as wives, mothers, and homemakers and find meaning in their lives by raising children and serving others. The following three women struggled with these issues. One was hospitalized and had shock treatments. Two were suicidal.

Scientists seeking a cure for schizophrenia experimented with chemically induced seizures, later replaced by their electroconvulsive equivalents. Shock treatments (ECT) did not cure schizophrenia, but often alleviated the symptoms of major depression for a while.

Norma Patterson

Norma Patterson, a retired businesswoman, owns an antique shop in Sweet Briar, Virginia. She is eighty-four. "I lost everything I had when the broker put it all in Real Estate Investment Trusts in the Fifties. As a woman, I wasn't expected to know anything about money. My husband was supposed to take care of things like that. Most of the psychiatrists I saw didn't pay attention to me. It was easier to send 'a hysterical little woman' for shock treatments."

I was married in 1939, the height of the Depression, and had three children by the time I was thirty. We struggled during the early years of our marriage. Bill was a womanizer. He had numerous affairs and, when I was forty, he left me for a younger woman. He got the divorce on his terms and was supposed to pay alimony and child support, but he never did. With no money and no job skills, I rented out the house and took the children to live with friends, watching their children in return for room and board.

Around 1955, I began to have stomach problems. I went to Bill's doctor who sent me to a psychiatrist without giving me a physical exam. The psychiatrist prescribed sedatives. When I couldn't get going in the morning, she gave me waker-upper pills and I got hooked. I became confused. I'd get home from the store without the groceries. I'd go to boil eggs and the pan would run dry. Eventually, she sent me to the hospital. The chief of psychiatry was the pits. He told me I needed a man and suggested the equivalent of "a single's bar," in today's terminology. He took me off drugs cold turkey and sent me for shock treatments. I must have had ten of those. I'd have ECT, go home and take care of the children, and then go back to the hospital for more.

Finally, my best friends took me to a different hospital where the attending psychiatrist saved my life. Dr. Bailer had them run tests, which showed I was anemic and my blood pressure was low. Other than the physical problems, he told me there was nothing wrong with me. I'd just been under too much stress. He urged me to contact my family. I hadn't wanted them to know, but when I called, my cousins came and took care of me and my children until I got back on my feet.

When I got out of the hospital, I was not fine, but I survived. My family and friends were my salvation. They helped me infinitely more than M.D.'s ever did.

To this day, Norma is angry about her treatment by a hospital psychiatrist who abruptly withdrew prescription medications and administered shock treatments, but never talked with her about her chaotic life situation. Most of our respondents wanted to read our accounts of their stories, but Norma did not. "It's too sad," she said.

The next two women, Mary Ann Kelly and Lisa Bea Weinberg, fit Lewis Wolberg's description of patients best suited for analytic psychotherapy and orthodox psychoanalysis. They were "capable of learning rapidly in the medium of an interpersonal relationship . . . [where] they analyze their dreams and other unconscious productions and come to grips with their anxiety without too severe resistances or too intense transference reactions."[9]

Mary Ann was caught in the convergence between the powerful societal expectations she perceived and her subjective view of herself as not being worth much.

Mary Ann Kelly

Mary Ann Kelly is a sixty-two-year-old theatrical producer who lives in London. "I began therapy the year the Russians launched Sputnik, but what I think about when I remember the Fifties is the nuclear arms race. People were trying to build bomb shelters in their basements. It was the time of the Cold War. The Russians were our enemies."

In the fall of 1957, I was a twenty-year-old secretary living in New York. I was engaged to Jeff, a student at an Ivy League medical school whom I'd met New Year's Eve. He thought I could be molded into what he wanted in a wife. "I'm expecting you to make me happy, dear," he would say. He put a great deal of pressure on me sexually and made it clear that I wouldn't need my Catholicism, which was then very important to me, once we were married. He wanted me to give up my job— which I loved—and go to work for an insurance company where the hours were 8:00 A.M. to 4:00 P.M., so I could get home and have his dinner ready every night. I began to feel terribly anxious that I wouldn't be able to fulfill his expectations.

One night we were in a restaurant on the second floor of a building. Outside, a street lamp cast a pool of light onto the sidewalk. It looked so warm and inviting, I had an almost irresistible impulse to jump out the window. I jerked myself back just in time and ran out of the building. When Jeff came after me, I begged him to take me to a doctor but he said, "Doctors see hysterical women all the time. What would we say was wrong?"

I knew I had to get help, so I went to the Cornell Medical Center where I was evaluated and referred to a psychoanalyst, Dr. Kiernan. I'd never known anyone who'd been in treatment and I didn't know what to expect. By sheer luck, I got the right doctor. I guess he was Freudian, but when I was in treatment I didn't know anything about the different theories and I wouldn't have cared. I felt so bad I would have thrown myself at the feet of anyone I thought could help me. I was in a very vulnerable position—but that's a time when you can change. Your resistance is low. But I was lucky. I got the right doctor.

Dr. Kiernan agreed to see me for $20 an hour. That doesn't sound like much today, but in 1957 I only earned $100 a week. I needed daily sessions during the first five weeks, so my treatment consumed my whole paycheck. I had to dip into savings to get by. As soon as I was stabilized, we cut back to twice a week and I continued therapy for three-and-a-half years.

In my Catholic circle of friends, psychiatry was viewed with suspicion so I made all my appointments before work and I kept my therapy a secret. I didn't tell my roommate and it was a long time before I told Jeff, even though Dr. Kiernan encouraged it. I never told my parents.

At the first session, I sat in a chair across from Dr. Kiernan's desk and told him what was going on in my life and what led me to want to jump out the window. He would listen and he took a lot of notes. It seemed that when I said a lot, he wrote very little, and when I said very little, he would write a lot. I always wondered what he was writing, but I never asked.

The situation with Jeff was what drove me into treatment, but I knew childhood experiences lurked in the background. What came out in therapy were the terrible conflicts I had with my family. I was the middle of five children in an Irish Catholic family of modest means and I must have been different from the beginning. I was the only one who liked classical music and I loved to read. I didn't look like my parents or my siblings and I wondered if I'd been adopted. I was the odd one and I became the scapegoat. Consequently, I developed a fantasy life which protected me. It came out of the movies, where I saw there was a world somewhere—California, I thought [laughs]—where things were very different from home. At the time, the only way I had to get out of my world was to go to the movies and fantasize. I got good at it.

I'd always had frightening nightmares, but early in treatment they intensified. I begged Dr. Kiernan to put me in the hospital, but he said he thought I should continue going to work. He prescribed a sedative—maybe Miltown?—but I didn't take it long. It helped, but the most effective thing he did was talk to me.

All my growing up years were absolute confusion. In Sunday School, I was taught that God loved you absolutely, that parents were God's surrogates on earth, and that you were destined for this ultimate reunion with God. But these teachings met with harsh reality. The nuns at school were often brutal and mean-spirited and I had no reason to believe my parents loved me. Catholic children were to be seen and not heard. Feelings were not discussed. My older brother, who was Mother's favorite, was violent and sadistically abused me. Because I never felt Mother loved or wanted me, I couldn't tell her what he was doing. I wanted to get away from home as fast as possible and I left when I was sixteen, but coming out of my family, I had no self-esteem. I was filled with guilt and self-loathing and I felt worthless. I thought I was ugly. When people seemed to like me, I thought it was because they didn't know me. I was sure they'd abandon me as soon as they did.

Once, I woke up from a vivid dream of my brother and rushed to my session. I got there just as Dr. Kiernan arrived. He still had his coat on. I sat down and boom, I just blurted it out. Talking to him about the dream and my feelings took such a weight off me. I learned that my dreams had meaning and were the keys to the past and what was troubling me.

After an insight like this, I'd think I was "cured" and talk about stopping. Therapy was expensive and my insurance didn't pay for it, but Dr. Kiernan would smile and say he didn't think it was time yet. He was right. If I'd stopped, I wouldn't have gotten to some of the hard stuff I needed to work out.

I began to get a handle on what was going on with me. I'd never had the courage to speak up for myself at home. I never said no because I thought the result would be awful. I was doing the same thing with Jeff. Dr. Kiernan had urged me to tell him I was in treatment but I was afraid he'd be angry, and when I told him, he was. Ultimately, I broke our engagement. Jeff's response was that it was too bad for me because if I didn't marry him, I'd probably never get married. [Laughs.]

Talking in therapy led me to experience my emotions. I felt this rush of anger, happiness, fear, anxiety—all the feelings I'd struggled to keep down. Dr. Kiernan told me I mustn't inhibit what I was feeling. If I was at work and got tearful, he said I should excuse myself, go to the ladies room, and cry.

Dr. Kiernan saw that some of my dilemmas had roots in Catholicism and suggested I talk to a priest, so I looked up a Father Andrew I'd heard on the radio. He was young and handsome. Just out of the seminary. I told him one of the things I needed to work on was my mother's always giving me the third degree: "Where are you going? Who are you going with? What are you doing?"

Father Andrew told me that as a self-supporting adult, I no longer had the obligation of absolute truth to my parents. "You have the right to live your life free of their interference," he said. I was astonished! Overjoyed! Father Andrew became a champion of social justice, a real guiding light in the community. He began to refer parishioners to Dr. Kiernan and Dr. Kiernan sent patients to Father Andrew. They worked together for years.

During therapy, I began to believe I could handle what life presented me. This next dream illustrates what I'm talking about. In real life, my roommate and I lived in a brownstone with two locks and a chain on the door. In my dream, a guy in the apartment above us was having a terrible argument with someone. I heard a crash—maybe a chair was thrown—and punching and swearing. Then their door burst open and I heard them fighting on the stairs, coming closer and closer. I rushed to the door and found two big holes where the locks had been. The chain was gone. In the midst of that nightmare, I thought, "Whatever is coming to my door, I'll just have to deal with it."

The other thing I learned—this was the turning point in therapy—was to stop fantasizing and live in the real world. When a guy said he'd call me, I had to stop fantasizing how "the relationship" would develop. It is sad and frightening to me, even now, that when I was twenty, I felt there was this other person inside me who would start the fantasizing. In treatment, I learned to stop it—that when a guy says he'll call, he's not talking about a lifetime commitment. [Laughs.] That brings me to how therapy ended. I was becoming more involved in my life and I met the man I ultimately married. I just didn't need treatment anymore. I honestly don't remember our last session.

There was a time when I thought Dr. Kiernan was the most wonderful thing that ever lived. He was quite handsome and I certainly had my share of fantasies about him, but he never talked about himself. I don't know if he was married or had children. He was even-keeled, never patronizing, and never sanctimonious. He had what really fine therapists have—something that can't be learned in school—an innate understanding of human nature. I always felt I was the most important person in the world to him in the hour I was there, and I knew I could trust him.

I entered treatment feeling that I was losing my mind. I would like to say loud and clear that without psychotherapy, I would never have gained the insights that enabled me to lead a happy, productive life. I married, had children, and developed a career I love. If I were twenty years old and seeking therapy today, I'd probably be put on Prozac and have six sessions with a therapist provided by the company's HMO. That would not begin to address the problems I had then.

I am a loving admirer of Freud, the audacity of his thinking and his courage. People who call him sexist are not taking into account that probably all European men of his generation would be considered sexist by today's standards. Freud was a product of his time—as we all are.

Mary Ann is one of the few respondents who comments on the impact of religion, saying that while it was once an important part of her life, it no longer is, but she got what she needed in treatment. "I never resumed therapy, but I saw Dr. Kiernan once years later when there was a death in my family. He helped me then as he had years before. I don't know where he is now, or even if he's alive, but I'll always remember him."

The next story is by a very up-front woman who entered analytic psychotherapy miserable and suicidal.

Lisa Bea Weinberg

Lisa Bea Weinberg is an over-seventy marathoner who lives in Palo Alto, California. "The most important thing that enabled the American worker to achieve middle-class status was passage of the Labor-Management Relations Act, known as labor's Magna Carta, by which unions became enfranchised. For the first time, workers were able to bargain collectively for wages and hours."

I went into analysis in 1957 when I was just past thirty, the ostensible reason being problems with my mother. During the Depression, my parents worked in sweatshops and fought for recognition of their unions. My father was fired because he was Jewish and my mother was told her ass would be kicked down the stairs if she went to the toilet. As a result, my politics are liberal and left-of-center. I am pro-union, pro-abortion, and anti-death penalty. Civil liberties are very important to me. I carry a copy of the Constitution in my purse.

My mother had to work, so I was placed in kindergarten at age three—in 1929, you could do that if you "knew someone"—and I stayed until I was six. My older sister would take me home after school. Did I feel deprived? Absolutely not. I tell my friends I graduated kindergarten *summa cum laude* in crayon management. When I developed rheumatic fever, Mother massaged my legs with ointment and wrapped them in flannel strips made of worn-out pajamas. She'd lie down next to me, placing my hands under her large breasts, and I'd snuggle into her body. She would sing old songs and tell me stories of her childhood in Norway. Heaven held no greater happiness. By contrast, my relationship with my father was distant. He always seemed to be telling somebody off and I never cared much for him. When I was ten and we moved to a new apartment, I was surprised that he came along.

Given my secure younger years, it may seem odd that I entered puberty desperately unhappy. I saw myself as the ugliest girl on earth. I wore braces and had a bad stutter. If people took time to listen as I stammered and blushed my way through a sentence, I thought they were feeling sorry for me. I hated that. It was easier not to talk at all, so I didn't.

In social settings, I never felt that I fit in, and as I got older I began to feel like an outsider in danger of being found out and asked to leave. Mother and I began to fight all the time and would go for weeks without speaking. I thought she no longer loved me and I became grateful if anyone, especially a man, paid attention to me. My love relationships became very self-destructive. While I never drank, took drugs, or went with a "fast" crowd, I'd had three abortions by the time I was thirty. I felt dirty. I hated myself for violating the standards by which I'd been raised and I was contemplating suicide. I'd lie in bed at night, sobbing, "Please, someone, help me!"

People at work talked about being in analysis. Said it was wonderful. I didn't know how to find a doctor and of course I wouldn't ask, but one day I saw an ad for a Jewish Social Service Agency and called and made an appointment. I told the evaluating social worker that I wanted a male analyst, thinking that since my problems were with my mother, a man would be more understanding. I'd go in a few times, explain how unreasonable she was, get some pointers on how to avoid arguments, and that would be that. The social worker gave me three names. I chose Dr. Joseph because his office was easy to get to on the bus.

My first appointment was on St. Patrick's Day. People on the street seemed so happy, wearing "Kiss me, I'm Irish" buttons, but I was miserable, ready to cry. I walked into Dr. Joseph's office expecting an old man, a Sigmund Freud type with a beard, and found—to my surprise— someone who looked young enough to date. At the first session, I sat across from him and told him my background and interests. He charged $25 for two sessions a week—peanuts today—but in 1957 I only earned $65 a week. I could afford it because I lived in a rent controlled, tub-in-the-kitchen, fifth-floor walk-up apartment—$32 a month.

That first session was a piece of cake. I left thinking it would be easy and quick, but it took seven years. Analysis became a way of life. I'd go right after work and I never told anyone. It wasn't stigma, just that most people wouldn't have understood and it would've been hard to listen to ignorant remarks about something so important to me. To this day, I can't stand it when people call analysts "shrinks."

At the second session, Dr. Joseph asked me to lie on the couch while he sat in a chair behind me, taking notes. I felt awkward the first time, but he was right. There was no way I could have opened up about the most intimate details of my life if I'd faced him. Every session began the same way. Dr. Joseph would put a clean paper on the couch and I would lie down. He'd ask if there was anything in particular I'd like to talk about. If yes, I'd take it from there. If no, he'd wait, silent, till my dreaded thoughts came to the fore and my words—and tears—would gush out. Psychoanalysis isn't called the Talking Cure for nothing. Dr. Joseph wanted to know of my dreams and I trained myself to wake up, jot them down in shorthand, and transcribe them the next day. He was a good listener who said very little and didn't make suggestions. That forced me to draw conclusions on my own.

Since problems with my mother drove me into analysis, I began to talk about her. She got me my first pair of ice skates when I was eight, took me to a frozen-over tennis court, skated with me to the center, and then skated away. "Come back! I'll fall!" I cried. She urged me to skate to her. I managed it and pretended to be angry, but I was secretly elated that I'd done it by myself. When I'd ask for ice cream, then only a nickel, Mother would tell me, "I have a nickel and some pennies. You can have the nickel or you can have all the pennies." "How do I know you have five?" I'd ask. "You don't," she'd reply, "but maybe I have more than five. Take a chance!" I always did and she never fooled me. Telling this to Dr. Joseph, I began to see how the skating taught me gutsy independence; the pennies were about trust.

Dr. Joseph was interested in my teenage years when things started to fall apart. I told him how jealous I was of Rosalie, my sister. She was pretty, popular with all the boys, and a flirt. She became pregnant when I was fourteen and made a hasty marriage, but it was a scandal in 1942 in our old-world, middle-class Bronx neighborhood. Mother saw Rosalie through the birth, giving the baby up for adoption, and she took out a loan to pay for the divorce. I hadn't realized how hard this must have been for my very proud mother until I lay on the couch and told Dr. Joseph. I had two more abortions during the early days of analysis when I was still miserable. This was prior to *Roe v. Wade*[10] so we're talking dirty, back-alley jobs. A lot of women died. I blamed Dr. Joseph. "You knew this would happen," I cried. "Why didn't you stop me?" He asked me why I was blaming him. I had no answer. He told me it was good I was expressing my anger, but that it was misdirected. He asked me to try to focus my anger on the people and circumstances that had caused my pain, and then he said, "Let's work together to find out why this is happening." It took more tears, more anger, and more time, but we worked it through and I never had another abortion. I was on my way.

Analysis was painful, but without it I'd never have gotten to the roots of my self-destructiveness. I fought with my mother because I'd been so lovingly tied to her and jealous when she gave herself over to my pregnant sister. Then Rosalie went her way and Mother was back—with a vengeance. She would not allow "Her Baby" to repeat Rosalie's mistakes. Dr. Joseph explained that my mother's motivation was love. "If people don't love each other, they don't care. There's no reason to argue if you don't care."

After about five years, I told Dr. Joseph I was ready to cut back on my sessions. I had learned to step back from emotionally charged situations and think before taking action, thereby avoiding a lot of heartache. He went along with this breaking away, which took another two years. Did I occasionally backslide? You betcha. But now I knew how to analyze the whys and wherefores and avoid making the same mistake twice.

One of the reasons my analysis went so well was that I was ready for help. I'm a good patient and will trust a medical doctor unless I find my trust ill-founded. Dr. Joseph never disappointed me. We never had a personal relationship, but I wasn't looking for a friend. I needed a doctor. In seven years of treatment I never called him at home, although he said I could. Years later, I phoned when there was a family crisis. A child answered the phone and I heard her say, "Daddy, it's for you." I remember being surprised to discover that he had a life of his own.

Today, I have a good, if not ideal, life. I'm a competitive runner. I love music, theatre, dance, any movie made before 1960, and I read everything from Shakespeare to Elmore Leonard. I write a bit and I've been published small-time. I never married but I enjoy the company of children, sometimes more than adults. If something must be done, I just get on with it. I don't wait for Prince Charming to come along.

Although Dr. Joseph held a central place in her life, Lisa Bea makes it clear that their relationship was never personal and that's how she wanted it. She refers to Dr. Joseph as "my analyst," but this was not a classical Freudian analysis. It was psychoanalytic psychotherapy, a variation on the analytic theme with fewer sessions per week (two as opposed to four or five). There was not as great a concentration on analysis of the transference, but, like analysis, the work was on the couch and dreams were interpreted.

Lisa Bea spent seven years with Dr. Joseph. In the next story, a college student negotiates three days a week in what is otherwise a classical Freudian analysis she is in a rush to finish.

Christine Brown

Christine Brown is a retired elementary school teacher in her mid-sixties. She lives in Sarasota, Florida. "I remember Korea. A friend of mine was sent even though he had already been in the Merchant Marine. I didn't think that was fair. And it wasn't even called a war—it was 'The Korean Conflict.' We lost a lot of men there. Another thing I remember in the Fifties is prominent people going on TV and talking about going to their analysts. It was a fad."

In 1952, I was a twenty-year-old sophomore at Marquette. I read Karen Horney's *The Neurotic Personality of Our Time* and thought, "This is me." I had no idea how to deal with things on an emotional level and my relationships were just a mess. I needed analysis.

My father agreed to pay for it, so I got a list of names from the American Psychoanalytic Association and interviewed a Dr. Craig. He must have been in his early forties, but he didn't seem old. He suggested four days a week, on the couch, and I wanted one or two. [Laughs.] We compromised at three days a week, $15 a session. That was a financial sacrifice for my parents with three children in college, and I was determined not to waste the money. I would work hard and finish as fast as I could.

Dr. Craig would listen while I related what was going on in my life and usually he wouldn't say anything. If I fell silent, he might prompt me, "Well, what do you think about that?" I wished he'd give me a little guidance. Sometimes I felt we made no progress for weeks.

I asked him what I could read to help me move along faster. He said you can't get it by reading a book, but that he thought I might like Lucy Freeman's *Fight Against Fear*. I still have that book. It's survived all our moves over the years. It's about a woman in analysis and it was popular in the Fifties. But Dr. Craig was right, you can't get it by reading a book.

We did a lot of dream analysis. In one, I was alone in a room with a gray, blobby thing inching along on the floor. Everything else in the room was green. Dr. Craig would not tell me what the dream meant. I had to interpret it myself. What I came up with was that the gray blob was my embryonic self and probably since I had begun analysis, I was changing. The green was associated with growth and hope. That first glimmer of self-derived understanding taught me what a breakthrough means.

Talking about this reminds me how young I was. Sometimes Dr. Craig and I would get to his office at the same time and go up on the elevator together. Alone. That would make me completely tongue-tied. I never fell in love with him, but he occupied a very special place with me and still does. I respected and admired him.

The thing about analysis is it's a professional relationship that is extremely intimate at the same time it's extremely remote. You have to tell the most dreadful, disgusting things about yourself and then be mature enough to scrape yourself together and go on with your life. When I think back on me as a twenty-year-old, I can see I was just too young. You need life experience I didn't have then to benefit from analysis.

Dr. Craig never talked about himself but if I asked him something, he'd answer. I wanted to know if he had children and he said he did, but then we had to go on and on about why I wanted to know and what it meant to me until I was sorry I'd asked. He knew I wanted to talk about anything but myself, so he'd turn everything back on me and that would force me to do what I'd come there for in the first place.

One time I didn't speak for the whole hour and neither did Dr. Craig. At the next session, I asked him why he didn't say anything and, as usual, he turned it back on me: Why hadn't I said anything? Why was I so angry? Those were important questions we didn't have time to answer. When I graduated, I married Rob and we moved to the West Coast.

I remember my last talk with Dr. Craig. I told him I was not attractive and he said something like "Quite the opposite is true." He always tried to instill some faith in myself in me.

Analysis was big in the Fifties and there was never any stigma as far as I was concerned. I just think it takes too long. It's an absolutely open-ended process and while that may be good for some things, it's not the only way to go. Some of the focused, short-term therapies are probably better for some problems. Still, psychoanalysis changed my life. It began a process that made it possible for me to have a life and enjoy it.

I was never able to hook in with another analyst, but about ten years ago a breakthrough occurred in a weight management program where I was in group therapy. I don't like group—it's just not my style—but that's where I finally understood what was going on with me. We had to talk about why we ate and it dawned on me that I'd grown up in a very angry family where a constant undercurrent of rage permeated everything. I'd been walking around in a cloud of anger—in charge of everything, responsible for everything, and furious. Well, I learned to let it all go—the control, the responsibility. That is when I found peace.

I wish I had achieved satisfaction earlier in life. I would have been a better mother. My children say I'm a great mother, but what do they know? [Laughs.] Marrying Rob is what saved me. I don't know that analysis had anything to do with my marrying absolutely the right person for me—but maybe. Or maybe it was just dumb, blind luck!

Christine describes a mixed reaction to her experience in psychoanalysis. A short-term, focused therapy finally worked for her, but she allows that without the analytic experience, she might not have been able to profit from it. This sort of delayed reaction to understanding is not uncommon. Self-understanding comes when one is ready because willingness to accept messages from within has to do with one's ability to deal with the flood of emotions that often accompanies a new insight.

The following vignette describes the impostor syndrome. Many people struggle with the incongruity between how they present themselves to others and how they regard themselves privately.

Bob Gordon

Bob Gordon is a sixty-nine-year-old land developer who lives in Denver, Colorado. "I went into land development in the Fifties. All the returning GIs needed houses or apartments. Later I got into HUD projects. Everything you hear about government contracts is true. The government has two speeds: slow and stop."

I went into a very competitive field and was quite successful from the beginning of my career, but I always felt I was hiding behind a false front. The tycoon image was not really me and I lived in fear that I'd be found out.

By the time I was twenty-five, my marriage was in bad shape and my relationship with my father, with whom I was in business, wasn't much better. Since I was quite successful professionally, there wasn't anyone I could turn to who would have believed I had problems. I had reservations about going into analysis because I didn't want anyone to think I was crazy, but I'd heard that analysis was supposed to make you a new person and change your life to a major extent. That's what I was looking for, so I made an appointment with a psychoanalyst, Dr. Leonard. The fee was $50 an hour and I wrote it off on my corporate account as an educational expense.

Dr. Leonard recommended working twice a week, face to face, for a few months to see if I was up to analysis. Then we went to four days a week on the couch. By the end of the first year, we could see that analysis was not working. There were long silences when I could not talk about my mother so we dropped back to two days a week, face to face again, and I discovered Dr. Leonard could talk! I found that what analysis could not do for me in a short time, psychotherapy did over a longer period. I saw him for about two years.

My problems with my mother were connected to my problems with my father. After his business collapsed, she considered him a failure. When I was about five, she would hold me up in front of her at the mirror. Wearing her night clothes and with her big, warm breast lying on my arm, she'd talk baby talk to me. "Bobby, widdle Bobby-Wobby, will you take care of Mommy when Mommy gets old?" What could I do? I would nod yes. It was exciting but it frightened me. I'd taken showers with my father and made the inevitable comparisons. How could I take care of my mother? That was his job. But my mother persisted with this mirror thing until I felt I had a special bond with her and had to perform for her. I would be her hero and make her life good to make up for my father's failure. Every time a good business deal went through, my first thought would be, "Boy, is my mother gonna love this!" It was the birth of the impostor syndrome.

In therapy, I learned how I compulsively repeated my errors, unconsciously wanting to spoil my successes because of guilt feelings. Dr. Leonard pointed out that I wasn't trying to replace my father and I wasn't an impostor. I was a smart, savvy businessman and that was okay!

Dr. Leonard died two years ago. He was a brilliant and practical psychiatrist and even after his death, he helps me solve problems. I have become not religious, but a spiritual person who asks his guides for help. Dr. Leonard is one such guide.

Putting the issue of sexuality aside, there are a number of similarities between Steve Semmes' concerns and what Bob Gordon calls his Impostor Syndrome. Both men describe a feeling of incongruity between their self-images and the images they present to others. Donald Winnicott wrote of the "true and false self"[11] and Karen Horney defined the "real and idealized self."[12] They both point out that without realizing it, some parents fail to recognize their children's individuality and uniqueness so that the children come to believe their right to exist depends on living up to the expectations of others. To Winnicott, this reactive over-compliance may create an experience of unreality for the person and a sense of futility about living a life that has personal meaning. In cases like this, the therapeutic task is to help the patient get in touch with the private world of subjective experiences that has been undeveloped or hidden even from the self. Karen Horney emphasized helping patients grow toward self-realization by discovering the unique aliveness of the real self, "the alive, unique personal center of ourselves, the only part that can and wants to grow."[13]

We end the decade with the story of a man who racked up more than thirty years of individual and group treatment.

Joseph Hans

Joseph Hans is a seventy-seven-year-old lay analyst from Philadelphia. "I went into therapy in 1951 during the Eisenhower Era. We Americans were the giants of the Earth in those days. We'd won the war. It was a peaceful and hopeful era, but not for me."

I went into therapy when I was twenty-nine because my two-year-old marriage soured and ended very quickly. I was a frightened kid, depressed, cut off from my emotions and in a lot of internal turmoil. My life was a mess.

I knew Dr. Fischer, who became my therapist, from the time I was a child. He was a family friend. I knew a lot about his personal life and preferences. He was not opaque and he diverged markedly from Freudian methods. I now question why.

I never lay on the couch and free associated or had analysis three days a week. This was psychotherapy, once a week in individual and once a week in group, from the spring of 1951 to January 1979. It cost $20 a session toward the end. Individual was hard for me. I thought I was a difficult patient. I had a lot of dog dreams. I identified with dogs as dependent and frightened. I felt like a dachshund—cut off at the knees. In reality, I was very quiet and frightened, like an abused dog, with my family. They never liked my being in therapy, but they liked Dr. Fischer.

Group therapy was very gratifying. There were ten or twelve people in group, men and women from my age up to their fifties. Different professions. Different problems. Dr. Fischer encouraged us to make friends outside group, and I needed that. In fact, that's where I met my second wife. Group was a little world of its own and that made it hard to break away from Dr. Fischer. When I left, I had to give up that little world, and one by one the friendships drifted away. Now I think Dr. Fischer made group into his personal cult.

I went into business with my father although I'd always wanted to be a writer. It was all right until he died, but I was never meant to run my own business and I failed within two years. By that time, I'd been in therapy twenty years. Dr. Fischer suggested I had two options: Go to work for someone else or train to be a lay analyst. I'd never thought of that and it appealed to me. I had remarried by then and my wife and I decided I could apply to the National Psychological Association for Psychoanalysis, which was founded by Theodor Reik, among others. You had to have a master's degree and I did—in English. While I trained, I saw patients at a clinic and made a little money there. Training was for ten years. I've always been a good student and I was delighted with it.

Dr. Fischer became my supervisor and I was his ardent disciple, but after twenty-eight years I could see I wasn't getting free of him. I wanted to take a year off, but he didn't want me to end treatment. Perhaps there was some theory he was following, but I couldn't see it. We ended on very bad terms. I never went back into treatment with him—in fact, I wouldn't touch him with a ten-foot pole—but I reentered therapy about 1981 to resolve my feelings of failure about the first therapy.

My second therapist, Anne-Lisa Pelier, was a classically trained analyst who had studied object relations. I liked Anne-Lisa. I always thought she looked like a gypsy dancer. Sort of an idealized picture of Mother from my childhood. She saw that all I really needed was room to talk about my first therapy and she didn't get in my way, although she occasionally made an interpretation. I don't remember any that were particularly dazzling or brilliant, but she would say cogent things. She saved my marriage by encouraging me to stay with it and not act out. I went to her twice a week for five years and it cost $60 or $65 a session. I had insurance in the Eighties. I think it paid 80 percent.

I got a lot out of psychotherapy. I have a much greater sense of who I am and what my thoughts and feelings are. I learned that I have more courage than I thought I did, and now I have great satisfaction in my work. When I was in business, it was all struggle and anxiety. I must have spent over $100,000 on treatment, but I believe psychotherapy made me the man I am and have been for some time. What else can you buy that's worth as much as a decent life?

While Christine Brown mentions that analysis was big in the 1950s and becoming a fad, not all the twenty-three respondents, eleven men and twelve women, who were in treatment during this decade were in classical Freudian analyses. Of the eleven stories in this chapter, one woman and four men were in psychoanalysis, but only two (James White and Bob Gordon) were seen at a frequency of four days a week on the couch. Jay Strickland, Christine Brown, and Steve Semmes were seen three days a week, a reduction from Freud's original six days a week, but still considered classical Freudian analysis in the 1950s.

It was becoming apparent that the analytic method was not the panacea for all forms of psychiatric illness, and psychotherapists in general began to modify their approaches to accommodate more complex problems during this decade. One variation was analytically-oriented psychotherapy used by Dr. Siegel in Ed Nathan's case. Hospital psychiatrists started using medications and electroshock treatments for patients suffering severe depressions or psychosis. Electroshock was championed as cheap and effective. Some neo-Freudians abandoned use of the couch and began using more supportive techniques: guidance, reassurance, environmental manipulation, and gentle persuasion. What seemed to make the difference between therapies that worked and those that foundered was that in successful cases, therapists were attuned to what their patients were going through and did not judge them or expect more from them than they could deliver.

As in Chapter 1, most of these people were in their twenties on entering treatment. Three were thirty or older. Two people (Jay Strickland and Steve Semmes) saw female analysts, and one of Norma Patterson's psychiatrists was a woman. Ed Nathan, Jay Strickland, and Bob Gordon were in touch with their therapists until their therapists died. Jay Strickland and Steve Semmes had social relationships with their therapists. The others did not keep in touch, but they remember their therapists fondly, except for Norma Patterson who was entirely disenchanted with the process.

Most of the twenty-three give therapy positive ratings. Joseph Hans had a negative reaction to his first therapist. He felt that Dr. Fischer kept him in treatment too long and turned the psychotherapy group into a cult, yet he was sufficiently impressed by the value of therapy that he entered the field, as did one other respondent from this group.

With regard to stigma, Jay Strickland comments that during the 1950s, he noticed a sense of suspicion about things psychological in some quarters but adds that the same is true today. For similar reasons, Mary Ann Kelly didn't tell her Catholic friends she was in treatment. Lisa Bea Weinberg didn't want to hear "ignorant remarks" about something she treasured, so she kept her therapy a secret, and Bob Gordon entered therapy thinking it was something only crazy people did, but Caleb Keep and Christine Brown were never diffident about being in analysis.

There is no mention of insurance reimbursements for mental health care and psychiatrists continued to be in short supply. They could make as much as $20,000 a year in private practice,[14] compared to the national average of $3,180. Health care costs continued to be a political issue during the 1950s. In 1950, the tab for medical care in America was $8.4

billion. People were shocked to find that by 1959, costs had soared to $17.2 billion, or $115 for every man, woman, and child in America.[15] Even so there were still sick people and dreaded diseases. About half of all Americans were covered by health insurance in 1950; 71 percent were covered in 1959. Physicians rebelled against the paperwork this created and started charging their patients an insurance filing fee—usually about $3.

President Eisenhower's reaction to soaring costs was to warn that socialized medicine would be the result if something was not done. During the Cold War, "socialized" raised the spectre of Communism.[16] But by the end of the decade, the nation's mood was relatively calm. Vice-President Richard M. Nixon had given his maudlin but supremely effective "Checkers" speech, *Brown vs. Board of Education* began the slow process of integrating the nation's public schools, and the civil rights and feminist movements were in their infancies. Jobs were plentiful, prices and inflation were low. Intellectuals decried "the silent generation" as passive conformists, but the system seemed to be working.

3   The 1960s: Improvisations on Treatment Variations

> There have in fact been investigations into psychoanalytic technique which show that, even within the same school, therapists differ widely in what they do. They vary not only in the beliefs which they hold, but in innumerable lesser ways ... in how often the patient is seen, in whether he lies on a couch or sits up, in the timing of interpretations, and in the degree of activity of the therapist.
>
> Anthony Storr

A GUIDE TO THE UNITED STATES OF THE 1960s

Population: 179,323,175

Average salary: $4,816 per year

        Coal miners: $5,367

        Farm laborers: $1,848

        Federal employees (civilian): $6,073

        Medical/health services workers: $3,414

        Public school teachers: $4,762

Inflation: 1.4 percent

Unemployment: 5.5 percent

Social welfare: $52.3 billion

Births/1,000: 23.7

Marriages/1,000: 8.5

Divorces/1,000: 2.2

Deaths/1,000: 9.5

Average household size: 3.34

Women in labor force: 32.3 percent

Cost of living: Birth Control: Enovid, the first marketed contraceptive, 55 cents a pill

Clothing: Jay Thorpe clear vinyl women's heels, $29.95; Florsheim calfskin men's oxfords, $29.95

Food: bread, 20 cents a loaf; coffee, 75 cents a pound; eggs, 58 cents a dozen; milk, 26 cents a quart; oranges, 75 cents a dozen; round steak, $1.06 a pound

Housing: 5 room, 2 bath apartment, Park Avenue, New York City, rents for $500/month

Transportation: Volkswagen Bug, $1,695 (1964)

Fun: Drive-in movies, Barbie and Ken dolls, singing in coffeehouses, talkathons, rock 'n roll

Pulitzer Prizes: Biography: Samuel Eliot Morison, *John Paul Jones*

History: Margaret Leech, *In the Days of McKinley*

Nonfiction: Theodore H. White, *The Making of the President 1960*

Sources: Robert Famighetti (ed.), *The World Almanac and Book of Facts, 1997* (Mahwah, NJ: World Almanac Books, 1997), pp. 325, 326, 318; 1962 was the first year Nonfiction was a recognized Pulitzer Prize category; Scott Derks (ed.), *The Value of a Dollar, 1860–1989* (Detroit, MI: Gale Research Inc., 1994), pp. 411, 412; Lois Gordon and Alan Gordon, *The Columbia Chronicles of American Life, 1910–1992* (New York: Columbia University Press, 1995), pp. 476, 484, 512; U.S. Bureau of the Census, *Historical Statistics of the United States, Colonial Times to 1970, Bicentennial Edition, Part I* (Washington, D.C., 1975), pp. 41, 49, 59, 64, 73, 132, 135, 213, 340; Advertisement in *The New York Times*, January 7, 1960, p. L9; January 10, 1960, p. L49.

More respondents commented on events during the 1960s than any other decade. John F. Kennedy, our youngest and only Catholic president, was shot on November 22, 1963. Everyone remembered where they were and what they were doing when they heard the news. Lucas Peabody, a physician, was on his way to his analyst's office. "I ran into his office, hysterical, shouting, 'Kennedy's been killed! Oh, that poor young man!' "

American involvement in Vietnam started out small in 1961 with South Vietnam's signing of a U.S.-Vietnam military and economic aid treaty. Euphemistically characterized as a "limited international conflict," the war escalated and raged throughout the decade. In 1969, there were 550,000 American troops in Vietnam. By the end of our "direct involvement" in 1972, 50,000 Americans had died.

We will begin with a classic analysis and move on to stories that illustrate variations and improvisations on the analytic theme. An anthropologist, Matthew Truax, went into psychoanalysis because of difficulties in interpersonal relationships and ended up training to become a lay analyst. This places him in a unique position from which to comment on what he sees as the assets and liabilities of psychoanalysis both as therapy and as a theoretical frame of reference for the study of human relations.

Matthew Truax

Matthew Truax, Ph.D., is an anthropologist in his late seventies. He lives in New York. "I thank God I experienced the Sixties. I was too old for the draft, but I was never one of the 'Old People' who hassled students for wearing their hair long—and I never wore a suit and tie to class."

In 1964, I was a forty-four-year-old college professor. I went into analysis because I was caught up in a marriage that had been extremely good but was falling to pieces. While it was not all my problem, I realized part of it was.

I was referred to a Dr. Harry Bernard. My first thought on meeting him was, "I wouldn't mind looking like that!" It was two years before I told him and we could start to analyze it. Once we exhumed it and worked it through, it seemed trivial. That was the biggest shock of the transference: "Is that all?"

I trusted HB—I always referred to him that way—instantly. He was about my age, but my father transference was set like a trap and it went off. HB seemed to be what I wish my father had been. My father was a good man. He protected me from being over-protected by my mother, who had lost a child before I was born. My father could have profited greatly from analysis, but given his age and the state of analysis in the 1920s, it could not have happened. He lived with his limitations, as most of us have to.

Toward the end of my analysis, thinking that if you have been cured by the witch doctors you must become a witch doctor, I applied to begin training to become a psychoanalyst and was accepted by the institute where I was a patient. This affected the analysis but we were able to work it out because while HB never said a lot, when he did he was straightforward: "Just because you know all the words, it doesn't mean you don't have to do the work." He was right. Another time he remarked, "You think you're smarter than I am, and you're probably right, but what's that got to do with it?" Answer: Nothing.

I trained for four years and got fairly fed up with some of the analysts because of their intense narrowness of interest. They were sealed up within a pretty tight frame of reference. Most of them could not give any other subject credit for being relevant to analysis. They did not understand culture and they refused to try. During one case conference, I remember an analyst describing his patient: "This man was so neurotic that he sat down to urinate." In the discussion that followed, I could not help noting that sitting to urinate can be cultural. In some parts of Africa, both men and women squat to urinate, except women with loads on their heads who urinate standing up.

The analysts under whom I trained thought Freud was a kind of God. In my view, Freud was a great thinker who was marked by the interests and attitudes of his time and place in history. I get as annoyed with critiques of him by people who obviously have never read him as I do with those who dare not criticize him. There was a tendency among the analysts I knew to say that if you criticized Freud, you had not been adequately analyzed.

When I approached the end of my didactic work, I was given the opportunity to take patients and I declined. The head of the committee asked why. I told him I did not have a drop of the doctor's need to cure or the adequate patience for patients. His response was, "I'm glad we're not going to turn a good anthropologist into a bad analyst."

My analysis was classical Freudian, on the couch five days a week for five years. Some of my academic friends who have been analyzed claimed they were in a "training analysis." I never did that. I was in a therapeutic analysis. I didn't wave it around, but my friends knew, just as they knew of my training. A couple of them suggested I was wasting my money but none thought I was crazy.

About money, I started at $25 an hour and went to $30 toward the end—the going rate at the institute at the time. It was all out of pocket—no insurance—but I did not find it a strain. You can always make money, but not time, and it took a lot of time. There was a lot of driving involved, but I learned to use the time to think—not worry—sometimes about the analysis, but more often about my work. I cannot imagine time better spent. I view my analysis as a liberation. [Matthew's voice breaks.] I find this interview more emotional than I anticipated. I am so grateful. HB allowed me to be me.

Was it worth it? It saved my life. I don't mean I would have died an early death without it, but I would certainly have lived a constricted life. Analysis saved the decent part of my life. I had to get out of that marriage. HB never told me that and he didn't help me do it, but with his help, I gained the information and courage I needed to do it by myself. One of the turning points in my life came when I finally told my mother I was getting divorced and she said, "We were wondering when you would get around to that." Her reply put one more stave in getting rid of my childhood image of her. It is sobering, now, to know what suppressed misperceptions can do to a person.

I know of no better road to self-awareness than psychoanalysis—but I also think it is an absolutely lousy form of psychotherapy. And analysis does not change your character. It changes the way you manage your character and it shows you what lies underneath the pieces of your character. I think I am the same person I always was, but smarter for having been analyzed. One of the benefits of analysis is that I think straighter than I used to. Once I got rid of the defenses, I had the freedom to think.

I believe that many—but not all—people who are analyzed are vastly better off for having been. However, I remember being taught that analysts have to be mentally healthier than their patients. No one is without troubles, but woe betide the patient whose problems are the same as his analyst's. When that happens, that patient is in deep trouble. I am grateful that whatever troubles HB may have had, they didn't keep him from helping me with mine.

I am interested in the study because I believe the psychoanalytic literature is full of ecological and sociological material of which most scholars are unaware. It has never been "mined." Analysts themselves do not see the importance of this material because their focus is so single-mindedly on the psychological aspects of the particular patient in front of them. They have great difficulty seeing beyond their own context as, probably, most people do. Also, having been analyzed, I am interested in what other analysands think they have gained through the process. What has analysis added to their lives?

Matthew criticized the analysts he trained under as being "sealed up within a pretty tight frame of reference." There is a reason: To consider the person in his or her situation forces scholars to cross academic disciplines and practitioners to think about alternative ways of treating psychiatric problems. That process moves psychoanalysis away from its self-definition as a science into an art form—which may be closer to the truth—but pioneers in the field asserted that psychoanalysis was a pure science. Freud and his followers were looking for cures, not social or cultural understanding.

"Once I got rid of the defenses," Matthew says, "I had the freedom to think." This shift in his tendency to intellectualize allowed him to discover his emotional life—one of the benefits of "an absolutely lousy form of psychotherapy."

Now we will hear more about analytic psychotherapy, unmarried couples living together, and a single woman who opted to adopt a child. Grace Renard was in treatment three times between 1966 and 1987. The psychiatrist she saw in her second therapy was influenced by the work of Heinz Kohut.

Heinz Kohut (1913–1981) received his medical degree from the University of Vienna, trained in neurology and psychiatry at the University of Chicago, and graduated from the Chicago Institute of Psychoanalysis where he practiced, taught, and was a training analyst. Kohut wrote about the importance of empathy and introspection in psychoanalysis, but his special interest was the treatment of narcissism, which spurred him to develop, along with others, self psychology. In sharp contrast to Freudians, self psychologists do not consider narcissism pathological; they view it as the backbone upon which an individual's psychological growth depends. For more, see the work of Edith Jacobson, Otto Kernberg, and Margaret Mahler.

Grace Renard

Grace Renard is a fifty-six-year-old photographer who lives in an artists' colony near Santa Fe. "My first therapy ended when I met Dave, this whacko Sixties type, and moved out here to live with him. The second ended when my therapist put a lot of negative spin on my desire, as an unmarried woman, to adopt a child. The third ended when I was ready."

In 1966, I was twenty-three, studying photography at the Guggenheim, and I had a job paying maybe $90 a week. I needed a therapist because I was in a state of high anxiety all the time. Friends suggested I see a Dr. Frankel over on Central Park West—the New York home of Freudian psychoanalysis. I remember walking into his office: very dark, Persian rugs, leather couch. He wasn't Viennese, but German. No beard. [Laughs.]

Dr. Frankel wanted me to come in three days a week at $50 a session. I agreed because I was young and needy and in great psychic pain, but I left his office worrying, "How can I get $150 a week for this?" I realized I couldn't afford it and I looked elsewhere.

Well, everyone is subject to the vagaries of luck the first time they go into therapy. I ended up with a Ph.D. psychologist on the staff at Beth Israel Hospital, Lucio Calabrese, this cute, young Italian guy. Instead of a suit, he wore white shirts with the sleeves rolled way up and a black skinny tie and black slacks. It cost something like $13 an hour and I went once or twice a week.

I come from a normal dysfunctional family. Have you read Alice Miller's *The Drama of the Gifted Child*? My third therapist suggested that book. I didn't know it when I was with Lucio, but that was my psychological agenda. I was an only child and I bent over backwards to satisfy a domineering, narcissistic mother. It perverted my personality and stunted my emotional growth. I didn't have a firm identity.

I'll never forget when I was leaving my first session, I told Lucio, "Now, look, I need you to know that sexual issues are not part of this and I didn't have any trouble with my family growing up." And he laughed! Not at me, but because it was funny. I am funny! Later, he told me that sometimes the things you say walking out the door are the most important.

I was with Lucio for about three years. I'm not sure how much psychological growth I achieved—I was very young emotionally, going in, and everything was very superficial—but I was able to hook into a process that made me feel I was moving toward something and that made me feel better. It might speed things up if a therapist could say, "Look, you have profound anxiety and here are twelve reasons for anxiety we can explore," instead of being completely nondirective all the time, but I wasn't ready for that when I went to Lucio. That came later.

Therapy with Lucio ended when I moved out here to live with Dave, this whacko Sixties type.[1] He wanted to get married and so did I, but I knew our relationship was all wrong for that. I kept having this fantasy that the wedding was scheduled for, let's say, noon on a Sunday, and right before I'd say, "I have to go to the drugstore," and get out and never go back. Dave was seeing a psychologist, so I went along once. I couldn't stand that therapist, so I tried one who was disappointingly faddish. He was sort of a "You-take-all-your-clothes-off-and-sit-in-a-dark-room" type—only you don't really take all your clothes off. I can't remember what it's called. Not Gestalt. Not Jungian. I thought it was bullshit. I'm not a faddish person and I didn't want any part of it, so I said, basically, "Fuck you," and left. Eventually, I left Dave, too, but we're still friends.

Then I shopped around for a psychiatrist and found Dr. Bernheim. By now it was the early Seventies. He was an analyst but this was not a Freudian analysis. We worked face-to-face. He would put questions to me and sometimes he would talk, but not much. When I first met him, I asked him what his goals were for me. Right up front, he told me he didn't have any goals for me; that when I was done, he hoped I wouldn't remember his name or the process. The only important thing was that I find my true self and function well. Another thing he said was that I'd know when I was done.

> *Self psychology* was born out of ego psychology. Ego psychologists trace the development of the individual within the framework of instinctual conflict, remaining true to Freudian drive theory. In the early 1970s, however, Heinz Kohut postulated a new framework centered on the emergence of a complex personal subjectivity within an interpersonal and cultural context, an Eriksonian idea. Kohut explored the phenomenon of selfhood: How does a human being become human? He ultimately broke with traditional drive theory and came to regard his explorations of the self as a distinct and separate psychology.[2]

I wanted a quick, complete cure, but I learned that you can't fix yourself in a superficial way. Working on identity takes a lot of time. I went twice a week over a period of almost ten years. Sometimes I would go for two years and then decide to take some time off, say six months, and Dr. Bernheim would go along with it. Then I'd go back, working at a different level. When I started—1973—it was expensive, $100 a session, but Dr. Bernheim never raised the rate and by the time it ended, I had a six-figure income.

I'd gotten by a lot in life on my personality and I tested Dr. Bernheim in my own individual way, which came into play like this: I was a middle-class person with upper-class aspirations. Smart, wily, and manipulative. It did not serve my needs to grow up and Dr. Bernheim knew it. He called me on my manipulative ways and it hurt. Another thing I'd do was put people on pedestals and have these intense relationships doomed to failure. Dr. Bernheim would have none of that and he told me so. He was a tough cookie and I was a little frightened of him.

I would talk through every session. Ramble, fill the space. I asked if I could tape the sessions and he said it was all right so I taped away and, with a two-hour commute, I had plenty of time to listen to myself—sometimes amusing, sometimes appalling. One of the most important things I did in that therapy was get to know me.

Certain themes come up in treatment. I was smart and capable and there wasn't a lot I couldn't have done—I'd thought about law school, the Peace Corps—and I attracted mentors. Influential people could see that I was a good investment, but having mentors kept me in a child position I didn't like. When Dr. Bernheim suggested I needed to explore this issue more, at first I'd intellectualize. The cognitive work helped me avoid the feelings. Then one day he said the same thing he'd been saying for seven or eight years and it finally connected to my gut so I could change. That happened over the rest of treatment.

As a high-functioning achiever, I'd built up defenses that allowed me to operate that way, but defenses are artificial constructs. I was a superstructure built on very shaky ground and I didn't feel real. To grow up and become real, I had to rebuild myself on a true foundation without artifice and to do that I needed a therapist to re-parent me. Dr. Bernheim became the good parent. The hardest thing was when my defenses and intellectual tricks were wiped away. I felt totally vulnerable. All I could do was cry. The work I had to do then was sometimes more painful than the neurosis, but as we worked, I began to think of myself in a different way.

By the mid-1980s, I was making $100,000 a year, I'd won a few awards, and although I was not married, I wanted to adopt a child. Dr. Bernheim had a mind-set that dictated that the only good family was a two-parent family and he put a lot of negative spin on my desire. The upshot was that from my newly achieved adult stance, I could see him as authoritarian. I realized I was not interested in becoming him or taking on his values or using up three hours of my day thrashing out why I did not agree with his values. Also, I had just turned forty and I wanted to get on with my life.

I have friends who've been in treatment twenty years and I hear them telling the same stories over and over. I didn't want to do that. I'd gotten all the information I needed in therapy. The task was to go out and use it to live a productive life, not to chew it over endlessly. I decided to end treatment. I'd left therapy a couple of times before, but this time when I said I was ending, I said it as an adult. I admit, I did it toward the end of the session. [Laughs.] I told Dr. Bernheim, "I'm not coming back. I don't know if I'm through with therapy forever, but I am done with here." He was, how shall I say? Diffident? Is that the word I want? I think he was surprised, and I don't know that he was pleased, but he accepted my decision. He called me about six months later to see how I was doing and I sent him a card when I adopted my child, but that's the only contact we've had.

Parenting my child brought up some tremendous issues left over from my childhood, so I sought further treatment about 1985. This time I knew more than when I was twenty: I wanted a woman within ten minutes of my studio and I didn't want endless on-the-couch therapy. I chose a psychiatrist on my health insurance plan and I went twice a week for two years. My co-payment was about $25.

Jenny was young and soft-spoken, very different from me. She wouldn't have been right for me before Dr. Bernheim because I was a different person then with different needs, but it was in this therapy that I finally got around to defining and working on goals.

I don't know what her theory base was—maybe humanistic—but she wasn't flaky or New Age.

> *Humanistic psychology* is now regarded as a third force in psychology after psychoanalysis and behavioral psychology. Its concern is with those qualities that differentiate humans from other animals: creativity, humor, psychological growth. Practitioners engage the whole person in the psychotherapeutic endeavor and help clients clarify their values and beliefs. They emphasize the future in contrast to the analytic concentration on the past, or the behavioral concern with the present. Humanistic psychotherapists are concerned with self-actualization (personal growth and development) rather than problem-solving interventions or symptom relief. For more, see the work of Gordon Allport, Abraham Maslow, and Carl Rogers.

I think she worked with each person the way that was best for that person. Flexibly. No cookie cutter format. Jenny and I talked. It was a conversation, back and forth. She'd offer advice I was free to accept or reject and she was supportive while I worked on my issues with my mother. Jenny's the one who recommended *The Drama of the Gifted Child*. She told me she didn't understand how I could even speak to my mother!

One of the major differences between my previous therapies and this one—and this may be an example of how I'd changed—is that I felt no need to manipulate Jenny. I could see her as a real person and I think she saw me that way, too. She was not my friend, but she did friendly things for me—like referring me to her gynecologist. When the two years were up, I knew I was ready to leave but the door was left open. If there were a crisis in my life today, I know I could go back.

Oh—the issue of names. I always called my first therapist "Lucio." He was a good guy—a safety net. Dr. Bernheim was always "Dr. Bernheim." I would call him that today if I saw him. He called me "Miss Renard" until the end of treatment when I'd grown up and he started calling me "Grace." Dr. Bernheim was a good and honorable man—not warm, but kind. And Jenny was always "Jenny." It was a relationship of equals.

So that's the story of my therapies and I think it's unique. Three different therapists with three different methods that were what I needed at three different periods in my life.

In Chapter 2, Bob Gordon talked about the impostor syndrome, the construction of a false self behind which the vulnerable true self hides. Grace didn't feel like an impostor; she didn't feel real. Her work was on identity: Who am I? Am I the parentified child of a narcissistic mother, the girlfriend of a whacko boyfriend, a successful artist who hides behind her mentors—or all these people? Grace's insight of tearing down a faulty superstructure and building on a new foundation is apt. Identity formation requires just that and it is every bit as difficult as Grace says—for the patient and for the therapist.

Our next artist had a problem with a part of himself he did not want. Again, he speaks of being in analysis when, in fact, the work was analytically-oriented psychotherapy, first with an analyst in training and later with a psychologist who had studied object relations.

Sam Temple

Sam Temple, a fifty-seven-year-old artist, is Grace Renard's neighbor. He was in therapy twice, from 1964 to 1966 and from 1972 to 1979. Sam's work has been exhibited in the Museum of Modern Art and the Georges Pompidou Museum. "When I was twenty-two, I was living in a slum cleaning bathrooms and loading a truck for the Salvation Army. As an artist, I felt I needed to know that side of life—the morbid world of North Beach and S&M magazines."

The first time I was in analysis was from 1964 to 1966 when I was a grad student in San Francisco. I was amazingly lonely living in a dollar-a-day hotel, but as an artist I felt I needed to know that side of life. It was a reflection of my own dark, weird world and I would paint it.

I was dreamy and predisposed to the arts from the beginning. To my mother, I was a miracle and whatever I wanted, she would happily provide. My father was a lawyer. Pragmatic. He never supported my artistic bent. I remember his comment at my first important one-man show: "That's good, but keep up your teaching certificate, just in case." I guess he came to terms with my success, but always in a niggling sort of way.

I went into analysis because of something that happened toward the end of college. I'd sublet an apartment from a six-foot-tall girl. Some of her clothes were around and I started putting them on. Her panties, her tights. I felt flushed and sexually aroused and it worried the hell out of me. Finally, I told a friend what was happening and he said, "Wow! You better see a doctor!"

I called one of the analytic institutes and just by the luck of the dice, I found Dr. Tanaka. She was a psychiatrist in analytic training, about my age. Small and bright. Japanese. I found her enormously appealing, very sexually stirring. The way she worked with me was she paid close attention to me. She watched me like a hawk, which increased my sense of self-reflection. I began to concentrate on myself the way she did. It was very organizing.

Dr. Tanaka and I met three or four days a week, face-to-face, and it cost almost nothing. Maybe $10? The institute had a sliding scale fee structure. Dr. Tanaka concentrated on my mind, my dreams, and my fantasies. "Uh-huh, uh-huh," she would say, and for a long time, she didn't interrupt me. Then she began to introduce ideas gently, with a measure of care. I saw myself as this all-American male who enjoyed sex with women but secretly liked to put on their underwear. It caused me great shame and I wanted to stop because it wasn't "normal," but I couldn't. It was a compulsion.

Dr. Tanaka was easy on me, unlike my father who was rather rigid in a Roman Catholic way. She didn't just pull up with a truck and dump terms like "fetish" or "transvestite" on me. She knew I was already feeling pretty abnormal. She wanted to hear my fantasies when I'd put on the panties and tights and I could tell her because she never looked away and she didn't seem horrified. Having someone who could stand to listen to stuff I didn't want to hear myself say helped me, if that makes any sense, but I kept on cross-dressing. I became desperate for the fetish to go away.

In the summer of 1966, I heard about a mind-altering drug, supposedly a miracle drug. A friend of mine helped me get it from a lab in Switzerland. I was probably one of the first people in California to try LSD. It vaporized my morbid fantasy world and the fetish disappeared. I don't think it was just the acid—I think it was a combination of LSD and therapy—but when the fetish was gone, my work changed from dark and foreboding to bright and hopeful. My friends said, "Wow! What happened to you?"

I told Dr. Tanaka what I'd done and that the fetish was gone and I didn't need further treatment. I was concerned that she might feel rejected, but she didn't. She wanted to convene a group of M.D.'s to talk with me about my experience and if I hadn't been going off to Europe for a year, I'd have done it.

When I was in analysis, all my friends were artists and most of them were in analysis. It wasn't seen negatively and I wasn't ashamed of it. The only thing I was ashamed of was the reason I was going. I didn't tell, and I don't tell, people about that. Yet here I am telling you—a total stranger.

This is what I think about the analytic relationship: It's a professional relationship within which there's a lot of caring. Dr. Tanaka was not my friend, but I know she cared about me. I didn't keep in touch and I haven't really missed her, but I've often wondered how she is, what she's doing. I wanted analysis to be a process I put myself through and when it was over, I could put it away.

In 1972, I was thirty and I'd gotten into a relationship with a woman, a TV producer. We were living together and things were great except we fought terribly. I found myself getting tremendously angry and feeling jaded about life. This time, I decided to interview possible analysts. The first was Jungian. I found her prone to pat thinking: "We will push everything through this sieve." The next person on the list was Dr. Winston. He was a psychologist probably eight or ten years older than I was. Right away, his aesthetic bothered me—his clothes—and I thought since he was a psychologist he might be marginal compared to a psychiatrist, but somehow I didn't bother to interview anyone else. I stayed with him seven years, three days a week. He cut me some slack in the beginning, charging me $40 or $50 a session. The last year of treatment, I'd gotten big as an artist and he took some of my art in payment.

I tested him mightily. "I can't stand what you're wearing," I'd tell him.

"Really?" he'd respond. "I kind of like it."

"I don't like your office, either. And you're only a Ph.D. How do I know you can help me?" He never got angry. I always thought he had my best interests at heart and I began to like him. After three or four years, I recommended him to my brother and his girlfriend and they started seeing him, too.

Dr. Winston was different from Dr. Tanaka. She concentrated on me and my mind, whereas he was into object relations. He asked me to tell him about my family and when I sketched it out, he said, "I see you did not mention your father." Treatment with him focused more on my connections to other people than it did just on me. My original complaint— fighting with the TV producer—took care of itself.

Object relations is a substantial departure from Freudian theory. Freud talked about the need to satisfy or inhibit instinctual drives, viewing people as primarily pleasure-seeking. Object relations theorists believe that people do not blindly seek drive satisfaction, but are programmed to seek appropriate objects (other people) and must learn to relate to their objects maturely. Melanie Klein's work bridged Freudian theory and object relations theory. For more, see Introduction to the Work of Melanie Klein by Hanna Segal, and Psychoanalytic Studies of the Personality by W. R. D. Fairbairn.

The way I see analysis and psychotherapy is that in the first year or two you do the official work. You are uniquely troubled and the doctor is really interested. It's like a movie. Then you do the hard work. You look at what you're really afraid of. What you talk about then is much scarier, because by then you're out of official explanations for yourself. I found it terribly hard. I'd tell Dr. Winston, "I'm afraid I'm gonna lose my marbles here," and he would tell me that I had strength and he was there to help me. He wouldn't let me lose it.

Dr. Winston had an inventive way of working with me. Sometimes we'd do sessions outdoors, sitting on the dock at his beach place. He came to several of my shows and once he gave me a gift. My friends said he shouldn't have done that, but it was between Dr. Winston and me and I think we kinda knew what we were doing. He was showing me he would do things for me that my father wouldn't. Toward the end of treatment, he suggested, "How about we stand up and I give you a hug?" We did and it proved very interesting. I had confused "sensual" and "sexual." Realizing that, I could then tease out how it was possible to have affection without it becoming sexual.

When we decided it was time to end, it took longer than with Dr. Tanaka. We did a retrospective of the analysis over the course of a year and it became clear that we hadn't left anything out. Then we said good-bye. I haven't kept in touch with Dr. Winston, although I think of him from time to time. Analysis, I think, should be a professional relationship built on the understanding that I am going to give you money to listen to me, about $50,000 in my case. There is a lot of human caring, but don't make it into pals. Dr. Winston and Dr. Tanaka were doctors whom I paid for the experience.

Years ago at night, I would be out on the street and I'd see a bus go by. There'd be maybe two or three men on it, each sitting alone, and I'd think, "My God, is that what's in store for me? In thirty years will I be like them?"

My parents divorced after all of us left home. They'd never been happy, although they were married for thirty-five years. I always wanted a great relationship and a life that made normative sense. Analysis gave me what I needed to attain those goals. My wife is a great life partner. As to normative sense, well, artists have to delve deep to create. When I'm painting, I go into a dream, but I'm able to tell myself when it's time to come up for air. I'm not one of the men on the bus.

Sam believes that the combination of LSD and his intensive work with Dr. Tanaka produced the result he desired. Perhaps, but sequence is not necessarily causation. During the 1960s, many people, including Harvard's Dr. Timothy Leary, experimented with LSD. The vulnerable, some of whom were adolescents, could be permanently damaged by a "bad trip." Further, there is no evidence that LSD or other hallucinogens or street drugs are, in any sense, "cures." Indeed, even prescription medications should be used only as necessary and with careful supervision.

Now we will hear from a man who also wanted to rid himself of a fetish. His classical Freudian analysis failed.

Peter Johnson

Peter Johnson is a sixty-six-year-old attorney. "The Sixties—well, that's when I went to Wall Street and that's why I went to the analyst. What I'm going to tell you—well, it's like the Dick Morris thing. I didn't want to lose my job."

In 1961, I was a young lawyer, married, father of two little children. My wife [Ellen] was sexually inhibited. Missionary position only and lights out. I had developed a fetish as a child, but I never did anything about it until the time I'm talking about when I started asking young ladies if I could give them enemas. I made the mistake of going to one of Ellen's ladyfriends, she told Ellen, and Ellen blew up. She told me I had to go to a psychiatrist right then, so I went to a fellow downtown, Dr. Chassin. His reaction was, "What's the big deal? What's everybody so steamed up about?" He explained that the anus is a sexually sensitive area and that some people like to have enemas and even anal intercourse.

I told him I'd been thinking about hiring a prostitute and giving her an enema, but I was concerned about what would happen to me professionally if anyone found out. Dr. Chassin said just to keep it down and be careful. I went to him three or four months, and basically he said there was nothing wrong with me. Before that, I felt like a nut case, really sick. He made me feel less like a pervert. I told myself, "I will not do this anymore. I will keep this a private fantasy." But I did it again, it got back to Ellen again, and she insisted I go to a different psychiatrist. I think she found him by way of our family doctor. And she came with me to the first appointment.

Emile Zolan was famous. He was a psychoanalyst who had studied with Freud and I think he was at least thirty years older than I was. Ellen told him what was going on. Dr. Zolan told me I'd lose my job if I kept it up. He said a classical Freudian analysis would cure me. He raved about it. Said it was the only way to go; other forms of treatment were useless. He said it would be five to six years of work, three days a week on the couch, and he charged $100 an hour! The whole thing, including Dr. Chassin, must have run me $40,000. It almost bankrupted me.

I told him I was embarrassed having to go to a shrink and I felt like a nut case. Dr. Zolan told me analysis was nothing to be ashamed of and that analytic patients were not nut cases. That made me feel better, but I still kept my analysis a secret. I made all my appointments for 6:00 A.M., and I never claimed a dime on my insurance. Only Dr. Zolan and Ellen knew. Oh—and his secretary knew—but we'll get to that later.

During the consultation, Dr. Zolan asked my wife how many times a week we had intercourse. I thought she'd pass out. He didn't know he was talking to Miss Prude. Then he asked where we had sex. Neither of us understood what he meant, so he explained he wanted to know if we ever had sex on the table or outdoors and he asked Ellen if she ever assumed the "doggie position."

On the way home, Ellen said she thought he was disgusting, but since I was the one who'd be going—not she—I had to start right away or she'd leave. So there were three reasons I went: I didn't want to lose Ellen, I didn't want to lose my job, and I wanted to get rid of the obsession. I reasoned that if I could just get rid of it—the fantasy or fetish or obsession, whatever you want to call it—I wouldn't have to worry about losing my wife or my job.

I was a reluctant patient, though. Sometimes I'd lie there and not say a word and Dr. Zolan wouldn't either. In three years, he only made half a dozen interpretations and one time, he fell asleep. I heard him snoring! I woke him up, and he told me he wouldn't charge me for that hour.

The way the sessions went was I would come into the office and he would nod to me. I'd lie down on the couch and tell him my dreams—if I'd had any. Sometimes I'd think, "What am I going to say today?" or "This is a waste of time." When I'd ask him questions, he'd almost never respond. I wonder if he had some reason not to answer me? I never challenged him, though. He was the guru. The big expert. I just kept going through the motions.

Today, I think the Freudian approach was the wrong way to go at my problem, but I'm not sure what would have been the right way. I can't say I didn't get anything out of it, though. One session in ten, I'd unload something important and get some understanding, but I never got rid of the fetish. Still, I got my behavior under control and that probably saved my career.

My upbringing was very Catholic. No sex outside marriage—or inside if you could judge by my parents. I don't think they had an active sex life. I certainly haven't, although I would have liked to. Maybe that's one reason I developed the fetish.

If I could talk to Dr. Zolan now, I'd ask him a lot of questions, like where do blue collar people go if they need therapy? They can't afford $100 an hour. Another thing: What was he thinking all those hours when I said nothing and he said nothing? Was it significant to him that I was clamming up?

And termination. I've thought about that for years. When my behavior was under control—which it was although I still wanted to give out enemas—I didn't think I needed to come back and I told him so. That was after about three years. Well, Dr. Zolan bounced up out of his chair and shook my hand. "Well," he said, "that's great!" And that was good-bye. I got the definite impression he was glad to see me go. That he had a feeling of relief. I think he was looking forward to hearing some fresh new patient's interesting new problem.

My mother died a few years ago and a memory came back. I never told this to Dr. Zolan because I'd forgotten it, but when I was about six, I developed a high fever and my mother called the doctor. Back then they made house calls. Dr. O'Brien was a big Irish guy and he wanted to take my temperature with a rectal thermometer. I yelled and kicked and tried to get away, but he held me down. Mother put the thermometer in.

About two weeks after termination, Dr. Zolan died. He'd had cancer but I hadn't known that. Anyway, I got his bill and there were some mistakes, so I went to see his secretary—Nancy—and she asked me if I'd gotten my problem taken care of. I was somewhat taken aback, but I told her, "Yes and no." She said the fetish was still there because it was sexually exciting and that to get rid of it, I needed "to slay the ghost"—that if I'd hired a prostitute and given her an enema, I would have seen it wasn't such a big deal and the obsession would have been over.

That makes me think about something else I'd always wanted to do: Walk on a glacier. On vacation one time, I did, and I thought, "This isn't much different from sliding around Madison Avenue in January." My curiosity was satisfied and I didn't want to do it again. Maybe it would have been the same if I'd hired a prostitute. I still wonder how Nancy knew all about it, though. Did she read Dr. Zolan's notes? Is that ethical? What happens to a former patient's records?

Today, I'm turned off by psychoanalysis. I don't feel I was damaged and there was some benefit in the shock value of realizing I really could not, as an attorney representing Fortune 500 companies, keep going around asking young ladies if I could give them an enema, but I was not cured. My behavior got under control but the fantasy never left. Today, I'm pissed off about all the money I spent and I want to damn the whole process. [Peter stops. He looks abashed.] Dr. Zolan's dead and here I am knocking his process.

This case demonstrates that analysis is not "the only way to go," particularly when dealing with a fetish. Dr. Zolan promised more than analysis could deliver. An orthodox Freudian who had studied with the master, he believed what he told his patient: that other forms of treatment were useless. We have since learned that while other treatments do not guarantee success, they can be useful.

Other respondents' analysts have prompted them when they fell silent, but Dr. Zolan was ill, fell asleep in session, and perhaps practiced longer than he should have. Some analysts and therapists die, never having divulged that they are ill, while they have patients in treatment. This leaves patients with questions that can never be answered.

Termination is a sensitive issue. Patients are frequently torn, wanting to stop without feeling unwanted. It is generally advisable to explore a patient's desire to stop and set a date far enough in the future to allow sufficient time to discuss the issue. Perhaps Dr. Zolan's illness played into his behavior. We will never know and neither will Peter.

The other issue is confidentiality. Physicians are bound by the Hippocratic Oath, which dictates that "What I may see or hear in the course of the treatment or even outside of the treatment in regard to the life of men, which on no account one may spread abroad, I will keep to myself holding such things shameful to be spoken about."[3] Other disciplines have similar codes. But confidentiality is not assured. Secretaries who type therapists' notes and have access to files are not bound by these codes, and the use of computers and electronic mail have added a new dimension of risk to privacy.

Paul S. Appelbaum, M.D., writes that confidentiality has always been considered essential for successful psychotherapy and is theoretically protected by the ethical codes of all the mental health professions, but this principle is riddled with exceptions. Courts may demand confidential information needed for judicial proceedings. Employers, insurance companies, and HMOs are not bound by the ethical standards of the helping professions and there are inadequate restrictions on what they can do with the information they are given.[4] To avoid intrusive review procedures, some patients don't use their insurance and pay out of pocket. Others forgo needed care.

Some therapists warn patients that they may have to divulge sensitive information, an act of honesty that nonetheless puts their patients in a bind—how much can they then disclose? Other therapists keep minimal notes and some read them to their patients. Even this well-intentioned move raises the spectre of big brother watching.

The next case is that of a teenager who entered a residential treatment center because she wanted to stop using heroin and other street drugs. She ended up falling prey to the director.

Kristin Palmer

Kristin Palmer is a forty-seven-year-old veterinarian who lives on a small farm near Eagle Pass, Texas, with her husband, several dogs, cats, and a few sheep. "Dr. Firestone, the head of the center, took us to Woodstock and then to the march on Washington to protest Vietnam."

When I was a kid, I tried to be perfect. Good grades, good behavior. But in 1968, when I was sixteen, my parents weren't getting along and there was a lot of tension in the house. I got into drugs—pot, speed, LSD, heroin—was sleeping around, and I started running away from home. I'd go to an apartment in the city and stay a couple of weeks with some older people who were drug dealers. Then I'd go back home for a while. My parents took me to a psychiatric institute where I met with a psychiatrist. He told my parents living at home was too stressful for me and recommended residential treatment. I found that idea very scary and ran away again, but this time the police came and arrested the people I was staying with and I had to go to court.

That experience made me think. While I was never an addict, I'd already overdosed on heroin a couple of times. If it were now—not 1968— I'd have AIDS. I realized I had to get my life together or I would die, so I asked my parents to take me to the residential treatment center. It was $600 a month and my parents were probably concerned about how they'd pay for it, but they never told me that. Fortunately, my father's medical insurance covered everything but food.

The "center" was just a big old house in the country where the psychiatrist, Dr. Firestone, lived with his family. His sister's yard backed up on his. He was probably thirty years older than I was, and he was in charge of the dozen or so teenagers living there. A few were wealthy, with last names you'd recognize as manufacturers of household products, but the rest were middle-class kids like me. A couple of the boys were hyperactive, but what most of us had in common was drug use, truancy, and running away from home.

It was a very unstructured environment. The only requirement was that everyone had to sit down together for dinner at six. Therapy was individual sessions with Dr. Firestone three times a week and there was group treatment, too, but none of the meetings were compulsory. We were free to come and go as we pleased, and I'm sure I missed some sessions. Early on, I'd go out and do drugs and then I was vastly ashamed. I don't think I told Dr. Firestone, but he probably knew.

Individual therapy was just talking to Dr. Firestone for fifty minutes. You could talk about anything. He didn't direct the conversation or pick up on themes, but he took notes for a book he said he was going to write. He told us we'd each have a chapter. I don't know if he ever wrote it. The therapy had no particular slant and I guess I wanted to give it one, so I started reading his books on Freud. I began to talk about my parents and my dreams. Still, I can't say this was really psychotherapy.

What I got out of residential treatment is this: I was removed from my home and I stopped doing drugs. In other words, I stopped acting out in what was essentially a holding environment. In that way, my life was profoundly changed for the better, but with very little oversight it became the most promiscuous time of my life. I was with two of the male residents as well as a guy who had graduated but came back. Another guy wanted to take photos of me, naked and having sex, but I chickened out, thank goodness.

Group treatment was once a week and the inpatient group of teenagers I belonged to could be confrontational. I cried when a girl I considered a friend called me a whore because I was promiscuous. There was another group for the older outpatients who didn't live at the center. They were not permitted to attend the teenage group, but we were encouraged to attend their group and Dr. Firestone had me take notes for that group. That made me feel important and in retrospect, I think he intended to make me feel special. I looked up to him and trusted him.

The first summer I was there, we went abroad. I don't know how he got the money, but twelve adolescents and Dr. Firestone and his family trailed all over Europe for a month. At the time, I wasn't taking tranquilizers. The idea was for me to learn to deal with life without ingesting chemicals—no pills, no needles—so I didn't get as much out of the experience as I might have if I hadn't been depressed, anxious, and fearful in strange places.

For all my drug and sex experience, I was, in many ways, this very naive kid, easily led and with little sense of self. In Yugoslavia, we came upon some total strangers—they were bikers—who wanted to take me up into the mountains. Dr. Firestone had started treating me more like an adult and less like the kid I was, and he let me go. I almost got raped. After that was the first time I had sex with him. It was during my individual therapy session on a boat going from Amsterdam to Bergen.

He just got up and locked the door. The sex didn't happen every day, maybe ten times, but he threatened me: "This would kill my wife, and I'd kill anyone who told her about it." Our sexual relationship was completely split off—we never discussed it in therapy or out of therapy.

I graduated from high school and left the center around 1971 when I went to college, but I continued to see Dr. Firestone maybe once a month for another year or so. My parents paid the $35 or $40 it cost, probably out of guilt, but they also wanted me to get well. When I transferred to a college out of state, treatment ended. We never had a wrap-up session. I just faded out.

For the next ten years, I was plagued by terrible anxiety. I had tremendous self-esteem problems and thought the only way I'd ever be somebody was by making perfect grades. I tried to memorize every detail in class—I started out as a math major—but my anxiety interfered with my ability to concentrate and recall. I would obsess, add a column of figures ten times. I got so stressed out it's a wonder I made it, but I graduated with honors, got married, and went to graduate school. The anxiety and depression didn't let up, though. I still felt little self-worth and decided to go to veterinary college, thinking that if I were a vet, I'd finally be somebody. Also, I think I identify with sick animals.

By 1986, my marriage was in trouble, mainly because of my chronic anxiety. My husband supported my desire to go for treatment and, since we didn't have insurance, we paid the $75 a session out of pocket. I certainly had symptoms of anxiety and depression, but I think the real reason I went was to understand myself, what happened with Dr. Firestone, and how—after twenty years—it was affecting me and my marriage.

I had never told anyone—not my husband, not my parents—what happened with Dr. Firestone, but I told my new therapist and she wanted me to report it. Talking to Dr. Martin about what happened opened up a lot of memories and associated feelings. As a teenager in need of help, I was taken advantage of by my psychiatrist. I have wondered if he went on and did it to others but by the time I saw her, he would have been in his seventies—or dead—and I decided not to report him. I was worried about how it would affect his family. I've always taken too much responsibility for others' feelings, and the gravity of what he did really didn't make much of an impact on me until recently. I guess that's because until now I didn't have enough self-esteem to believe that others should not be allowed to hurt me. I didn't feel that I had a right to get angry.

In 1988, I started taking Prozac. It's been tremendously helpful. I think there is a biological component to my anxiety and depression. I have a lot of relatives who are similarly cursed. On Prozac, my anxiety level finally diminished and my personality emerged. Without being occupied with anxiety all the time, I was able to do some cognitive work with Dr. Martin. I became able to feel, and I came to understand and accept my feelings.

I haven't been in treatment for years, but I remember Dr. Martin fondly. I've written her a few times to let her know how I'm doing. She was a good listener, very accepting, and I didn't worry about what she thought of me the way I did with my husband and family and friends. Your study interests me because I want to be helpful to others, tell my story, and give my experience more significance than a tawdry case of sex abuse. But part of me wants someone to recognize Dr. Firestone.

This case makes us cringe. Dr. Firestone violated Kristin, but he also violated the Hippocratic Oath: "Whatever houses I may visit, I will come for the benefit of the sick, remaining free of all intentional injustice, of all mischief and in particular of sexual relations with both female and male persons, be they free or slaves."[5] He also broke the law: "A male or female is guilty of rape in the third degree, a Class E felony, where . . . being 21 years old or more, he or she engages in sexual intercourse with another person, to whom the actor is not married, who is less than 17 years old."[6] And he violated his profession's code of ethics. Psychotherapists of every discipline are bound by a code that prohibits sexual relations with their patients.

Returning to the issue of sexual identity, our next teenager feared she might be gay. She was seen by psychiatrists at a clinic for eight months, going once a week, face to face.

Josie Schiller

Josie Schiller is a legislative aide who lives on Capitol Hill. She is fifty-three. "I remember the riot in Watts and I remember when Betty Friedan's book came out. I know there were The Beatles when I was in therapy—1963—but in my immigrant status, I was not the 'typical American teenager.'"

I'm in the middle of five children with two brothers and two sisters. For the first twelve years of my life, we lived in Hungary. My father was a furrier and Mom was a housewife. It was an ideal situation with lots of cousins, aunts, and uncles.

I went into therapy when I was seventeen because of a homoerotic experience which occurred when I was ten. I "played doctor" with another girl, and while I knew what we did wasn't exactly kosher, it didn't really bother me until a homosexual murder took place in our town. Everyone started talking about the strange and terrible things homosexuals did. I became determined I would never do anything like that again. Moreover, I wouldn't even think about it.

We moved to Venezuela in 1958. Many Jews had fled to South America to escape the Nazis and some of our family was there. Caracas was exotic and exciting, but I didn't speak Spanish and, a kid from a Jewish family of modest means, I somehow ended up in a Catholic school. While we were not observant, we were Jews and I was confused by all the crosses. I'd never seen one before. I learned Spanish, but I didn't make friends as easily as I had in Hungary. Also, I was just beginning to mature physically and found myself intimidated yet flattered by the catcalls and whistles young women were subject to while walking anywhere in the city.

A year and a half later, we moved to Miami, right in the middle of the school year. I didn't speak English and my Spanish had a heavy Hungarian accent. I'd just turned fourteen and I was getting pimples. My mother wouldn't allow me to shave my legs or armpits and I was forbidden to wear makeup. [Laughs.] I had not only international angst but teenage angst as well. I was an outsider.

While I was learning English, I was sent to a special school to catch up on American history. That's where I met Lisa. She was from South America, so she spoke Spanish. She was Jewish, too, very bright, and an outsider like me. We became fast friends. I learned that Lisa had been going to a therapist since first grade. The concept of psychotherapy was totally unfamiliar to me, but Lisa filled me in.

Then it was ninth grade and I fell in love with the most popular boy in high school. I was still constantly observing myself and it confused me that if I was homosexual, why was I falling in love with Tony? He already had a girlfriend, but I was sure we would be married one day. My delusion went on nearly two years. I'd follow him around and one time he looked at me. I quickly looked away. I obsessed about that for days, thinking he wanted a clandestine meeting and I'd blown it, so I put a note under his car's windshield wiper: "I'm sorry. Josie."

Later that week when there was no one around, I asked him if he'd gotten the note. He hesitated, probably wondering what the hell I was talking about. That made me think he was denying "our relationship." I turned on my heel and walked away only to go into an emotional tailspin. My homosexual fears overwhelmed me. I managed to go to school but I couldn't sleep, my hands shook, and I began to think about suicide. I'd never told Lisa about Tony and certainly not about Hungary, but she could see I needed help and she gave me the phone number of the clinic where she was a patient. I made an appointment for that Friday after school.

Mr. Luben, the intake worker, was tall and soft-spoken. He asked why I came and I told him I feared I was a homosexual. It was the first time I'd said the word out loud and I began to cry uncontrollably. I told him about my fantasy romance and what happened in Hungary. He asked if I'd considered suicide. When I said yes, he told me he'd arrange for me to see a psychiatrist that Monday. Since I was only seventeen, I would be seen in the child clinic by a Dr. Gold. Mr. Luben told me not to talk to anyone about what I'd told him and he gave me his phone number and told me to call if I had questions between then and Monday. Well, I couldn't lie to my parents, so I told them I was going to the clinic where Lisa went because I was unhappy. They disapproved intensely. No daughter of theirs was crazy. They didn't want me to go and they would not pay for it.

Monday came and I went to see Dr. Gold. I told him my parents wouldn't give me any money and he told me it was important for me to pay something, but that the clinic had a sliding scale fee. I would be charged $5 a session. $20 a month was a fortune, but I was determined to do it, so I got a part-time job at a pastry shop after school.

Sessions with Dr. Gold were face to face and went something like this: I'd come in and go on and on, unloading. Dr. Gold would smile and be receptive and I'd feel totally understood. Toward the end of the hour, he would signal me, "We have ten more minutes." That gave me time to wind down. He never cut me off abruptly.

Why was he so good for me? Well, he was an artist. He was very, very good at what he did. [Josie begins to cry.] When I told him what happened in Hungary, he said, "It's all in the realm of experience." That one sentence took all the guilt away. All the weight and shame of seven years was gone when I could think of it that way.

Shortly after that, I fell in love with a boy at the pastry shop. He was an Orthodox Jew and while I was Jewish, I was not Orthodox, so he couldn't date me, but he seemed to be flirting with me. I checked it out with Dr. Gold and he smiled. "A woman knows these things," he said. Statements like that confirmed my identity as a desirable woman.

When we took vocational aptitude tests at school, my scores scattered. The guidance counselor was at a loss, not knowing how to direct me. "This means I'm not good at anything," I told Dr. Gold. "Or," he said, "You are good at everything." He had a way, using very few words, of showing me there are always two sides—at least—to everything.

After only three months, I turned eighteen and Dr. Gold had to transfer me to the adult clinic. I told him how much he meant to me—how crazy I was about him. "There is a certain simpatico between us," he agreed. He always treated me as desirable but he never did anything even slightly out of the way. I think he was sensitive, but he was also matter-of-fact. I was transferred to the adult clinic where I saw an intern until I graduated from high school. I don't remember much about the intern—not even his name—but of course I didn't like him. I couldn't accept a replacement.

I think of Dr. Gold with love to this day. I wanted either to be like him or marry someone like him. My husband's a psychologist. I have tremendous respect for the profession and what it takes to be a good therapist. I believe it's as much an art as a science.

Another thing I remember from the day I entered therapy is that I didn't want to be assigned a woman or a man shorter than I was. Now I associate that with the lack of respect I used to have for myself as a female. My mother reinforced my perception that women weren't as able as men, but she was a product of her time. "Ask your father," she'd always say. "He's so much smarter than I am." Later in life I learned that my mother's self-effacement belied a strong will and a self-respect my father honored. When I understood power structures better, I was ready to accept that as a woman, I could be equal to a man.

My whole identity was at stake when I went to Dr. Gold. The issue was not just fear of homosexuality but my fear that as a woman, I was doomed to be second to men. That's why I didn't want a woman therapist or a man shorter than I was.

Therapy saved my life when I was a teenager. It made me feel worthy and likable and taught me to interpret my life in a way that was not self-destructive. It's a first-rate educational process with, hopefully, an excellent professor who gives his undivided attention to a class of one.

Carl Jung died in 1961, but like Freud, he had established a school of psychology and had ardent disciples. While it has never been a huge force in the United States, the Jungian movement took off during the 1960s.

Carl Gustav Jung (1875–1961), a Swiss psychiatrist, received his medical degree at Zurich in 1902. Freud was interested in Jung's word association research, probably because he thought it might support his own. Jung joined Freud's inner circle and became the first president of the International Psychoanalytic Society in 1911. Theoretical differences concerning the importance of the sexual drive, the contents of the unconscious, and the significance of current life situations led to the demise of their relationship in 1914 when Jung left Freud and founded his own school of thought, Analytical Psychology.

A minister's son, Jung was interested in myths, dreams, and religion. He theorized that the unconscious has two layers: the personal, an individual's repressed or forgotten experiences, and the collective, a structure common to all human beings. The latter is composed of archetypes—symbols from humanity's collective past—transmitted from one generation to the next in the same manner as physical traits. Jung was surprised to find that one culture's symbols are strikingly similar to another's; crosses, circles, alphas, and omegas, for example, are cross-cultural shorthand. Jung believed every person's lifelong task was to seek harmony between the conscious and unconscious in order to achieve wholeness and peace. Therapy could help people with that task—note that Jung never said "cure." For more, see June Singer's *Boundaries of the Soul.*

April Silver

April Silver is fifty-one. She manages an art supply store in Berkeley, California. "In 1968, the Vietnam War was raging, anti-war protesters were marching, and hippies were out with their flowers. Social upheaval was in full swing."

When I was a twenty-year-old college student, I started experiencing terrific anxiety and I blacked out. When I woke up, I thought, "This is it. Get over to the counseling center and get some help." I took the first available therapist, a clinical social worker.

Clinical social workers have master's or doctoral degrees in social work; at least two years of clinical social work practice; and, in states that require licensure or registration, the appropriate certification. They practice with individuals, families, or groups whose functioning is threatened by social and psychological stress or health impairment.

Miss Allen was quite a bit older than I was then and she had studied Jungian psychology. We began working twice a week, trying to get to the source of my anxiety. Treatment at the college psychological center was free to students.

I didn't know what to do with my hands during sessions, so I started bringing in clay and molding it as I talked. Sometimes I created grotesque figures and Miss Allen would ask me who they reminded me of. I started having vivid dreams and drawing pictures of the people in them: a mean old hermit and a sprightly little girl. Miss Allen viewed my drawing and painting as important additions to the therapy. I would tell her stories about the people in the drawings. The hermit lived in a hut and threatened to shoot anyone who came near. The little girl wanted to approach him but was afraid. I learned that these were archetypal images. Each was an aspect of me horribly at odds with the other.

Jung taught that every problem has an archetypal core and human beings can achieve transformation by trying to find the sources of their problems in archetypes. Conflicting archetypal energies were the source of my anxiety. The clay figures, my drawings, and the study of my dreams all got into the mix of what I was trying to communicate and understand. I also began a journal. Miss Allen helped me connect my fantasies to fairytales and legends, looking for the archetypes. I saw her once a week until I graduated, and when I moved home, we corresponded. I think she went out of her way to keep in touch with me. She cared about my well-being and was interested in me.

One of the strengths of Jungian work is that it helps you define the forces of the human psyche, understand the figures embodying archetypal energy, and conceptualize the energies at play. What to do about what's troubling you is another matter. I believe other clinical approaches might be better for certain problems, but Jungian work is a good place to start.

Two years after I graduated—1972—I was teaching, but I found myself becoming anxious again. I decided to look for another Jungian analyst and found a Dr. Rogers through friends. She was quite a bit older than I was. Honest, bright. I went to her once a week for several years, and it cost something like $65 a session. My insurance covered most of it. Dr. Rogers helped me deal with my anger toward the mean old man— who was my father—and she did it in the here and now. She offered me an umbrella and I beat the hell out of a beanbag chair with it. Let me tell you, that exorcised my demons. My anger was gone. That's a here and now technique Dr. Rogers incorporated into her Jungian approach, and for me, it worked. I didn't get rid of all my problems with anxiety in that treatment, but the work was a good sequel to what I'd had before. I remember Dr. Rogers as one of the best therapists I saw.

My Jungian therapists loaded me down with literature, everything from Jung to Horney to Kohut. You learn a lot, analyzing and identifying, but it can become an intellectual pursuit. That's part of my criticism of pure Jungian work. If you remain on the intellectual level, it's difficult to get your problems worked through and change your destructive behavior.

I'd like to talk about some of Jung's concepts and how they relate to my particular situation. Jung believed that in addition to the personal unconscious, all living things share a collective unconscious which is passed down from one generation to the next. You can think of humanity as a river. We form the river at the same time that we are separate parts of the river which is us. See how it's circular? We have to accept our interdependence, just as we have to accept the different parts of ourselves. Understanding that the parts of me and the rest of the universe were all part of the river was the first step toward helping me overcome my sense of alienation and develop a healthier perspective. My anxiety diminished when I felt more grounded.

I married, had children, and by 1980, was involved in the computer industry in Silicon Valley. I began experiencing job-related anxiety and started searching for another therapist. I saw several—not Jungian—over the next five years. Some of them were what I call "Talking Head New Age Flakes." They want to know how you're feeling. Well, I'm not interested in that. I want to know how to work with how I'm feeling. That's where psychotherapy seems to fall short. You can understand your behavior and your feelings, but the goal—for me—was how do I channel my feelings into constructive behavior. That's the hardest part.

When you come in and you're in crisis, I think it would be better to have a therapist who would say, "Let's see what we can do to get you out of this," but I've never encountered anyone like that. The Talking Heads want to discuss your dreams, parrot their own book learning, and issue pseudo-wise edicts that contribute nothing. Marriage and family therapists want you to vent. They seem to think expressing anger will bring about a miraculous cure.

In 1986, I had my worst experience with a therapist. She was a woman I looked up to as older and wiser, but she put me down from the start. When I asked what model she was working from and what her strategy was to produce change, she reacted with indignation. "It is part of your maladjustment that you are asking such impertinent questions," she told me. I stayed almost a year with that abusive charlatan and I paid her a lot of money, something like $100 a session. I was victimized and I allowed it.

After a good, solid twenty years of psychotherapy, I began to think a talking cure does not exist and the so-called "profession" was full of frauds and flakes. It finally dawned on me that nobody was going to do it for me; I'd have to do it myself. That is when I saw a notice for five group sessions with an art therapist. My instincts told me to take that course.

Art therapy is an activity that involves both art and therapy. According to Judith A. Rubin, a former president of the American Art Therapy Association, art therapists must know art—the media and processes and their nature and potential. They must understand the creative process—the language of art, its symbols, forms, and content. And they must know therapy—psychodynamics, interpersonal relationships, the treatment relationship, and the mechanisms that help people change.[7]

The course cost about $50 and there were eight women in the group. Mrs. Whitman was a good therapist because what she did was client-centered, not therapist-centered. She was also a good container. A psychic container keeps you from foundering—collapsing into the deflated self—or inflating into arrogance and thinking you are a god. Jung said any person who aspires to be God will be destroyed.

Mrs. Whitman encouraged artistic expression in a client-centered experience followed by a mutually supportive group feedback session. She was nonjudgmental and could insert herself into the group and redirect energy when that was needed, like when one student drew a disturbing picture of herself that almost conveyed a death wish. Mrs. Whitman got us away from reacting like: "You are weird!" or "You are defective as a human being!" She got us to think about owning all the parts of ourselves, good and bad. Then that woman could embrace her drawing and own it as one part of who she is. She didn't have to split off the part she saw as toxic. That's transformation.

For me, the destructive energy of my negative archetypes was reinforced by my job. After Mrs. Whitman's class, I left Silicon Valley and went back into art. It was a financial sacrifice, but my life is worth it. I changed religions, too. I was raised Protestant but I've become a practicing Buddhist. Meditation gives me a sense of peace.

My archetypal energies—negative and destructive or positive and life-affirming—will always be with me, but the negatives can be transformed and counterbalanced by other psychic forces. The destructive energy of the calcified old man can be changed by inducing him to be receptive to the positive energy of the vibrant, loving little girl, thereby integrating the disparate parts of the segmented self. Archetypes can evolve and be rechanneled into acceptance. It's an organic process.

Therapy has changed a lot since Jung was alive. I believe he was the quintessential archetypal loving father, not the masculine all black or all white patriarchal father we have today. I was driven crazy by the patriarchal, power-hungry society we live in. Last year, I heard a Native American Ph.D. psychologist from Harvard, who is also a shaman, talk about the collective unconscious. The buffalo is the man and the man is the buffalo. It's the circle again.

Much as I feel some of my therapists have not helped me, I believe in the value of therapy. Maybe I should have been a Jungian analyst. Maybe in another life.

While self-understanding is a primary goal of Freudian and Jungian psychoanalytic approaches, the means for reaching the goal are different. Freudians pay special attention to dreams and the transference responses to the analyst, whereas Jungians are interested in the spiritual aspects of their patients' lives and encourage them to keep journals. But what does one do to change self-destructive behavior and rechannel energy in more positive ways? Like many who keep looking for that wise elder to provide the answer, April learned that she alone was responsible for managing her life.

In the next case, a young man enters a private psychiatric hospital for treatment of acute anxiety exacerbated by his use of alcohol and the drugs prescribed by his "kindly old doctor."

Alan Rhodes

Alan Rhodes is a sixty-eight-year-old advertising executive who lives in Baltimore, Maryland. "I remember taking the bus back to work after a session. I noticed groups of people clustered around cars listening to the radios and I wondered what was going on. It was November 23, 1963, the day President Kennedy was killed."

This all started when I was thirty-two with symptoms I didn't recognize as particularly important. Nervousness at work, anxiety, a difficult boss. The history of it is that I had an only brother, four years younger, who died of leukemia in 1955. I had fought in Korea and was getting out of the Air Force at the time. I was also just coming out as a gay man. I had thought my brother would marry and provide our parents with grandchildren, something I knew I would not be able to do. This all came out in analysis. A little further background: I'd been at Columbia, but in 1956, someone offered me a modeling job. I did that for about four years and became quite successful, but modeling is a fast life-style and I started drinking too much.

Anyway, at first my symptoms were minor. I didn't have a doctor so I went to a friend's doctor. A kindly old man who prescribed Miltown. I went along on that for a while and continued drinking. Then, in the summer of 1962, I began to be very uncomfortable descending into the subway. I started having dizzy spells walking down the street and I'd think things were dropping onto me from buildings. I thought I could overcome it myself—I tried to keep a stiff upper lip—but when I went back to renew my Miltown prescription and told the kindly old doctor the new symptoms, he prescribed Thorazine. That must have been when it first came out.[8] I took 300 mg of Thorazine and drank to calm myself down, but I was so hyper that when the phone rang, I'd jump. I couldn't sleep, so he prescribed sleeping pills.

One morning, getting ready for work, I went to shave and managed to lather my face but then I could not move my arm. Somehow, I managed to call a friend who came over and took me to my parents' home. I had literally ceased functioning. They got me into Austin Riggs Hospital quickly—I bypassed the waiting list—and I spent two months there, the minimum stay. It must have cost something like $4,000 a month in 1962. My medical plan paid 80 percent and my parents picked up the rest.

I remember the drive up to Stockbridge. Was I thinking about being on my way to a mental hospital? No. I was looking around at the gorgeous fall colors. Perhaps that is simply part of my nature. I've always been an optimist. Mother believed in keeping a stiff upper lip and I do, too. I always thought I'd get through it. But when we got to the hospital,

I couldn't sit still. I was in a state of acute anxiety with a pulse of 160 and during the intake evaluation, I kept jumping out of my seat. I apologized to the evaluating doctor, who took it well. I told him I was gay, and he said he hoped I would not "do anything" as a gay man, whatever that meant.

The first thing they did was try to get me off the Thorazine as quickly as possible. It was complicated because I was also taking sleeping pills with a large quantity of alcohol. Interestingly, they worked on the prescription medications but no one ever challenged the drinking. Austin Riggs is an open hospital where patients come and go as they wish. We were allowed to keep liquor in our rooms, so I went to the local liquor store and got a bottle of Scotch to calm my nerves. I couldn't sit down long enough to eat a meal, but two women patients were very comforting—their attitude was "been there, done that." They didn't find my behavior peculiar at all.

The only mandatory meeting every day was my individual psychotherapy session and I know I went, but what did we talk about? I really don't remember. I know everyone was assigned a chore, like mopping the floor, and I guess you had to make your bed. Otherwise, there was a lot of socializing. When I was there, and this may still be true, Austin Riggs was one of the best psychiatric hospitals and many of the patients were quite wealthy. They'd talk about other institutions they'd "visited," comparing and contrasting Menninger, the Institute for Living, Chestnut Lodge, and Shepherd-Pratt. Rumor had it that Judy Garland had been bounced from one of them for giving too many parties.

When the two months were up, it was hard for me to contemplate leaving. I can understand how people become institutionalized—I was afraid all my symptoms would come back. The doctors at Austin Riggs arranged for me to continue treatment as an outpatient and I began seeing Dr. Weitzner, then head of Psychiatry at Beth Israel, three days a week. It was about $40 an hour. Insurance paid for most of my hospital stay, but it didn't cover this, so we had to cut back to once a week after the first six months.

I saw Dr. Weitzner for two years. He was a classical Freudian analyst, probably in his mid-forties when I met him. I can remember excruciating silences as I was lying on the couch. If I asked him a question, he would respond, but tersely. He wanted me to do the talking. I was like a child with him, seeking approval. Sessions were at his apartment and while I was waiting one day, his wife walked in. She looked like Sophia Loren. Gorgeous. I certainly reacted to that—and to his going on vacations. Part of it was jealousy, but another part was my fear that I would not be able to reach him if I was in trouble.

I was also very jealous of my forty-five minutes. Once I had managed to remove the barriers to revealing my innermost thoughts to another man—it would have been easier for me, as a homosexual, with a woman—the essential bond was established. My relationship with my father was a noncommunicative one, so being able to talk freely with a male was a deeply satisfying experience.

At the end of therapy, when I'd resolved my guilt feelings about not being able to give my parents grandchildren, Dr. Weitzner asked me to consider continuing therapy in order to change my sexuality. I don't remember being offended. I just told him no, that would not be possible. He didn't press the issue, but it was clear that he genuinely thought he could do it. That's another example of the homophobia of the time and how it affected my life. Still, I feel that psychoanalysis and Dr. Weitzner saved my life. I mean that literally. I think I was fragile enough that I could have become dysfunctional again if he had not been there to help me. It was not so much what he said as my perception that he cared about me. He was a rock I clung to during a turbulent time in my life.

I didn't feel stigmatized then, and I don't now, by having been in therapy or by having been hospitalized. In fact, I wrote a play, which has been staged, about my experiences at Austin Riggs.

Ken Kesey's *One Flew over the Cuckoo's Nest* was popular reading at the time Alan Rhodes was hospitalized. A few years later, the movie, starring Jack Nicholson, portrayed psychiatric inmates as victims of an insane, inhumane, authoritarian system. Intellectuals such as Michel Foucault and Ervin Goffman, and psychiatrist Thomas Szaz, asserted that psychiatric illness was a myth. There were only deviants or people with problems in living. Arguments like these, plus the introduction of antipsychotic drugs like Thorazine, set the stage for the massive discharge of mental hospital patients into their unwilling and unprepared communities. Newly established Community Mental Health Centers were called upon to care for a far more disturbed population than had been envisioned,[9] and there was never a cohesive plan to implement this brave new idea. The hope that the deinstitutionalized could function with a lot of help and support from their communities was too difficult to achieve.

Thirty-eight people who answered the query were in psychiatric treatment during the 1960s—eighteen men and twenty women. Of the eight whose stories make up this chapter, five responded positively to treatment. The three negative responses were from Peter Johnson, the analytic patient; Kristin Palmer, who was sexually abused by her psychiatrist; and April Silver, who found some helpful therapists, some charlatans, and psychotherapy not all that she thought it would be.

Freud's 1919 prediction was coming true. Mental health services were becoming available to people with modest incomes, but only fairly healthy people could benefit from the classical psychoanalytic method. Therapists who were classically trained had to adapt their techniques to conditions they had not met in training, and they found it necessary to alloy the "pure gold" of analysis with the "copper" of direct suggestion to treat alcoholism, drug addiction, compulsions, suicidal tendencies, and incapacitating anxiety, none of which are amenable to quick fixes. Trends in treatment included more face to face work, fewer sessions per week, interpretations that approach direct guidance, and more activity on the part of therapists.

Respondents were between sixteen and forty-four-years-old when they entered treatment. Matthew Truax and Peter Johnson were in formal analysis; Grace Renard and Sam Temple were in analytically-oriented psychotherapy with psychiatrists and psychologists. April Silver spent a quarter of a century with mainly Jungian psychologists, but also saw a clinical social worker, and finally met her goals with an art therapist. Kristin Palmer was at a residential treatment center for teenagers who used illegal drugs or had problems at school or with their families. Our other teenager, Josie Schiller, received supportive psychotherapy from a psychiatrist at a clinic that offered sliding-scale fees based on income.

Matthew Truax paid $25 to $30 an hour—the "going rate," he says. He is one of the few to comment on time as a cost: "You can always make money, but not time, and it took a lot of time." Four people paid between $5 and $13 an hour at institutes with sliding-scale fees based on income. April Silver's treatment at a college counseling center was free. Kristin Palmer's father was insured and his plan paid for 80 percent of her residential treatment. Alan Rhodes' inpatient treatment was also covered at 80 percent; his family paid the remainder. The highest fee was paid by Peter Johnson: $100 an hour in a three-days-a-week analysis. "It almost bankrupted me," he says.

Matthew Truax didn't feel he needed to keep his analysis a secret, but he didn't "wave it around," either. Sam Temple's only sense of stigma was related to his reason for being in treatment. Peter Johnson was so concerned about confidentiality that he didn't seek insurance reimbursement.

Only Sam Temple and April Silver saw female practitioners during the 1960s. (Grace Renard saw a female psychiatrist in the 1980s.) Josie Schiller and April Silver are the only respondents who comment on the influence of religion or spirituality. Josie was influenced by Betty Friedan's book, *The Feminine Mystique*. Dismissing the happy housewife paradigm, it was a 1963 best seller and sparked the feminist movement in the United States.

In 1965, at the dawn of the Great Society, federal legislation in the form of Medicare for the aged and Medicaid for the poor was enacted. Overall, the 1960s witnessed an enormous investment in government public health activities. In 1960, Federal agencies spent $414 million on medical/health programs—$2.25 per person. In 1969, the figure was

$1,316 million, or $6.38 per person. This steep increase paralleled the increase in total national health costs: $26.9 billion in 1960, and $64.1 billion in 1969, greater by far than the rate of inflation.[10]

The first year of the decade was Eisenhower's, the last was Nixon's. The eight years between were the Kennedy-Johnson years. Between 1960 and 1965, salaries were up 20 percent and the gross national product—the total value of goods produced—increased by 36 percent, fueled significantly by defense and space programs.

In 1960, Congress passed a general aid to education bill and a civil rights act that authorized the Justice Department to protect black voters' registration rights. In February of that year, the now famous lunch counter sit-in by black students took place in Greensboro, North Carolina. Late that spring, President Kennedy, in a speech to University of Michigan students, proposed, almost casually, the creation of the Peace Corps.

Civil Rights, feminism, the Cold War, and Vietnam were the great issues. The murders of John F. Kennedy, Robert F. Kennedy, and Martin Luther King, Jr., punctuated the decade with blood. Nonviolence was denounced by black power militants, middle-class white hippies, and left-wing academics. Rage and alienation produced bombings, trashings, and riots, especially as the draft threatened affluent young men. Antiwar demonstrations took place in forty cities and there was a large scale riot in the Watts area of Los Angeles. Against this background, we move into the 1970s.

4   The 1970s: Eclectic Treatments and the Golden Age of Group Therapy

But since the 1960s, a gradual disillusionment began to set in. Psycho-analysis promised more than it could deliver. Freud himself said that psychoanalysis was good only for "ein kleine Neurose"—a small neurosis. But it was turned to as a cure for all kinds of schizophrenias, psychoses, drug addictions, affectlessness and whatever.

Abram Kardiner

A GUIDE TO THE UNITED STATES OF THE 1970s

Population: 203,302,031

Average salary: $7,679 per year

        Coal miners: $9,790

        Farm laborers: $3,787

        Federal employees (civilian): $10,921

        Medical/health services workers: $6,593

        Public school teachers: $8,299

Inflation: 6.5 percent

Unemployment: 4.9 percent

Social welfare: $145.9 billion

Births/1,000: 18.4

Marriages/1,000: 10.6

Divorces/1,000: 3.5

Deaths/1,000: 9.5

Average household size: 3.14

Women in labor force: 36.7 percent

Cost of living: Clothing: Gimbel's platform sandals for women, lizard grain, $23; Edwin Clapp shoes for men, $41.90

Food: bread, 24 cents a loaf; coffee, 91 cents a pound; eggs, 61 cents a dozen; milk, 33 cents a quart; oranges, 86 cents a dozen; round steak, $1.30 a pound

Housing: Four-bedroom, two-bath colonial, Scarsdale, New York, $65,000

Transportation: 1971 BMW Bavaria, $4,987

Fun: Mood rings, pet rocks, skateboards, disco fever, and "Pong," the world's first video game

Pulitzer Prizes: Biography: T. Harry Williams, *Huey Long*

History: Dean Acheson, *Present at the Creation: My Years in the State Department*

Nonfiction: Erik H. Erikson, *Gandhi's Truth*

Sources: Robert Famighetti (ed.), *The World Almanac and Book of Facts, 1997* (Mahwah, NJ: World Almanac Books, 1997), pp. 325, 326, 381; Scott Derks (ed.), *The Value of a Dollar, 1860–1989* (Detroit, MI: Gale Research Inc., 1994), pp. 469, 470; Lois Gordon and Alan Gordon, *The Columbia Chronicles of American Life, 1910–1992* (New York: Columbia University Press, 1995), pp. 570, 623; U.S. Bureau of the Census, *Historical Statistics of the United States, Colonial Times to 1970, Bicentennial Edition, Part I* (Washington, D.C., 1975), pp. 41, 49, 59, 64, 132, 135, 213, 340; Advertisement in *The New York Times*, January 2, 1970, p. L17; January 4, 1970, p. R7; January 18, 1970, p. L18; Peter Bohr (ed.), *Road and Track's Used Car Classics* (Santa Fe, NM: John Muir Books, 1987), p. 111.

The introduction to *American Decades, 1970–1979*, asserts: "It is easy to dismiss the 1970s as the decade that never happened. . . . Feminism, drugs, progressive education, busing, pornography, exotic religions, paranoia, welfare, ethnic politics, long hair, blue jeans, platform shoes, and amphetamines lingered from the 1960s. . . . The 1970s, it seems, have little to define them except, perhaps, their nothingness."[1]

Yet it is hard to view Kent State, the raging anti-war protests, the end of the Vietnam War, *Roe v. Wade*, and Watergate as marginal or nondefining events. Separately, and certainly together, these events wrenched and agonized the nation in unprecedented ways, and their effects still reverberate.

Take Watergate. It is shocking to recall, even a quarter of a century later, that seventy Nixon aides were found guilty of criminal acts. The precipitating event was the clumsy burglary of the Democratic National Committee offices in the Watergate building. It led to the first resignation of a U.S. president, who was advised by his supporters to resign or be impeached and probably convicted.

Sandra and Gavin Hilgardner

Sandra and Gavin Hilgardner, both fifty-eight, were in group therapy from 1972 to 1980. Gavin is CEO of a hotel chain. Sandra is a fashion designer. Gavin: "While we were in group, the whole Watergate thing took place. Haldeman, Ehrlichman, and the others took the rap and Nixon got off scot-free." Sandra: "Well, he did have to resign the presidency, Gavin. That's not exactly scot-free." Gavin: "She's just saying that because she's a Republican."

Sandra: This took place in 1972, when therapies like Primal Scream were in vogue.

> *Primal scream therapy* is a method of psychotherapy in which patients are encouraged to re-experience painful, repressed emotions from their childhoods. The theory is that once emotion is recovered and completely expressed, in a primal scream, patients will be able to integrate split-off parts of themselves and function at a higher level.

We found the group through friends. It was modeled on Daytop, the famous drug/alcohol treatment program, but no one in our group had substance abuse problems. One of the similarities between Daytop and our group was that Daytop was a confrontational model, and this group could be extremely confrontational, or extremely supportive.

Gavin: Rob, the person who ran the group, was a counselor who had worked for a psychiatrist running groups. He was a strong, controlling, charismatic leader. That can be good, but it could be a negative factor in the group process. It was okay to have conflict with anyone else in the group—in fact that was encouraged—but not with him. He said it was okay to confront him, but when I did, he asked me if I'd like to step outside.

Sandra: In some ways the group was like a cult. A lot of groups in the Seventies were like that. We were encouraged to make friends within the group and to socialize with our group friends—to consider the group our family. Some people were encouraged to cut off their families of origin completely. Rob would invite the group—we're talking twenty to twenty-five people—to his summer home for parties or use the group setting, his Manhattan brownstone, for a Friday night party. And if you didn't go, the other group members might ask why you weren't there with your friends. If you missed a group session for any reason, you were grilled by the other group members. If you were late for group, there was a lot of discussion of whether it was for psychological reasons. That part was quite coercive.

The group spent a lot of time together. Couples would go to group once a week together and once a week by themselves. Gavin and I were in individual therapy with Rob, too. Each group was an hour and a half and then every month or so there would be a group marathon. Those began about 6:00 P.M. Friday and lasted until 1:00 A.M. Saturday, and from 9:00 A.M. Saturday to midnight.

Gavin: There was a lot of love and support in that group. Rob put together a good group.

Sandra: A lot of good stuff came from being in the group. Learning your feelings and the defenses you used. Learning to be more open with your partner and friends in a way you'd never been before. Gavin and I were like the rest—we came to the group because we were not satisfied to go on day after day living with the same problems.

Gavin: People came in with problems and others in the group would confront, explore, build them up. Support them. Whatever you needed seemed to come from the group.

Sandra: People came with baggage from childhood—their parents, siblings—all that stuff comes out in group. You can express your feelings freely. You can be angry and shout and the reaction of the group is, "That's okay. It's only a feeling." Any feeling at all, about anything, was explored, discussed, and not judged by the group. Once you admit a feeling that frightens you—hatred, fury—and go through the feeling for as long as it takes, scary and painful as that is, you become free of its power over you. Going through a feeling is talking about it in group— experiencing the feeling to the maximum in a supportive setting. When you are free of its hold on you, you no longer need to waste psychic energy suppressing it, and you have all that energy for other things. When its power over you is gone, you can experience other feelings— love, happiness—in a way you could not before.

Gavin: There were a lot of wonderful things about the group. People who were natural leaders emerged. If Rob was not there for some reason, one of them would lead, or the group would run itself until Rob arrived.

Sandra: Rob might be upstairs in a one-on-one—which made a lot more money for him—and somebody else would lead the group—and pay for it, too. [Laughs.]

Gavin: And it cost a ton. $20 or $30 a group and $120 for marathons. The money didn't bother me. What I found negative was "group think."

Sandra: Yes. Like if the leader decided someone was erratic or screwed-up or not acceptable, then everyone in the group came down on that person. Looking back, I feel some of that was quite destructive for some people. Rob related to people who were weak and in trouble. He could be nurturing, warm, and accepting of those types but not people who were stronger and more assertive.

Gavin: After eight years, we decided we didn't need group anymore. We told the group we were leaving and . . .

Sandra: The silence was deafening. It's not that you couldn't leave—you could—but if they thought a member was running away from something or that you were still screwed up and shouldn't leave, the group would confront that. And all the people who had been your friends could band together and cut you off if you left without their approval. I remember being terribly anxious about leaving the group. Even afterward, I wondered for weeks if I'd done the right thing.

Gavin: Rob was a screwed up dictator but the group process was wonderful.

Sandra: I got a lot out of it. Made a lot of friends. People from all walks of life attended group. Some very successful business and professional types, people from the theatre, and some blue-collar workers. One thing I didn't like was that whole families were pressured to attend. I didn't think it was so good to use some of the language or discuss sex in front of teenagers, and Rob let that go on. In fact he encouraged it. People would vent their feelings totally. In retrospect, I was brainwashed into thinking it was fine, but now I don't think that part was such a good idea.

Gavin: If there was an argument between two people, group members might egg one on, or confront the other, or stop the argument. The group might ask civil questions like, "What's causing you to feel this way?"

Sandra: People would get in touch with their pain and anger. That would cause deep crying and sobbing—that's what I mean when I say "working." That's dealing with feelings. After that, the person would go around the group and each person would hug him. I wasn't used to that, and at first it bothered me, but it is a liberating type of thing.

Gavin: I was uncomfortable with the language: "bullshit," "fucked up," "cunt." [Gavin and Sandra both laugh.] I didn't think that language was necessary. [They laugh again.]

Sandra: There was a seductiveness about the closeness of the people there. If you were needy and wanted love and to be close, you could get that in group. I think we and our friends in the group needed each other emotionally. It wasn't a friendship based on shared interests and values.

Gavin: We got our four closest friends out of the group and we're still friends even though we left almost twenty years ago. I can't over-emphasize the positive aspects of group—but I notice that many of the marriages that came out of group have fallen apart. It's almost as if there are two worlds—the world of group and the normal world. Maybe their marriages just couldn't last in the normal world without group.

If the 1940s were the heyday of Freudian psychoanalysis, the 1970s must have been the golden age of group. Twenty-eight out of the fifty-six people interviewed, a far larger proportion than in any other decade, were in some form of group psychotherapy. Some were in small groups that resembled the dynamics of the family. Others were in single-sex groups, self-help or support groups (A.A. and Recovery Inc.), marathon group therapy, and groups coming out of the human potential movement (Trigant Burrow's Lifewynn and Michael Murphy's Esalen Institute). There were groups with more than one leader, and—as with Sandra and Gavin—groups for the nonaddicted modeled on drug treatment programs like Synanon and Daytop.

Classical analysis was alive and well, however, and several respondents told us that insurers, such as Blue Cross/Blue Shield and Aetna, picked up 80 percent of full-scale analyses, five days a week on the couch, for as long as it took. Connie was in analysis for six-and-a-half years.

Connie Claybrooke

Connie Claybrooke is a fifty-two-year-old city councilwoman from Amarillo, Texas. "I protested the war, burned my bra, and had sex in the backseat of a Mustang. [Laughs.] If I'd thought of anything else rebellious, I'd have done that, too."

In 1974, I was twenty-seven. My four sisters were married and had kids, and I had just finished law school. I made law review and clerked for a Houston judge, but I couldn't land a job with a top firm. As a woman, I was treated condescendingly, like a glorified paralegal. It made me furious, but I could have tried harder to get along. I had a chip on my shoulder. Anyway, after the first year, I thought of going back to school for a doctorate—I had a master's in economics—but I knew that would be a cop-out.

Not only did my work life suck, but my love relationships were rotten. One night, my roommate and I were watching TV and I was complaining about life in general when an ad came on where this guy is talking to his shrink. We looked at each other and laughed, but it started me thinking. No one in my family ever went to a psychiatrist, as far as I know. Catholics go to priests. But I decided, why the hell not? I asked around, got a couple of names, and made an appointment with Dr. Thornton. He was a psychiatrist, about thirty-five. Tall, blond. He asked why I needed psychotherapy and I told him that if I didn't get some help, I'd kill myself. I told Mother I was seeing a shrink and she was horrified, but she gave me the money, about $50 a session, probably out of guilt. "Don't tell your father," she said.

I saw Dr. Thornton on and off for three years and I made progress, but I knew there were fissures and schisms within me that psychotherapy could not reach. Dr. Thornton agreed that the work we'd done together was a good preliminary for analysis, which is what I decided I wanted, and he gave me the names of the three best analysts in the area. We parted friends.

The first analyst I interviewed was too entreating. He leaned forward in his chair too much. The second, Dr. Garland, was a supervisory analyst old enough to be my father, but I never thought of him as a father. I thought of him as an old man and I said so. For all his credentials, he had the ugliest office in the world and his clothes were just awful. I told him—not at the first session!—that his socks should be long enough that when he crossed his legs there wasn't this big gap between his socks and his trouser cuffs. I didn't interview anyone else, though. I stayed with Dr. Garland. One reason was he asked me about drug use. I want to make it clear that I haven't done anything like this for years, but in the Sixties, I smoked and sniffed and snorted everything. He asked me if I'd done LSD, angel dust, speed—I was impressed that such an old guy could just name them off—and the questions he asked about my involvement in the drug scene told me he knew something about the average hippie's psychology.

We agreed to begin a classical Freudian analysis. I would come in five days a week, lie on that frayed orange couch, tell him everything I thought—no holds barred—and I'd pay $70 an hour for the privilege. My insurance picked up half, but I was in analysis six-and-a-half years, so the whole thing must have been over $100,000. It was worth every cent. Compared to analysis, psychotherapy is Wonder Bread. In analysis, you learn what real bread is.

When I went into analysis, I was depressed, angry, and prone to fits of rage. I didn't know what happy was. I was the youngest by seven years of five girls. Mother was forty-one when I was born and she didn't want another baby. Especially a girl. She told me she'd considered an abortion. Fortunately, I had my sisters. Before I was old enough to go to school, I was depressed every day from September to June when they would go off to school and leave me with "The Witch."

While Mother hated me, I was my father's special baby. I was named for him and I was the apple of his eye. He'd had tuberculosis before I was born and hadn't been expected to live. When he got well and I came along, he felt he had a new lease on life and he spent a lot of time with me. Dad taught me to play catch when I was about two. I was always good at sports and as soon as I could walk, I was swinging a baseball bat. When I was a teenager, I played touch football with the boys.

I started analysis testing Dr. Garland for all he was worth but he never retaliated. He just sat there and waited while I tore at him. I'd heard analysts were only supposed to say, "Um-hmm, um-hmm," but when I said something funny, he'd laugh. I liked it that he thought I was funny but I knew he wasn't supposed to laugh, so I told him his technique was awful. I criticized him constantly and when I got going, I could really heap on the shit, but he never struck back. He was always neutral. I even taunted him for that. "Mr. Neutrality," I called him.

Analysis really began when I forgot he was in the room and started talking about whatever came to mind. I talked about my mother. She'd wanted to be a concert pianist but she gave that up to get married. Lying on the couch, I would say these things up into the air and Dr. Garland might say, "Um-hmm," or he might say a little more. Depending on how I was that day, I might like that or it might enrage me and I'd attack him as useless or worse.

It was easier to talk about being special to my father and liking sports. That made me think about playing fair and competition. All the things I said were related but it was up to me to find the connections with minimal guidance. That's why analysis works—for those who can tolerate it—and I almost couldn't. I needed to understand how the things I said fit together and what it meant to me. If Dr. Garland had said, "That means so-and-so," that would have been what it meant to him. And who gives a damn what it means to him? It's what it means to me!

Halfway through analysis I moved in with Danny. We got married later. We bought a house with potential, but it needed a lot of work and the dust and commotion during the renovation were terrible. Walls got torn out, junk was all over the place, and when digging out the basement began, I couldn't stand it. Danny pointed out the similarities between what was happening to the house and what I was going through in analysis. The house and I were both getting new foundations.

Analysis was terribly difficult and painful. If the first task is understanding, the task for the rest of your life is to live with what you learn. I went into analysis wanting to find out my mother loved me, and I left analysis knowing she didn't. She was an angry woman, humorless. I think one of the reasons she hated me is that I was blessed with a sense of humor. I know now that she was treated for depression. After she died, we found bottles of antidepressants hidden all over her house. She'd been taking them for years. If I'd known that, it would have helped me understand my own depression sooner. I still don't know why she kept it a secret.

Analysis saved my life. Without it, I might never have married, and that would have been a real loss because my husband and I have an absolutely show-stopping marriage. Sure, he tries to dump shit on me sometimes, but I don't have to take shit from him or anybody else. Analysis made me stronger. It taught me to evaluate my motives and other people's motives. When I ran for city council, the opposition spread the lie that I was sleeping with my campaign manager. Because of analysis, I can take the snide and untrue allegations of political life in stride.

Once my rage was gone, I didn't need Dr. Garland anymore and I told him so. When we said good-bye, I told "Mr. Neutrality" I bet he'd miss his clothing critic. I also thanked him. Come to think of it, he's probably the first person—except my father—I ever thanked for anything.

Connie absorbed her parents' two perceptions of her. Her mother found her hateful and her father found her wonderful. Analysis enabled her to integrate these polarized extremes as she learned that her unbridled anger did not destroy "Mr. Neutrality" and it wouldn't destroy her, either. Connie could then rechannel her free-floating, self-destructive aggression into the constructive energy she uses to get what she wants out of life.

Francine Donovan's analytic experience did not turn out as well. She entered a classical Freudian analysis as a depressed teenager with an eating disorder, and six years later she completed analysis, depressed and with an eating disorder.

Francine Donovan

Francine Donovan is a forty-three-year-old journalist who lives in Chicago. "During my analysis, Nixon was impeached. It was very disillusioning and caused a great deal of cynicism."

When I was a freshman in college, I was depressed and had an eating disorder. This was 1974. My mother and my father, who was a physician, sent me to Dr. Belmont, an analyst they found through a friend. My father paid $50 a session for my treatment.

Dr. Belmont seemed old to me—he was losing his hair—but I was only eighteen. He might have been fifty. He had a European background and was very formal. He told me very little about himself in the course of the six years I was in analysis, but I guess he liked classical music. He kept *Opera News* in the waiting room and had the radio tuned to the classical music station. I knew he was married and had one or two sons.

The first time I saw him, he asked me why I thought I was there and a childhood incident popped into my head. When I was four years old, I was taking a bath and felt a sharp pain in my vagina. My father stood me on the toilet and examined my vagina. I also remembered that when I was eight, I had a discharge from my vagina and was examined by my pediatrician. He thought I might have pinworms and told my parents to check my genitals every night with a flashlight. As it turned out, I did not have pinworms, but I found the whole thing very upsetting. The idea of worms was horrible to me and I imagined that I did have worms.

After the initial interview, I lay on the couch and free-associated four days a week. Dr. Belmont asked about dreams. I remembered a dream of being in the shower with my father when I was a child. Some sexual images. I never resolved whether it was a dream or really happened.

Dr. Belmont was a strict Freudian. A great deal of emphasis was placed on sex. At the time, I was afraid of boys, afraid of sex, very repressed, and still a virgin. A lot of sexual images came out in my dreams, but, at first, I was totally unaware that they were sexual and I was shocked and horrified by his interpretations. He said this was my Oedipal stuff—a typical Freudian interpretation. His tenet was that I'd wanted to have sex with my father. This made me feel ashamed, but to Dr. Belmont, it wasn't a big deal. It didn't matter to him if it was a real experience or not. It was "what it means to you."

I had become anorexic when I was fifteen. I'd always been thin, but I thought I was fat so I began to diet, lost a lot of weight, and stopped menstruating. Eventually, I told my mother and she took me to an ob-gyn who prescribed hormones, which made me hungry and very emotionally upset. I gained about thirty pounds in a month. It was horrifying. The eating disorder kept going back and forth from starvation to bulimia, but I'd gained a lot of weight by the end of high school.

I began analysis the second semester of my freshman year in college, depressed and with an eating disorder, and I left analysis six years later, depressed and with an eating disorder. I think my problems were a reaction to things going on in my family, such as my parents' marriage being in bad shape and the fact that I had a very incestuous relationship with my father. None of these things were addressed in analysis.

When we began, Dr. Belmont told me a typical analysis lasts three to five years and that I had what he called a "happy neurosis." Unfortunately, it was not happy for me. It was horrendous. I was hospitalized three times, began cutting myself with razor blades, hoarded prescription pills intending to kill myself, and abused drugs and alcohol. I was prescribed Valium, Dalmane, and antidepressants. I hated analysis and wanted to quit. Dr. Belmont told me I had a negative therapeutic reaction.

The first two of my hospitalizations were in a regular hospital on the psychiatric unit, but when I was twenty-one, there was no room at that hospital so Dr. Belmont sent me to one of the institutions where the chronically mentally ill stay. It was like the movie *The Snake Pit*. They took all your clothes and the doors were locked. People were walking around talking to themselves. I knew I didn't belong there and I vowed, "I will never let things get to me like this again." I called Dr. Belmont and he got me out of there that night. I dropped out of school for a while after that, but I stayed in analysis, and when I went back to college, I took a reduced load. It took me seven years to graduate, and by then I was twenty-five.

During the analysis, Dr. Belmont put me on Imipramine. That helped. I'm probably genetically predisposed to depression. One of my grandmothers was hospitalized for depression and had shock treatments. I believe my father is a depressive, and my mother was depressed when I was a child. When Dr. Belmont and I began to plan for termination and set a date, I was petrified. I seemed okay on the outside, but I knew I was only patched up. Underneath I was not all right.

About a year after analysis ended, I was still depressed and I went to a cognitive therapy center. The cognitive work was about "changing the tapes in your head." I didn't stay long and I can't say I got a lot out of it, but it wasn't damaging. Still, I hadn't gotten free of my eating disorder, so in 1984, four years after the analysis, I went back to Dr. Belmont. I had taken an overdose of my antidepressant and been hospitalized again. I wanted to know why I was not better. I could not understand, since I had been analyzed, why I was still so sick. He told me that eating disorders are like addictions and can take on a life of their own. He said something like, "I can't do anything more for you. You had a thorough analysis." I felt like he was telling me I had to go it on my own.

I had idolized Dr. Belmont—both loved and hated him, but mostly, I loved him. When he got me out of the snake pit hospital, I thought he was my savior. When analysis ended, I begged him to at least shake hands good-bye and he did. I've had no contact with him since that one time after one of my suicide attempts. I don't even know if he's still in practice.

In 1987, I went to a drug and alcohol treatment center called Confront. Not for drug and alcohol treatment—although I did have those problems—but to work on my eating disorder and my continuing unhappiness. Confront was what I needed. It was all about expressing feelings in a supportive group setting. They also had marathons—very intensive work that took place over a weekend. The difference between this work and analysis was that in analysis, I was the problem. I was marked as the defective person in my family and I was treated in isolation. No one else in the family was in treatment. In group, I learned to express my feelings with other people and hear their feelings and stories. I found out I wasn't alone and I wasn't unique.

The group was run by a certified alcoholism counselor who was also a clinical social worker. There were about eight people, all women, and it was only about $10 for a two-hour session. I liked the leader very much. She was tough, strong, and compassionate. I did some individual work with her and kept in touch with her for a couple years afterward.

After Confront, I stopped starving myself and binging, and feelings began for me. I started to eat normally for the first time in twenty years. I got a new job and moved to a new city, but after the first six months, I was feeling suicidal a lot of the time. One morning, I couldn't stand it any longer and I said to God, "I just can't do this anymore. I give it up to you." Two days after that, I told someone, for the first time, that I had an eating disorder. She said, "You should go to Overeaters Anonymous. I've been there." The spiritual experience took place on a Sunday and I told my friend on Tuesday or Wednesday. The next day, I went to O.A. and a woman got up and told my story. She was anorexic and bulimic, too. But I found O.A. too filled with people who were still addicts and hooked on weight and diet. That wasn't what I needed. Overeating isn't the same as anorexia and bulimia. Eventually, I had to leave. The talk about food and weight was too much for me.

In 1991, I realized I had been abusing alcohol and drugs for years and I went to A.A. I made friends there I see to this day, and I still go to meetings several times a week. My seven-year anniversary was just this past Monday. I have not been bulimic for seven years, and I haven't had a drink or a drug, either.

When I was a college student, I was tied down by the analysis. It took so much time I couldn't go anywhere or do anything else. My life revolved around the sessions. I was isolated and different from my peers. In all those years, I never met one other person who was in analysis. Back in 1974, there was not much known about eating disorders. Now I think analysis was the wrong type of treatment for me. It just prolonged my suffering. I think I overcame the analysis—isn't that something to have to say—through my own strength. I was a person who was badly put together with cracks in my self, cracks inside me, and analysis made it worse. It made me even more confused and mixed up inside. It was through my own strength and, finally, through the help of God, that I survived analysis and, ultimately, the eating disorder.

Another thing about analysis—Freud was not a religious man. He called religion a "mass delusion." I had a belief in God growing up and I brought that belief to analysis. Dr. Belmont never directly said that I shouldn't believe in God, but there was a silent disapproval I sensed whenever I talked about God. I think now that the belief I had in God as an eighteen-year-old was precious and could have helped me, but analysis completely squashed it. I didn't recover until that day seven years ago when I couldn't go on and cried out to God for help. I believe my healing started at that moment.

Comparing the results of the last seven years of therapy and being in A.A. with six years of analysis: Now I feel like a real person. To be free from depression, from my eating disorder, from alcohol and drugs, to live life like a normal person, is unbelievably precious to me.

Anorexia, which involves starvation, is said to be rare in the United States. Its prevalence is estimated at between 0.1 and 0.6 percent of the general population, but it is thought to be several times higher than that among adolescent girls. Bulimia, in which people eat large amounts of food and then either cause themselves to vomit or use laxatives and diuretics, is perhaps two to three times as common as anorexia. We live in a culture obsessed by physical appearance. Some women, even some men, want to be as thin as fashion models.

Current approaches to the treatment of anorexia and bulimia include hospitalization for anorexics, medication (sometimes Prozac) for bulimia, and behavioral and cognitive therapies for both conditions. Patients may not want to enter group treatment, but those who do frequently say they benefit from being with others who have wrestled with the same problems. Anorexia and bulimia are, as Dr. Belmont told Francine, like addictions. They are difficult to eradicate, and like other psychological problems, they become worse when the individual is stressed. They are insidious and can reappear over the course of a lifetime.

Randy Castleman

Randy Castleman is a sous chef from Boca Raton, Florida. He is fifty-five. "Like many people with eating disorders, I love to cook. I studied French cooking at The Four Seasons and would go home and make these marvelous gourmet creations I would not touch."

I am an only child. When I was eleven, my parents divorced. Mom left me with Dad. That was an unusual arrangement and particularly hard for me as I'd been closer to her than to Dad. He was a commercial photographer away from home a lot, and I really didn't know him very well.

Mom told me she was leaving when she and I were at the beach one weekend. We took a walk and she started asking if I could understand how unhappy she was in her life, emotionally and sexually. I had no idea what to say. When she said she was leaving, I was distraught. I begged her to stay, but she kept telling me to try to understand how unhappy she was. There didn't seem to be much I could say in argument. When we got home, Mom left a letter for Dad on the kitchen table and drove off in the family car. Dad arranged for a neighbor to watch me after school. Mom moved in with her boyfriend, Albert, and married him when I was twelve or thirteen. I idolized Albert. My happiest times were the weekends I spent with them.

As a kid, I was chubby and other kids would tease me and call me fat. When I was about sixteen, I got a crush on a girl in my class. She was going steady, but since her boyfriend was off at college, she went to the movies with me a few times. She made it clear, though, that she would not be my girlfriend. I thought if I lost weight I'd win her, so got a calorie book and memorized it. I based everything I ate on that book. I eliminated lunch and then breakfast, and I got into physical fitness big time. I could climb ropes and do hundreds of situps. I lost about forty pounds, and not eating became an end in itself.

By the time I went to college, the anorexia had evolved into bulimia. I started gorging and purging in secret, and I began to punish myself. I wouldn't eat anything all day and I'd take the stairs, no matter how many flights, from one class to another. I studied all the time, I made no friends at school, and the only places I ever went were to museums with Dad. Then he died. I dropped out of college then and, living on my inheritance, I began to study French cooking. I taught myself French and got my first job cutting up crudités and worked my way up to sous chef.

I went on with the same problems, sometimes better, sometimes worse, until I was about thirty. I was isolated, partly because of my eating disorder, and I was depressed. I didn't have a girlfriend and I was still a virgin. On New Year's Day, 1974, I made a conscious decision that I would finally lick this thing. The following week, I went to a community mental health center and was assigned a therapist, Dr. Olson. She was a Ph.D. psychologist. It was a lucky assignment. She was the right person for me, about my age, maybe a bit older, and I developed the requisite crush on her.

Insurance from work paid for most of my treatment. Boy, those were the good old days! I went once a week and it might have cost me all of $20 a session. [Laughs.] I made a lot of progress with Dr. Olson. That was my golden age of psychological growth. We looked at my food fixation and my repressed sexuality. My body image. My isolation. My feeling that I was worthless if I was not perfect. Dr. Olson gave me behavior modification assignments. I was to write in a notebook everything I ate. I told her I never ate breakfast or lunch and she told me to choose one thing, eat it, and write it in the book. I remember the first entry: "Breakfast—stirred one level teaspoon of sugar into my coffee." I'd take the notebook to sessions and we'd review my progress week by week.

At one point, I went on vacation. Alone, like always. I bought Dr. Olson a present—a little basket of potpourri. She took it and said something like, "I've been meaning to ask. Are you falling in love with me? It's okay, you know. These are good emotions that are coming out and will be transferred onto someone else someday." That was the perfect thing for her to say. It let me know she accepted my feelings. She was not repulsed. That's when I started feeling some kinship with the rest of the human race. It was the first step on a long, twisty road with lots of pitfalls and relapses, but at least I was on the road. We began to work on how food-starved and sex-starved I was, and how I mixed the two up.

Dr. Olson encouraged me to get involved with other people. To get me out of the house, Dr. Olson used the same technique she'd used with food. I was to choose one thing, do it, and tell her about it. After two years of therapy, I met a woman at a party. Jill. We liked the same music. Read the same books. After we'd dated a while, Jill was at my place for dinner and we started kissing. At thirty-two, I finally lost my virginity. We were married that spring.

Therapy ended when my eating habits were more normal. Eating disorders tend to be chronic, however, and I've had relapses. Fortunately, Dr. Olson told me the door is always open. I've been back, and I'll go again if I need to.

Our next patient tells what it was like to cope with a major psychiatric illness while she was caught up in the drug culture of the 1960s and 1970s. This complex case required intensive psychotherapy, medications, and psychiatric hospitalizations. Maggie was treated by a young psychiatrist just out of his residency.

Maggie Glass

Maggie Glass is a fifty-four-year-old artist who lives near Lake Tahoe, California. "I entered treatment in 1974, the time of the Pop Art explosion. Andy Warhol's soup cans, Roy Lichtenstein's comic strips—but what I remember from the Seventies is the mental hospitals I was in."

My mother was depressed, messed up, and abusive. I turned to alcohol and drugs, married when I was eighteen, and, lonely only child I'd been, I had two babies right away. When they started getting difficult—turning into people—I got a lot worse. My husband kicked me out when I was twenty-nine. I had no friends, nowhere to go. My mother, my husband, even my kids were against me. I was desperate, suicidal, and lost.

Somehow, I called the county mental health clinic. I've never been one to ask for help, and I'd never had any kind of mental health treatment, so I don't know how I came to make that phone call. Maybe I saw an ad somewhere. The receptionist told me they didn't refer by phone, but I guess I sounded so desperate she gave me three names. The first one I called, Dr. Crispin, responded. He was a psychiatrist about my age, not long out of his residency. By sheer luck, I got a great doctor. I stayed with him ten years.

I didn't have any money but I had MediCal. Back then, it seems to me I had a chance that is no longer available to people. MediCal couldn't have paid much—maybe $25 an hour—but you could stay in treatment as long as it took and I didn't have a co-payment. Today, managed care pays about $25 an hour and cuts you off after ten sessions. What would have happened to me? Short-term stuff just wouldn't have done it. That's one of the reasons I'm interested in this study. I believe it is potentially valuable to people who need mental health coverage.

The reason Dr. Crispin was so good for me is that unlike everyone else in my life—including me—he was completely nonjudgmental. I was terrified when I made the appointment to see him. My life was just in shreds. The first session, I remember I spewed for forty-five minutes and then I felt this enormous relief. It was, literally, a physical sensation of weight that had lessened. I felt better.

I saw him three days a week in the beginning because I was very intent on killing myself. It was, like, out of my hands, this unconscious drive to die. I made many, many suicide attempts and I was in psychiatric hospitals many, many times. When it's happening, you think you'll never forget, but I really don't remember how many times now. I know I was in twelve different facilities more than once and two state hospitals. Those are real hell holes. Dr. Crispin came to see me except when I was at Napa. I don't blame him—that was a 140-mile round trip.

Soon after I started treatment, Dr. Crispin felt the hospital was the safest place for me and he sent me to Mt. Zion for two weeks. That was a very good private psychiatric facility—probably similar to Menninger—but I don't think that program exists anymore. When I was there, it was clean and there was a good patient/attendant ratio. It was a gentle, nurturing environment with only fifteen or twenty patients. The only thing I didn't like was group therapy. It was so hard talking about myself to total strangers.

A lucky thing happened at Mt. Zion. I didn't have any friends, but in the emergency room I met a young intern and we became friends. It was Jaime who told me, after many, many of my suicide attempts, "If you can't get yourself squared away, I am not going to be your friend anymore." That jolted me. I knew he meant it. January 1976 was the last time.

Looking back on the first two years with Dr. Crispin, I was staying alive, that's all. It sure wasn't psychoanalysis, and I did an embarrassing amount of game-playing. Dr. Crispin explained to me later that my emotional maturity had been arrested by life events. He was simply a very good human being. He'd always take the things I gave him—things I made, like drawings, papier-mâché animals—and he saved them, just like you do with a kid. He didn't "analyze the meaning of the gift," either. He knew why I gave him those things.

It took me about three years to get on my feet. During that time, I'd draw and paint some. I'd gone to an art institute before I had the kids, but I never got a degree. Somehow, I landed a drafting job in 1978 with Blue Cross/Blue Shield benefits. That paid for 80 percent of my treatment. I was only going once a week by then, so it cost about $80. Still, I was only earning $500 a month—a fifth of my income was going for therapy.

Was it worth it? It saved my life. It was worth every minute and every penny. When I started with Dr. Crispin, I hated myself. I'd been judged "bad" and "flawed" and I'd taken in that perception, but Dr. Crispin didn't view me that way. He said that I was different from the people who judged me so harshly, and that "different" was not "bad." I was out of a mold they could not understand. Over time, I learned to take in his perception of me. I learned to accept and value myself and I learned to manage my life. I achieved freedom from all the things that were knotting me up inside, including the angst brought on from believing that other people's perceptions of the reality of me were correct while my own were not.

I'm very cautious about what I tell others about having been in therapy. Most of the people I've been around in work situations are not very secure and are inclined to pass judgments. They think something must be very wrong if someone has seen a psychiatrist for ten years, so I might talk about the benefits of therapy and recommend it, and I might let it be known that I've been in therapy, but I never say for how long.

I worried for years about how treatment would end. I feared a sort of "This Is Your Last Visit" end. What happened was a natural process where I found I didn't need to come in every week. I'd decide I could go maybe two weeks between sessions. Then it was more like a month. Finally, I knew I didn't need Dr. Crispin as a therapist anymore. He was sad and glad about that and I was, too. It was like going to school. Ten years of my life and a consistency I've never given any other endeavor.

When I stopped, the only thing that worried me was would I be able to come back if I needed to. He told me the door was always open. The first few years, I'd go in about once a year. Now I send him a Christmas card and write him every three or four months to let him know how I'm doing. I always include some drawings.

I learned a fair amount about Dr. Crispin over the years. He was in analytic training when I started. Freudian. Now I think he'd say his theory base is eclectic. I know he went through his own analysis while he was working with me. I could tell when he wasn't being himself— he'd slip on his unresponsive "cardboard man" face. We tried the couch a few times but it didn't work for me. We both felt I needed the eye contact.

We clashed, early on, about my need to be alone. Dr. Crispin would push me to make more friends, but I'd been a latch key kid. I was good at being alone. He didn't understand then—but he does now. I still don't have more than a handful of friends. After my divorce, I was single for twenty years. I just remarried. Since we're not social friends, I hadn't thought of inviting Dr. Crispin to the wedding, but when I told him I was getting married, he asked if he could come.

All through treatment and beyond, I was depressed, but I was against the idea of medication. I'd had enough trouble with drugs. Also, I was stubborn and I wanted to whip this thing by myself, but three or four years ago, I started spiraling down and my depressions got closer and closer together. I tried Zoloft and it helps. I guess that's another thing I can attribute to treatment: I have the ability to assess and accept my needs.

Maggie cites Dr. Crispin's nonjudgmental style as the primary reason she could work with him. He treated her better than she treated herself. Her overly severe conscience gave her only one choice—to end her own life—and she tried to escape that thought through the use of alcohol and drugs. She had what we call today a "dual diagnosis," meaning she had two psychiatric diagnoses: depression and chemical dependency.

Dr. Crispin did not dig into the unconscious reasons for the gifts Maggie gave him. He accepted her offerings just as he accepted her, unconditionally, and began to work building trust from the ground up. Maggie's description of her therapy as being like going to school for ten years is apt—it provided a structure for as long as she needed it, and she lived to graduate.

The next young woman had an attachment disorder, experienced mood swings, and used street drugs like pot and LSD.

Frieda Sager

Frieda Sager, forty-eight, lives in New York City. She and her husband are high school teachers. "In 1976, my parents and I drove through Washington, D.C., and for the first time in my life, I saw homeless people living under bridges. I told myself 'If I don't get better, I'm going to end up like that.'"

I believe I have a unique story. I was in psychotherapy with Adam Silvio for ten years, beginning in 1977. I can tell you right now, the work I did with him saved my life. I come from a typical Jewish household where, growing up, things looked good on the outside. Big house in the suburbs, two cars, but Mom was depressed and my dad had a difficult temperament. He was honest and good, but he could be very controlling and he would lose his temper. Mom had post-partum blues and was hospitalized when I was two months, eight months, and three years old. That early period is the time when a baby bonds with its caregiver and develops object permanence, but that didn't happen with me. I was well cared for, but I couldn't have understood why my mother was gone or known that she'd come back, and to make matters worse, we had to move several times because of Dad's work.

Somehow, I was an excellent student through high school and I was a pretty, popular cheerleader, but just like my family, it was all superficial. I was really an at-risk kid, a facade with no solid underpinnings and a whole lot of anxiety. I entered Kent State in 1969—really too big a school for me—and the shootings occurred my second semester. I was going to the administration building to drop a math class when I heard what sounded like cherry bombs going off. I went to look and there was blood everywhere, National Guardsmen running around, people screaming. For the longest time I thought that scene was the trigger for my future mental illness. I'd smoked pot, but after that, I started using psychedelic drugs. For the person I was then—without a firm core, not integrated—LSD is a recipe for disaster. I became quite unstable and my parents had to hospitalize me. I was on a locked ward in a state asylum when I was nineteen.

After a few months, I was discharged with a recommendation for family counseling and we went to a Gestalt therapist a few times, but Dad ended up telling the therapist he was crazy. That treatment form just didn't work for us. My parents probably should have looked for something else, but they weren't sophisticated enough to think, "Well, our daughter has just come out of a mental hospital and she ought to have some sort of psychiatric aftercare." And I didn't know how to get it by myself.

Over the years, I was in and out of college. Sometimes I'd have a job, but a lot of times I'd do nothing but get wasted on LSD and other drugs. I had a real shaky adult transition and floated close to being a street person. When I was twenty-six, Mom got in touch with a community mental health center and I agreed to go. I was assigned a doctor. The clinic where he worked had a sliding-scale fee and when I didn't have $20, my parents gave me the money. They wanted me to get well.

I'm not a religious person. I'm sort of a Zen Buddhist-atheist-agnostic, but if there is such a thing as God or providence, I credit whatever that is with allowing Dr. Silvio's path to cross mine. He was a psychiatrist just a little older than I was and he was trained as a psychoanalyst, but the work we did was face to face and interactive. He had studied John Bowlby's attachment theory, which explains the young child's bonding process, and he was an expert at using a humanistic, eclectic approach.

John Bowlby (1907–1990) was an English psychoanalyst and theoretician who studied medicine and psychology at Cambridge, joined the Tavistock Clinic in 1946, and was associated with that institution until his death. Bowlby disagreed with certain psychoanalytic ideas, believing that children's real experiences with their parents, not fantasies, were greatly underestimated in accounting for the development of personality disorders and neuroses. In 1950, he studied children left homeless after World War II, concentrating on very young children's responses to separation from their primary caregivers. He developed *attachment theory*, the theory of the relationship between the infant and his or her primary caregiver, which draws upon ethology, control theory, psychoanalytic theory, and developmental and cognitive psychology. This has led to its criticism by Freudian purists. Bowlby's work is explained in his trilogy, *Attachment* (1969), *Separation* (1973), and *Loss* (1980).

I believe he opened a door that helped me see into my problems for the first time when he told me, "No, it didn't start with Kent State, and no, it didn't start with LSD. It started long before that." We looked back at my early childhood and my family system. My parents are good people and they did their best, but they were immigrants, and like other children from homes like that, I became confused when things at my house weren't like at my friends'. My parents had trouble communicating and I heard some inappropriate dialogue with a lot of shouting. So there was the attachment disorder, the cultural part, the anxiety and depression, and the drugs.

I was still an addict when I started with Dr. Silvio and he knew it, but still he took me on. Sometimes when I'd have an argument with my parents, I'd wait until everyone went to bed and get out my stash and get stoned. Then I might have the police escort me to the hospital. Dr. Silvio told me, "Look, you've got to start taking care of yourself." He doesn't usually do a lot of medicating, but in my case he prescribed a low dose of Valium and told me to take it every day whether I thought I needed it or not. That kept me low-key enough that I could live at home and not buy into family arguments. Another thing he did was send for my records and review them with me. I'd had shock treatments when I was twenty-one, one of my milder diagnoses was "Personality Disordered," and the most serious was "Paranoid Schizophrenic." All Dr. Silvio said about that was, "I've never cared much for labels."

There was a point in treatment when I developed a father transference to him. An unethical practitioner could have taken advantage of me, but because of how Dr. Silvio is, the feelings I had for him could unfold in a very safe way so that I could learn from what was happening and complete treatment with him as my psychiatrist who became my friend.

During the time I was with him, I entered a rather prestigious university, but four months before I graduated I had a setback and ended up in a state hospital. The doctor there suggested I try Lithium. I began taking it and when I got out of the hospital, I joined a support group for manic depressives. I met two of my closest friends in that group. We are in touch to this day.

Treatment ended in 1989 when I met Len. We got married and moved here. A few years later, I stopped taking Lithium. I'm not in any form of psychotherapy now but I attend yoga classes. Yoga gives me a sense of peace.

For a person like me, with severe, deep-rooted problems, therapy takes a long time. The structure of self anyone needs to develop normally was not inside me due to disordered bonding resulting from my mother's being away during crucial periods of my infancy and early childhood. I was an adult with childhood attachment problems.

I would not be where I am today if it were not for Dr. Silvio. He always told me I was courageous—that I had pulled myself up by my bootstraps. I had never thought of myself that way. He was the first person who said to me, "You have a story and I want to hear it." His finding me worthwhile, being interested in me—well, when someone you respect respects you, you can begin to respect yourself. I began to regain my dignity and I started to get well.

The work I do now is with kids at risk the same way I was. I know their pain because I've been there. I know why they can't trust. I could say I "found" stability, but it would be more accurate to say I built my own foundation with Dr. Silvio's help. I remember telling him, "You really helped me." He replied, "You helped yourself."

I write to him a couple of times a year to let him know how I'm doing. I want to add my story to your study to thank him—I hope he'll read this—and to say again that I truly believe I've been given a second chance.

Frieda Sager's story is similar to accounts given by other young people caught up in the drug scene of the turbulent 1960s and 1970s. Familiar with Bowlby's studies of attachment and loss, and acquainted with the works of Fromm and Sullivan, Dr. Silvio was able to integrate useful ideas from several sources in a broad-based, eclectic approach that could accommodate Frieda's complex illness. However, his success was determined in large part by his ability to gain Frieda's trust. He began to accomplish this when he let her know, simply and honestly, that he was interested in the story of her life.

Dr. Crispin and Dr. Silvio developed a dynamic understanding of their patients' needs, remained responsive to what their patients had to say about themselves, and were up to date on new medications. Use of tranquilizers like Valium, mood stabilizers like Lithium, and—later on—antidepressants like Prozac, intensified the disagreement between those who believe that mental illness is primarily the result of one's biological makeup (a chemical imbalance) and others who see mental illness basically rooted in psychosocial factors. Psychiatrists of the latter persuasion usually do not prescribe medications, but Maggie's and Frieda's doctors did—to their patients' advantage. There are no hard and fast formulas for treating cases like these. The work is hard and it requires flexibility.

Our next patient describes treatment of depression with and without medications. Henry Hamner saw a psychiatrist first and then went to a psychoanalyst. The psychiatrist prescribed medications. The analyst believed medications mask a patient's emotional life and asked him not to take antidepressants while he was in treatment with her.

Henry Hamner

Dr. Henry Hamner is a seventy-year-old political scientist, college professor, and former dean of his school. He lives in Providence, Rhode Island. "At home, I learned to be responsible. To work hard and achieve. What comes to mind when I think of the Seventies is that's when I came to understand that I did not wish to continue as dean, even though I would lose the perks that went with the job and take a considerable decrease in salary. The decision to quit was a significant part of my 'emancipation.' "

During most of my adult life, I have experienced anxiety and depression requiring medical treatment. My first overwhelming anxiety attack occurred when I was attending a conference in 1962. As dinner was being served, I suddenly felt short of breath and my heart began to pound. I thought I was having a heart attack.

A couple of years before that, I remember spending an afternoon in my study with the drapes drawn against a beautiful, sunny day. I contemplated suicide, but as a practicing Catholic, I could not kill myself. I lost more and more weight, completely unaware of it, until I was walking down the street one day and my slacks started to slide down. I went into a shop and bought a belt. The waist was 27 inches. I've kept it as a reminder. My normal waist size is 34 inches.

It never occurred to me to consult a psychiatrist, although I think there is a history of depression in my family. My father, a hard-working man, took to his bed for about two weeks during the Great Depression. I was eight at the time and his collapse terrified me. It was never called *depression*, but I believe it was just that.

The weight loss is what finally drove me to my internist who performed a thorough physical. He could find no reason for it and suggested that I consult a psychiatrist. I was dean of my school and, while desperate for help, I was not anxious for others to know, but it was impossible to keep it a secret. What surprised me is how supportive people were. This was the Seventies and attitudes have changed, but I still tell people that fear of stigmatization should not prevent their seeking help for mental illness.

The psychiatrist I saw put me on Librium and later, Tofranil, an antidepressant. This chemical caused a change so great it was almost a miracle. I stopped brooding. I could eat and sleep. I have continued on Tofranil, almost without interruption, notwithstanding its side effects: dry mouth, constipation, bleeding nose, cold hands and feet. I was able to work and raise my family, which I might not have been able to do without it. Last year, I tried Prozac, but it didn't help. I will put up with Tofranil's side effects.

While the medication he prescribed helped me, I still question what I got out of my first experience in psychotherapy. I saw Dr. Anderson for a few years and perhaps our commonalities sidetracked us. His widowed mother lived with him and his family, just as mine lived with us. When I did not improve, he would change the medications or up the dosage, but the therapy didn't give me a sense of why I was depressed or what to do about it.

I became a walking pharmacy. In place of Librium and Tofranil, he put me on Valium, Mellaril, Desyrl, Sinequan, and Lithium, one after another. I remember having horrific dreams of being lost in large cities, going from one place to another, never able to find my way. I stopped psychotherapy.

By 1975, I decided I wanted a thorough workup and I went to Menninger, where I was evaluated over five days by a team that included a psychiatrist, a psychologist, a social worker, and an internist. They would have seen my whole family if I had been able to arrange it, and my insurance paid for it all. The Menninger report was: Plain, garden-variety depression. I was given the names of four psychoanalysts near my home, all formerly with Menninger, and I began working twice a week with a woman, Dr. Remey.

She was a little older, married, and had a son in high school. A South American, she spoke Spanish. I understand Spanish, so that was a positive tie, and the fact that she was a woman was reassuring. She told me she wanted to see what I was like off medications and asked me to stop the Tofranil while I worked with her. I complied for the two years, 1975 to 1977. She asked me to keep a daily log of indicators of depression. Did I listen to music? Did I swim? I loved music and swimming, but when I was depressed, I didn't want to hear a sound, and I couldn't summon what it took to get to the pool. I was also to log my diet, sex life, and anything else I considered significant.

Psychotherapy with Dr. Remey was a voyage of self-discovery. I learned how my father's extreme sense of responsibility for me, my siblings, my mother, and his own widowed mother influenced my development. Both his parents died young and he was put in charge of his younger siblings. He described his mother as a saint. I learned to be as over-responsible as he was. Dr. Remey characterized me as "God" and a saint. I was to be counted on at home, church, school, and work. No one who came to me would ever be turned away. The smallest complaint from anyone meant I had to do my duty: Set matters straight. In therapy, I learned that I had choices and could not be responsible for others' lives. I learned to say no.

Significant as those achievements were, psychotherapy has its peaks and valleys as well as its plateaus. When I wasn't making any headway and was still depressed, I'd lash out in frustration, "Why are you wasting our time?" "Because I care about you," Dr. Remey said. I liked her but I never fell in love with her. I regarded her as a professional I saw for something like $50 or $75 an hour. My insurance didn't cover outpatient psychotherapy.

Therapy ended when I was offered a chance to be a visiting professor at a prestigious university on the east coast. It was the professional opportunity of a lifetime and I jumped at it. When I returned home, Dr. Remey had left the area and I never saw her again. I regard the time I spent with her as the two toughest, most difficult years, but they gave me a discipline that has enriched my life and permitted me to have a life that was right for me. I could never have resigned as dean if I hadn't worked with Dr. Remey, but my depression continued and I soon went back on Tofranil. I also began to attend a weekly Recovery, Inc. group for people diagnosed with a mental illness. It was valuable in that I learned I wasn't the only one.

Before the Menninger workup, I would not fly unless I absolutely had to. That was a real problem because my work required a lot of travel. To get through a flight, I'd start drinking bourbon and taking tranquilizers at the airport, whatever the time of day, and I'd drink all through the flight. When the plane landed, I'd almost fall off. I couldn't drive over bridges. I'd go blank and my wife would have to take over. I was so claustrophobic I could not swim unless I was in the outside lane, and if my children did anything even remotely dangerous, I'd make them stop. I don't understand why, but after I was fifty, these things simply went away. I hadn't changed medications so it can't be that, but I was suddenly able to do all the things I'd put off—downhill ski, scuba dive.

I applaud efforts to educate the public about mental illness and its treatment. Unhappily, three of my children have suffered depression, which has severely impacted their lives. They are not cured, but, like me, they have been treated. If you read *Molecules of the Mind*, you get a sense of God as a chemist, if there is a God.

Psychoanalysts have been slow to endorse the use of medications because some of their patients have progressed without them and medications have side effects that some people find intolerable. The following two cases describe treatment by social workers, who are not permitted to prescribe medications. Psychotherapists with a background in clinical social work have been involved in mental health as far back as the 1940s, working for public agencies, community clinics, or hospitals, specializing in treating individuals, families, couples, and groups. A number of social work schools were influenced by Freud and Rank. Others, cool to psychoanalytic ideas, favored sociological and family systems theories. By the early 1970s, clinical social workers were entering private practice to work with patients referred to them by psychiatrists and other physicians. Julia Mason was referred to a social worker.

Julia Mason

Julia Mason is a forty-five-year-old caterer from Los Angeles. "I can't think of anything that was going on in the Seventies. I guess it's too depressing to remember."

I started therapy in 1978 when I was twenty-four. My first therapist was a social worker. Phyllis was about fifty and married to a psychiatrist. I was referred to her by the doctor I worked for because I was depressed and crying at work every day, but the real reason I went was that I felt shame and guilt about everything and it kept me from really living.

I went to Phyllis once a week and I usually sat in a chair, but sometimes I lay on her sofa. It was freeing not to see her. It helped me not censor myself. In my family, we learned to read minute cues and I'm sensitive to other people's reactions. My mother was depressed and I learned to behave according to the cues I perceived.

Mom was hospitalized a number of times for depression and had shock treatments in the Fifties. Dad was distant and not strong enough to deal with what was going on, so he blamed my sisters and me. There were five of us. He'd say Mom was in the hospital because we fought all the time. I blamed myself that she was sick and I couldn't make her better and make all the problems go away.

I got some good from my first therapy. I began to have some perspective and not feel so chained up, but after two years, I thought I'd achieved all I could with Phyllis. She charged $50 or $60 and my insurance only paid half, so it was expensive. I also began to wonder if she was as good as I'd been led to believe.

I looked around for another therapist and found Mary Kelly through a friend. Mary was a clinical social worker about my age. We had a lot in common, both being raised Catholic and having fallen away from that. When I'd talk about something painful, I could see she understood how hard it was for me. When I remarked about that, Mary said it was probably because our psychologies were similar. I didn't get that kind of empathy from my parents.

Again, therapy was expensive. I never finished college and I don't make a lot of money. It was $50 a session in 1981 and my insurance didn't cover treatment by a social worker. As much as I liked Mary and as much as therapy helped, there were times I felt like quitting, but I knew deep down that would have been a disservice to myself. It's a no-brainer to see that when there's more work to do, you have to explore whatever would make you want to quit. For me, one thing was stigma.

Everyone in my office knew I went to my "shrink" every Tuesday night and I didn't want their pity. Now I think people who go for therapy exhibit strength. They're trying to do something about what's going on inside themselves.

About 1983, I moved to Boston for a better job. I saw a psychiatrist once a week for the five years I was there. He charged a lot more than Mary—$80—but it only cost me $10 because he was on my health plan. Dr. Kenney was much older, a Harvard-trained Freudian. I was impressed by all that, but I don't remember much about the treatment. When I had a chance to return to L.A., he wanted to spend a lot of time on "What is your real reason for going?" I wasn't hiding my real reason. I was from L.A., I only went to Boston because of my job, and I wanted to go back home. Finally, I said, "I'm going back and that's that."

As soon as I got back home, 1987, I started up with Mary again. She had raised her rates to $60 while I was gone and my insurance still wouldn't pay for it, so it was hard but I managed to afford it. It was the best money I ever spent and in the long run it turned out okay because she never raised her rates for me and my financial situation got better over the years. I was with her for ten years.

Sometimes therapy was painful, but Mary seemed to know exactly how far she could go before she went over the line and I'd be angry and shut down with hurt feelings. I learned to tell her when she hurt my feelings or made me angry. I hadn't done that in my family. Speaking of family, Mary saw my sister for awhile when I was in Boston. Sheila thought Mary was a good therapist, but tough. When we talk about Mary, Sheila gives examples of how Mary told her, basically, to cut the crap. Mary never did that with me.

I started antidepressants about three years ago when I hit the wall. Couldn't function effectively, cried all the time, couldn't get out of bed. For years, Mary had wanted me to try medication, but I never wanted to take pills. She compared depression to diabetes, saying, "If you were diabetic, you'd take insulin, right?" So I went to a doctor who put me on Elavil, but I hated it and stopped after six months. A couple of years later, when my mother died, I got depressed again, and by then Prozac was on the market. I've been taking it ever since and I'm willing to stay on it.

I've had a weight problem most of my life. I've never been anorexic or bulimic, but I overeat. Mary's the one who suggested I join an eating disorders group. That made me think, "Oh, my God! Not a group!" My core issue is shame and I didn't want to reveal myself in front of a group of people I didn't know. At first, I'd cry the whole time, but group has turned out to be phenomenally good for me. I've been going four years now. [Julia begins to cry.] This stuff means so much to me. I learned that

I don't have what it takes to make every situation in everyone's life perfect, but that doesn't make me shit.

Three years ago, I told Mary I might be ready to stop seeing her. I was in group by then and my life was going reasonably well. I'd made a lot of changes and they seemed to be lasting. Mary agreed that I was probably ready, but she said she'd like to take a few sessions to wind down. At the last session, she hugged me good-bye.

I got a lot out of therapy. I can express myself easily now and it's so natural, it's hard to remember how it was before. And I can ask people for help. When my mother died, I asked one of my girlfriends to stay with me. I doubt I would have felt comfortable even accepting that a few years ago. Another change is that while I never went back to organized religion, I have become a spiritual person. I believe we all have a spark or a soul. I believe there is good energy and bad energy, and we can make good choices or bad ones. Worrying does no good.

For psychotherapy to work, the bottom line is you need to find the right therapist, be willing to work, and be as honest as you can. Mary changed my whole life, but she wouldn't say it that way. She would say we did it together.

Julia's therapist saw Julia's sister in treatment and when the sisters compared notes, Julia saw how different their perceptions of the same individual were. Generally, therapists will not work individually with members of the same family or even with intimate friends because no two relationships are alike, but in Julia's case it did not make a difference. Mary encouraged her client to join a group run by another therapist and Julia has benefited from that work.

By contrast, Lucy Katz's therapist saw many of her clients' relatives and friends in individual and group therapy. She appears to have fostered her clients' dependency and exploited them to build a multipurpose practice in which she combined personal and professional relationships.

Lucy Katz

Lucy Katz is a forty-eight-year-old opera singer from San Francisco. "All I remember about the Seventies is it was the end of disco fever. I was glad. I hated that. Otherwise, I have few memories of the time. I suspect that is because of the therapy."

I was in graduate school in 1976, preparing for a recital. It was the most important thing in my life and I let my other studies go. As a result, I got one bad grade, and that was enough to make me want to quit school. I went to the student counseling center and was assigned a psychiatrist at a local institute. I liked him. I saw him over the summer and into the fall, going once a week. I guess the most valuable thing he did was teach me auto-hypnosis. That's a relaxation technique and it helped when I was so anxious I couldn't sleep. It cost about $3 a session, it was helpful—I still use it—and I got what I needed in a brief period.

That fall I turned twenty-six and I met Jeff, my husband-to-be. We moved in together the following year. I loved Jeff and I wanted to stay in the relationship, but we had a sexual problem. I don't want to give the impression that I'd had a lot of previous experience—I hadn't—but I knew what an orgasm was and I wasn't getting there with Jeff. We went to the social worker who had been Jeff's therapist when he was a teenager. I had no misgivings about seeing someone Jeff already knew, but even if I had, I would have done it. I was desperate.

My worst fear was that our problem was hopeless, but Mrs. Fogel was reassuring. She assigned us sensate focus exercises—giving each other messages and abstaining from intercourse for a week or so. I guess it helped. We became more comfortable with our bodies and being together, but from the start, I was identified as the person with the problem, and I really bought into it.

After we finished couples therapy, I started seeing Mrs. Fogel in individual therapy and when she suggested I join her women's group, Jeff said I should, so I did. He was in her men's group. That was $35 a session for each of us in addition to $40 for my individual therapy. Mrs. Fogel also conducted couples' group marathons several weekends a year. They were $100 when we began and about $200 nine years later. The situation is even more complex when you consider that within the groups there was an "In" group and an "Out" group. Members of the "In" group were invited to Mrs. Fogel's beach house. Jeff and I never made it to that level. We knew we were excluded, but we weren't the only ones.

The women's group met for two hours every Monday night. There were six other women in group. You could talk about anything you wanted, but discussing anyone else's business outside of group was strictly forbidden. The other main rule was you had to be there come hell or high water. "Unless you are dying," Mrs. Fogel would say. The group rate was the same for everyone, but individual rates varied. We weren't supposed to discuss our individual rates.

We were encouraged to make friends and socialize outside group and I tried, but it was hard for me, and just like in couples treatment, I became perceived as the person with the problem. I found it very hard to talk about my sex life, so I was always the last one to speak and the others would pick on me. I am sorry to admit that when someone else was getting the same treatment, I'd join in. Mrs. Fogel didn't do that, but she didn't discourage us. It was all supposed to be in the name of helping another group member. I began to feel compelled to reveal details of my sex life I would never have told anyone.

While this was going on, I began to have vivid nightmares. I would dream I was being pressed to death. That's what they did to Blessed Margaret Clitherow, an English Catholic martyr. She was forced to lie on her back with a heavy door on top of her. Then a group of people piled on stones, heavier and heavier, until the life was crushed out of her. I dreamed the group was doing that to me and the more stones they piled on, the happier they were. They kept saying to each other, "I think she's dead now!" like they were doing a good thing. I kept trying to tell someone—myself, I think—that I was still alive. There was always a corner of myself I never gave away—that's the part of me that was still fighting. [Lucy begins to cry.] Actually, I was luckier than another group member who got so sucked in that she gave herself away to the group. I got kicked out of group before Melinda left, but we kept in touch.

The group experience basically devastated me, but I thought all this therapy would cure me and save my relationship with Jeff. I tried hard to be a good patient, whatever that is. Perhaps some of this need goes back to having been reared Catholic on a diet of the Baltimore Catechism. I was to be a good, compliant girl. To defer. I thought it was my own fault if I was mistreated. I had no self-esteem at all.

Jeff and I were married in September 1984. We invited Mrs. Fogel and the group members to our wedding and they all came. The greatest regret of my life is that we did not invite many of our family members. I wrote my family a terrible letter. I said I hated them. I can't blame the group for that letter. They didn't encourage me to do it, but it's amazing how like a cult group became. After what happened to us, I can understand extremes like Waco and Heaven's Gate. The formation of a cult is a very slow process. It reminds me of the story about how to boil a live frog. If you put the frog in a pot of boiling water, he'll jump out. You have to heat the water very slowly.

My behavior in group—not talking—eventually got me thrown out. Mrs. Fogel said I was being disruptive by not talking, which made it impossible for anyone else to get anything done, so about six months after Jeff and I were married, I was emancipated from group. This coincided with Jeff's coming home from his group and telling me he wanted me to move out. I didn't fight him because I was convinced I was a bad person and deserved it. I was too proud to beg and I thought if I did what he wanted, we might get back together someday.

Mrs. Fogel wanted me to meet with all the people in both groups, except Jeff, as a kind of farewell and I guess my brain clicked on around then. I wasn't married anymore, so I went in unafraid and dignified. The members asked me what I wanted from Jeff and I said, "Just for him to say the separation was not entirely my fault." The group seemed to respect me for that. They seemed surprised, too, as if they were seeing me for the first time.

I stayed in individual therapy with Mrs. Fogel, feeling afraid and inadequate after the separation, and I became even more dependent on her. She was the one fixed point in my life. I'm rather proud of how I conducted myself after the separation, though. I didn't become ill and I got plenty of support from my sister and two dear friends not in group. Three months later, Jeff called and told me he couldn't live without me and I went back to him. He had graduated from his group by then and he told me I could quit seeing Mrs. Fogel. You'd think that would have been music to my ears, but I was so hooked, I continued to see her secretly—sometimes twice a week—for another year. It's really crazy. I have never felt about anyone the way I felt about Mrs. Fogel.

Then I had lunch with Melinda and she told me that while she was in group, she had basically been functioning as Mrs. Fogel's appointments secretary, social secretary, and had even gotten her a couple of speaking engagements. Essentially, she'd become Mrs. Fogel's agent. I was shocked, but at the same time I thought, "Wow! Melinda must have been in the 'In' group!" That conversation took place in March 1988, and afterward, I sat down and wrote Mrs. Fogel a letter saying I couldn't lie to my husband anymore and I didn't want to see her anymore. Mrs. Fogel didn't write back or call me. It was over.

But it wasn't over in that my reaction to the end of those ten years was like PTSD [Post-Traumatic Stress Disorder]. I was relieved not to have to go to sessions anymore, but I would have flashbacks to the worst ones and I couldn't turn off the scenes in my mind. After two or three months of considerable pain, I went to a behavioral therapist. She encouraged me to rebuild my life—resume the things I'd stopped—and she assigned mental relaxation exercises for when I had flashbacks. You relax your whole body by concentrating on something else. She also had me do an exercise where I would deliberately recall a particularly bad time—saturate myself in the feeling—and then let go of the feeling and replace it with a pleasant one. She encouraged me to talk about my experiences with Mrs. Fogel and the group.

At first it was extremely difficult for me to put into words what had happened, but when she said I had been "exposed and humiliated," the floodgates opened. I talked a lot and I cried a lot and it really helped. That therapist was a truly nice, caring person and if I ever needed to go back to her, I know I could. She's the one who told me a lot of people think Freud was a crock and didn't know anything about women. [Laughs.] During the behavioral therapy, I began to sing again. Right now, I'm in rehearsal for *Don Giovanni*.

During the behavioral therapy, I began to think about the money, the time I'd wasted, the pain I'd endured, and I finally had the nerve to acknowledge my anger at Mrs. Fogel and Jeff and myself. The sequel to all this is that my husband and I are still together. We've worked out our differences as well as any couple ever does. I came to realize I have a right to my anger as well as all my other feelings. My sister helped me get back together with my family. She's the one who told me, after the separation when I thought it was all my fault, "Well, you know, these things are never just one person's fault." That helped me feel less like throwing myself in front of a truck.

Mrs. Fogel's training may have been Freudian, but Freud did not advocate marital counseling or group treatment. Those therapeutic methods were developed later by psychotherapists representing a range of theoretical ideas. Whatever her theoretical orientation, Mrs. Fogel violated the code of ethics for clinical social workers because she engaged in dual relationships—she participated in two or more roles with one person. The code prohibits entering into or promising personal, scientific, professional, financial, or other relationships with a client or patient if it appears that this might impair objectivity or exploit the other party. Lucy's experience illustrates that the power differential between psychotherapists and patients can be harmful when it's used by self-aggrandizing therapists who are careless about maintaining clear boundaries.

The last case for this chapter is the story of a young feminist. Twelve years after publication of Betty Friedan's *The Feminine Mystique*, Patricia Woodruff began psychotherapy.

Patricia Woodruff

Patricia Woodruff is a fifty-one-year-old psychotherapist from Wellesley, Massachusetts. "The Seventies was the beginning of talking about possibilities and potentials for equality between the sexes. We haven't come a long way since then. Men remain sexists at heart. They give lip service to equality."

When I was twenty-seven and getting ready to separate from my husband, I consulted a therapist. This was in 1975. It was a horrible, humiliating experience. The therapist pathologized me. He insisted that the problems in my marriage were all my fault. I felt he didn't understand or even hear me. After two sessions, I didn't go back. Interestingly, I felt I was doing something wrong by ending treatment. That says a lot about how I was at the time. I had a lot of negative inner talk going on.

Then Bill and I sought marriage counseling. We went to Dr. Black, a Ph.D. psychologist. He was probably my contemporary, or perhaps a bit older. He sat with his arms wrapped backwards over his chair, and he didn't bother to try to make Bill or me comfortable. It was a very cold,

clinical assessment. I spoke first. I said I was lonely in my marital relationship and that our fights were never resolved. Bill countered that he
found me intimidating and said I complained too much. Dr. Black replied, "I can see where you'd find her castrating." Since I was well-
schooled to believe all the problems resided in me, I didn't argue.

The next morning, I told Bill I wasn't going back to Dr. Black. I'd find
another therapist, but if that didn't work out, our marriage was over. I
went to a psychologist our neighbor recommended—a hypnotherapist.
The initial evaluation was conducted by the guy's assistant. She took me
into a room with what looked like a dentist's chair. I sat there with
headphones on listening to music to get into a hypnotic state. There was
no communication. I was then led to the doctor's inner sanctum. Seated
on his throne, he told me the evaluation would be $100 and to make an
appointment with his secretary for the following week. No discussion.
No advice. That was it.

I didn't complain because I didn't have that kind of voice or authority
then. He was the professional, but hypnotherapy seemed like a scam and
Bill never supported the idea of therapy. He said I was making a mountain out of a molehill. We had to pay out-of-pocket because our insurance
didn't cover it, and it was a financial strain at the time so I cancelled my
appointment with the hypnotherapist. He didn't call to ask why. I
thought that was because I was such a sickie he didn't want me as a
patient. Now I think he was simply indifferent to my suffering and didn't
know how to form a therapeutic relationship.

My first two therapists wanted me to adjust to an intolerable situation.
That has nothing to do with growth. It simply maintains the dysfunctional status quo. My life didn't change until I got out of that marriage.
Then I went back to school for a master's in women's studies. The director of the program was a feminist and much of the work we studied
came out of the Stone Center at Wellesley. I learned that women need
connection and men are socialized not to. People get screwed up because
of their relationships, which, in our society, maintain the incest model.
When I went for therapy, if the therapists had seen me as a person—
had cared about my well-being in a relational context—it would have
jeopardized the patriarchy. That is why they could not help me.

The relational model, which is the work of Jean Baker Miller and others,
posits that an inner sense of connection to others is a central organizing
feature of women's psychological development. Miller writes that psychoanalytic thinking has accepted without question the Western notion
that becoming self-sufficient is the goal of human psychological development. The degree to which we can achieve separation and independence is the standard by which we should define ourselves as
healthy human beings. Such traditional ideas neglect or misunderstand

many aspects of women's experience. Connection, the experience of mutual engagement and empathy, is a continuing source of psychological growth. Disconnection leads to anxiety, isolation, and depression.

As I see it, therapy needs to include philosophy and spirituality. It needs to address questions like, "What makes a good world?" and "What makes me happy?"—not, "Why am I not happy?" The mental health field has changed now that there are more women therapists. Women have a greater understanding than men do of gender differences, the power structure, and the spiritual issues that make men and women different.

Fifty-six respondents, fifteen men and forty-one women, saw analysts, psychiatrists, psychologists, and clinical social workers during the 1970s. They were between eighteen and forty-six years old when treatment began. Seven people were in classical Freudian analyses. Twenty-eight were in some form of group psychotherapy.

In the first of the ten stories in this chapter, Sandra and Gavin Hilgardner talk about couples group therapy. They were bemused by Ron, the charismatic, controlling group leader with whom they were also in individual treatment. While they appreciate the love and support they received in group, they note that it was insular and like a cult. Gavin says, "It's almost as if there are two worlds—the world of group and the normal world." Joseph Hans (Chapter 2) makes the same observation. Lucy Katz, who survived lengthy individual and group therapy, remarks, "It's amazing how like a cult group became. After what happened to us, I can understand extremes like Waco and Heaven's Gate."

Others remark that group was valuable. Henry Hamner attended a weekly Recovery, Inc. group for people diagnosed with a mental illness: "I learned I wasn't the only one." Francine Donovan learned the same thing in Confront. She is also a longtime member of Alcoholics Anonymous. Frieda Sager joined a support group for manic depressives and found her two closest friends. Julia Mason found an eating disorders group "phenomenally good for me." But Maggie Glass didn't like group. "It was so hard talking about myself to total strangers."

Randy Castleman, anorexic, bulimic, and depressed, was treated by a woman, a Ph.D. psychologist, who used a combination of techniques, including behavioral/cognitive therapy, an innovation further described in Chapter 5. Henry Hamner was depressed and contemplated suicide before beginning therapy but, "As a practicing Catholic, I could not kill myself." His analytically-oriented therapy was with a female psychoanalyst. Julia Mason, who describes herself as spiritual if not religious, was treated by a female social worker for depression. Lucy Katz, depressed and unable to achieve orgasm with her boyfriend, also saw a female social worker. "Reared Catholic on a diet of the Baltimore Catechism," Lucy has since left the church.

Frieda Sager, who had an attachment disorder and was treated for depression and anxiety, says, "I'm sort of a Zen Buddhist–atheist–agnostic, but if there is such a thing as God or providence, I credit whatever that is with allowing Dr. Silvio's path to cross mine." Francine Donovan has this to say: "Freud called religion a 'mass delusion.' I had a belief in God growing up and I brought that belief to analysis. I think [it] could have helped me, but analysis completely squashed it. I didn't recover until . . . I couldn't go on and cried out to God for help."

Six of the ten people who were treated for depression eventually began taking antidepressants. Henry Hamner credits Tofranil with miraculously changing his life. He doesn't like the side effects and neither does Julia Mason, who takes Prozac, but they find the benefits of their medications outweigh the adverse side effects.

Patricia Woodruff, who tried individual therapy, marriage counseling and hypnotherapy, rated her treatment experiences negatively but subsequently went into the mental health field. Five respondents (Connie Claybrooke, Randy Castleman, Maggie Glass, Frieda Sager, and Julia Mason) gave their treatments outstanding ratings. Five others (Sandra and Gavin Hilgardner, Francine Donovan, Henry Hamner, and Lucy Katz) describe mixed responses. Only Maggie Glass and Frieda Sager keep in touch with their former therapists.

The climate of the time was such that both Democrats and Republicans favored comprehensive treatment of mental illness. Psychotherapy became culturally acceptable, but even so, most of the people in this chapter felt uneasy telling others they were in treatment. Maggie Glass, who used alcohol and street drugs, attempted suicide and was hospitalized repeatedly, never mentions she was in treatment for ten years because she fears people would then regard her as "crazy." Sam Temple (Chapter 3) will tell people he's been in therapy but not why. He says LSD was a boon, but Frieda Sager ended up on a locked ward in a state psychiatric hospital after experimenting with LSD. Francine Donovan used alcohol and drugs, hoarded prescription drugs and tried to kill herself by overdosing on them, and was hospitalized more than once.

Sandra and Gavin Hilgardner estimate that group sessions ran $20 or $30 apiece and group marathons were $120. Lucy Katz and her boyfriend each paid $35 a session for group therapy, an additional $40 for Lucy's individual treatment, and $100 to $200 for group marathons. Connie Claybrooke's psychoanalysis was $70 an hour. Her insurance paid 50 percent and placed no restriction on the number of sessions. Francine Donovan's analysis, for which her father paid, cost $50 an hour. Randy Castleman remembers the 1970s as "the good old days" when his insurance cheerfully paid for most of his cognitive/behavioral treatment without imposing any limit on the number of sessions.

Maggie Glass's therapy was covered by a state program for the needy. Frieda Sager went to a community mental health center with a sliding-scale fee. "When I didn't have the $20, my parents gave me the money." Henry Hamner's insurance plan paid for a full workup at the Menninger Clinic but did not cover outpatient psychotherapy which cost him $50 to $75 an hour. Julia Mason paid $50 a session because her insurance did not cover treatment by social workers. Patricia Woodruff paid $100 for an initial psychiatric evaluation by a hypnotherapist's assistant because her insurance company would not.

During the 1970s, the cost of medical care rose faster than the cost of living. "By 1979, the total cost of medical care reached $212.2 billion, or 9.1 percent of the GNP . . . an increase of almost 20 percent [over 1970]."[2] One family in five had no health insurance and one family in four had insurance for hospitalization but not for outpatient expenses. Americans believed there was a crisis in health care because of escalating costs driven in part by Medicare and Medicaid expenses—humanitarian acts of Congress which brought some people into the health care system for the first time.[3]

Like President Eisenhower, President Nixon said something had to be done or the system would break down. In 1973, the Health Maintenance Organization (HMO) Act was passed. An HMO is a prepaid group practice in which people, or their employers, pay a monthly premium for comprehensive health services. HMOs try to keep costs down by encouraging preventive services, such as inoculations, and by ceilings on medical costs.[4] Physicians are on salary paid by the HMO, and patients receive hospital coverage, laboratory tests, and prescription drugs at little or no additional cost.[5]

While HMOs are less expensive than traditional insurance plans, patients may be treated by whoever is on duty—not necessarily their doctor of choice. Further, HMOs will not pay for the services of doctors who are not members of the plan, and many medical services must be pre-approved by HMO non-physician staff. Still, by the end of the 1970s, nine percent of the population belonged to HMOs.

While "relationships" were mentioned in previous chapters, in the 1970s the word saturates psychiatric jargon: people enter therapy because of difficulties in interpersonal relationships. Patricia Woodruff comments, "I was lonely in my marital relationship," and "People get screwed up because of their relationships." Connie Claybrooke's "love relationships were rotten." Lucy Katz wanted to "stay in the relationship" with her boyfriend. More about relationships in the next chapter.

5 The 1980s: The Centrality of the Relationship

Although it was slow, at last attention moved on to the vital interchange between the two participants in the clinical venture. . . . Allegiances led to antagonisms and controversies flared . . . yet for all of those who established and defended fixed positions, there were others who strove to integrate. Because of the considerable advances made in the last half of the twentieth century, the analytic field is no longer described as the mind of the patient inspected from the remote detachment of the analyst like a test tube viewed at arm's length by a white-coated scientist.

Warren Poland

A GUIDE TO THE UNITED STATES OF THE 1980s

Population: 226,542,203

Average salary: $15,721 per year

        Coal miners: $24,555

        Farm laborers: $7,434

        Federal employees (civilian): $21,206

        Medical/health services workers: $14,728

        Public school teachers: $15,438

Inflation: 13.5 percent

Unemployment: 7.1 percent

Social welfare: $303 billion

Births/1,000: 15.9 (smallest birth rate increase since the Depression)

Marriages/1,000: 10.6

Divorces/1,000: 5.2

Deaths/1,000: 8.8

Average household size: 2.76

Women in labor force: 47.7 percent

Cost of living: Clothing: Andrea Pfister patent leather women's flats, $190; Bally men's oxfords, $154

Food: bread, 51 cents a loaf; coffee, $2.98 a pound; eggs, 84 cents a dozen; milk, $1.04 a quart; oranges, $1.37 a dozen; round steak, $2.37 a pound

Housing: Split level, 3-bedroom, 2½ bath, Scarsdale, N.Y., $115,000

Transportation: "Previously owned" 1978 Mercedes, silver, 30,000 miles, $19,500

Fun: Cabbage patch dolls, Rubik's cube, CD players, aerobics, break dancing

Pulitzer Prizes: Biography: Edmund Morris, *The Rise of Theodore Roosevelt*

History: Leon F. Litwack, *Been in the Storm So Long*

Nonfiction: Douglas R. Hofstadter, *Godel, Escher, Bach: An Eternal Golden Braid*

Sources: Robert Famighetti (ed.), *The World Almanac and Book of Facts, 1997* (Mahwah, NJ: World Almanac Books, 1997), pp. 325, 326, 381; Scott Derks (ed.), *The Value of a Dollar, 1860–1989* (Detroit, MI: Gale Research Inc., 1994), p. 521; Lois Gordon and Alan Gordon, *The Columbia Chronicles of American Life, 1910–1992* (New York: Columbia University Press, 1995), pp. 664, 672; U.S. Bureau of the Census, *Historical Statistics of the United States, Colonial Times to 1970, Bicentennial Edition, Part I* (Washington, D.C., 1975), pp. 59, 74, 372, 398, 490; Advertisement in *The New York Times*, January 4, 1980, p. A21; January 6, 1980, p. A40; January 29, 1980, p. B15; January 3, 1981, p. A38.

Rarely has our economy simultaneously experienced both unemployment and double-digit inflation, but that was the situation in 1980. Increasing budget and trade deficits rocked many Americans' belief in the viability of our economy. On the home front, mortgage rates exceeded 20 percent, the divorce rate shot up from one in three marriages in 1970 to one in two. Single-parent families increased 50 percent and the number of unmarried couples living together tripled.[1]

In November 1980, Ronald Reagan became our fortieth president, thrashing Jimmy Carter, 43 million to 35 million votes. Our first divorced president was rarely seen in church, yet he appealed to family values and his proclaimed apparent piety captivated fundamentalists, who had overtaken mainstream Protestants in sheer numbers, as well as other conservatives. Ronald Reagan looked and acted like a president.

Reagan's strategy to restore the economy involved cutting social programs and reducing income and capital gains taxes, thus stimulating capital investment and job creation. Coupled with lower taxes, military expenditures soared, rising to $303 billion a year by the end of his second term—half a million dollars a minute. The huge gap between income and outgo could only be closed by borrowing, and so it was. The strategy was not immediately effective; the first two years of Reagan's term witnessed a serious recession. In 1983, however, the economy revived and remained relatively healthy until 1987 when the stock market crashed but slowly recovered. By the end of the 1980s, taxpayers were paying billions in interest to the government's creditors, and more billions to bail out savings and loan executives who had foolishly risked—and in some cases embezzled—their depositors' money.

Notwithstanding the federal government's efforts to limit doctor and hospital fees, Medicare expenses ballooned to a point where they were the third largest budget item, exceeded only by defense and social security. In 1980, our society spent $250.1 billion on health care. In the last year of the decade, we spent $604.3 billion, a staggering 242 percent increase, far outpacing inflation. Two figures sum it up: In 1980, the average American adult or child spent $1,059 on health care. By 1990, the tab came to $2,566.[2] A semi-private hospital room averaged $127 a day in 1980 and $250 a day in 1988. The consequences were enormous. Businesses cut back on employee medical benefits, outpatient clinics and same-day surgical centers proliferated, and insurance companies imposed restrictions on covered types and permissible length of treatment.

In the 1970s, some respondents valued their connection to religion. Now we begin to hear from the disaffected. Philip Bohrer, a forty-two-year-old surveyor from Pittsburgh: "Christianity was a real bummer for me. I still generalize that Jesus Christ was a great guy, but Christianity is a negative influence. As a child, I'd see Sunday School teachers smoking, or shouting and cursing at football games, and even slamming their children about. It's hypocrisy."

We begin with the stories of two men and a woman who found analysts able to adapt their treatment styles to their patients' needs. In the first case, a Roman Catholic priest is in therapy with a Polish Catholic survivor of the Nazi concentration camps.

Father SJ

Father SJ, a fifty-five-year-old priest, teaches Catholic mysticism, spirituality, and the Old Testament at an east coast university. "The Eighties were the beginning of the conservative era and here I was, a former Sixties radical, supervising ultra-conservative twenty and thirty-year-olds. If they'd known about my past [laughs], they'd never have listened to me!"

I went to a psychoanalyst for a modern reason: I wanted to be more

effective in my work. It was 1982 and I'd been appointed to a sensitive
job counseling men going into the priesthood. One of the issues was
celibacy. I was thirty-eight and examining my thoughts about vocations,
my relationships with authority figures, and my own sexuality. Priests
and nuns have to deal with an area of their lives they sometimes think
they can conveniently lock up and shelve. My ostensible reason, then,
was a screen for wanting to examine my own issues.

I'd heard of the unconscious and I was aware that in my own life
some things just did not fit, but it came as a shock that there could be
forces and motivations within me that influenced my life without my
conscious knowledge. I even considered going to a woman analyst.
[Laughs.] What an avant-garde idea for a priest!

A psychiatrist at the school where I taught recommended an analyst
originally from Poland. Dr. Otto had been imprisoned by the Nazis during the war and was probably sixty, a practicing Catholic, pro-life and
pro-democracy. He had a charming accent and excellent verbal skills. I
was impressed by his ability to put just the right word on the experiences
I described. He was interested in priests and sisters, and I know he was
acquainted with Catholic mysticism. Some of my favorite authors' works
graced his bookshelves, along with the collected works of Freud and
Jung.

Dr. Otto had an office in the psychiatry department of a local hospital
where I saw him once a week. I liked the guy, but when things I was
not comfortable with started opening up, I wondered how much to trust
him. I'd met a nun and I thought we had a special spiritual relationship
but I learned it was not platonic. Living on an instinctive level and following the genetic script, I thought Elizabeth held every good thing in
life for me, but during the first six months of therapy, I realized that if
I kept this up, I would have to leave the priesthood. I had to make a
decision I did not want to make, and at that point I thought it would be
great to step off a curb, get hit by a car, and not have to face myself.
Analytic psychotherapy is not pain free.

But you can't hide in therapy forever. There is only so much information you can get and then you have to make a decision. Leaving the
priesthood was not an option, and continuing down the path I was on
would have meant I'd have to lead a double life, which would have been
catastrophic. Elizabeth's life and my own came to a fork in the road and
I took a different path.

I sometimes look back on the decision I had to make when I was thirty-
eight. My faith taught me that if you live your life according to the rules
and are a good person, conflicts can be resolved in a good way, but I
learned that we humans are sometimes presented with choices and none
of them are what we want. I paid a high price for the priesthood. I never

imagined I'd be faced with something like that, but God works that way. This is a mystery.

After I made my decision, Dr. Otto said we could call the work complete, but I took that opportunity to renegotiate treatment. The focus shifted to an examination of my unconscious as well as the problems my counselees brought in. Dr. Otto became my supervisor as well as my therapist and our work continued eight years longer. If I hadn't had health insurance—my plan paid 80 percent—I couldn't have done it. The charge for individual psychotherapy was $80 an hour in the beginning and $110 at the end.

This therapeutic endeavor was one Dr. Otto and I undertook together. I did not lie on the couch and free associate. Dr. Otto was an active therapist who spoke at least half the time. His comments in the "Aha!" moments I experienced when I suddenly understood something important would lead me to a deepened comprehension. He tried to help me connect childhood memories to my current behavior. For example, my mother had to be hospitalized when I was five. She had tuberculosis and died when I was ten. What I learned from my mother's death, a belief that became imprinted on my unconscious, is that women won't be true blue, faithful friends. They will leave you right when you need them.

My father was the strong silent type and gave little affection. After Mother died, he began to work more and was gone a great deal. Dr. Otto pointed out that he might have felt he was left holding the bag. Whatever my father's reasons, when I was a young teenager I needed a man to emulate, and he wasn't around. I learned to respect authority but I didn't learn how to handle conflict. I became ingratiating toward male authority figures and when that resulted in approval—especially the Bishop's!—I'd be in heaven, but when things would go wrong, I'd bend over backwards too much.

Dr. Otto helped me find the origins of this personality pattern. I had depended on my father for everything—food, clothing, shelter—and having lost my mother, I certainly didn't want to lose him. I felt on shaky ground once he remarried and started having a new family. Consequently, I was not able to stand up to him when I was thirteen or fourteen, the time when boys become notoriously rebellious. I did my rebelling later on and it cost me.

After I completed training at the seminary, I sought permission to live and work in the "real" world for a year. This was unheard of and the Bishop—the head honcho—denied my request, but I went ahead and did it anyway. Over the course of that year, I became wiser, more stable, and better attuned to the world parishioners live in, but the Bishop regarded me ever after as a rebellious independent and withheld some choice assignments.

Dr. Otto was a devoted Catholic, but he spoke of the church in a way that exposed his knowledge of the unconscious repression it fosters. I envied the active sex life I imagined he had, but he would say he admired me and what I was trying to do with my life. He was a trusted confidant, as honest with me about myself as anyone could have been.

With a friend you have to hold back, but not with Dr. Otto. We worked on how I felt inside when I'd hide behind other people and let them make my decisions. How I had developed sexually, yet put a lid on my feelings. Dr. Otto gave me feedback and information I could act on.

After sessions, I would review what we talked about and try to remember what he said. Insights come and go. You have to be aggressive and look for opportunities to practice your insights. Integrate what you've learned into your life. I believe prayer is the great integrator. It has become more and more important to me.

When Dr. Otto retired, he told me I could call him any time. I have not, although there have been times when I have wanted to, but I feel a strength in managing my own life. I think he would be proud to know that I can deal with my feelings and crises better because of him.

I find the common impressions of therapy are stereotypical. It is neither a panacea nor a useless band-aid for the self-absorbed. Therapy is hard work and a lifelong endeavor one must ultimately carry out alone. I got to know who I am, what my motivations are, and I continue to use and refine that knowledge. I have examined my own suffering and I try to make it available to others to help them with their suffering. This has helped me put my pain into a larger context.

When I was in therapy, no one but the referring psychiatrist, Dr. Otto, and Elizabeth knew. I've had no reason to tell anyone—but you—in the years since, but I've recommended analysis and psychotherapy to students and parishioners. I continue to study Freud and Jung, and I think I might have liked to be an analyst as well as a priest. Freud, I believe, was a great man but also a creature of the century in which he lived. We all are.

Our next story is of a young woman in cognitive-behavioral treatment with a psychologist who was also a pastoral counselor.

Lynn Ellison

Lynn Ellison is a forty-seven-year-old secretary who lives in Hartford, Connecticut. "I got a B.A. in Business Administration going to school at night while working full-time. I was climbing the ladder rapidly when, in 1980, I was laid off with my entire department. I really identified who I was with what I did, so it was a huge loss."

The background to being laid off is I was in a serious automobile accident two years before that—I was in critical condition and nearly died. I have a metal shaft in one thigh. I was in physical therapy for a long time and I still do special exercises to maintain mobility.

My parents fought constantly while I was growing up. They separated when I was fourteen and Mom had a cerebral hemorrhage and died that Christmas Eve. Dad came back, but he didn't know how to raise me and my sister. He was overly demanding, and Ellen and I could never measure up to his expectations. We grew up thinking we were never good enough. I became very critical of myself and everyone else.

I finally found a job as a secretary, a real comedown, but I had to make a living. I thought I could get myself together and find a better job, but when I'd get home from work, I'd sit in my apartment and cry. I couldn't seem to snap out of it. Then my grandfather, the only parent-type relative I was close to, died.

My sister was in therapy with a Ph.D. psychologist and when she went on vacation she suggested I take her appointments while she was gone. I had never been in counseling, but I went and I thought it helped. Her therapist said he couldn't see me and my sister at the same time, so he referred me to the psychologist he'd trained with who was also a pastoral counselor.

Pastoral counselors are members of the clergy. Programs in pastoral counseling are offered in seminaries, and many members of the clergy have taken formal courses in mental hygiene taught by psychiatrists. Graduates receive diplomas or certificates and are permitted to work with mentally ill patients.

Dr. Loring was forty-two. I know because after treatment, I went to his birthday party. He wasn't old enough to be my father, but he sort of took on that role. He called what he did cognitive-behavioral therapy. What that boiled down to was teaching me coping skills I should have gotten from my parents.

Behaviorism was introduced in the United States in 1913 by psychologist James B. Watson, who believed that all of human behavior is a physiological response to external stimuli. Since observable responses can be measured scientifically, behavioral psychologists can validate their studies with a certainty that is not possible among therapists who deal with affects (feelings are not always easily observable and quantifiable). In the mid-1960s, behaviorist B. F. Skinner wrote that almost all emotions were conditioned responses and as such could be learned or unlearned. That was the beginning of behavior modification therapy.

The field developed rapidly during the 1960s and 1970s in opposition to psychoanalysis. The cognitive approach was developed by

Aaron Beck and others for use in the treatment of depression. Beck's thesis was that cognitive processes (thinking) affect behavior and behavior will change if one's thinking changes. This type of therapy is a short-term, problem-solving model that teaches rational coping skills for dealing with personal problems. Cognitive-behavioral treatment does not consider the unconscious workings of the mind or place much importance on a person's emotional life, concentrating instead on correcting dysfunctional, self-defeating behavior.

At the first session, Dr. Loring gave me a test and told me it suggested I wouldn't stay in treatment. He warned me it would be hard. A few months later, I started to complain, "This isn't working. I'm still depressed. Why is this taking so long?" I tested him like that all through therapy, but he never asked why I was showing up every week if therapy was useless. I think he knew I would have used any excuse to stop because I was miserable and opening up made it worse. I wanted depression to be like a sore throat. You go to the doctor and he gives you pills and it goes away. I thought it might go faster if I came in twice a week, but that just made it worse. There wasn't enough recovery time between sessions when I was starting to deal with my anger toward my father for expecting too much and with my mother for dying. That was the hardest part.

Dr. Loring asked me to bring in pictures of me as a child. He'd look at them and say things like, "That little girl looks like she's having a good time." He was helping me see the other side of my childhood— that it hadn't been all bad. He liked another picture where I was bossing my sister around. "Now, there's an assertive little girl," he said. I had trouble being assertive. When someone disagreed with me, I'd get cold and shaky. I learned that dissent frightened me because I was afraid I'd be abandoned. Dr. Loring taught me how to think a situation through, not to immediately tell myself, "You can't handle this." That's the "changing the tapes in your head" approach and it helped me.

When I started therapy, I'd try to make things look perfect on the outside because I couldn't do anything about how I felt inside. I'd line up all the cans in the pantry by content and fold all the dishtowels into perfect squares. That would make me feel better. I made a list of things to talk about in therapy. A real breakthrough came when I was able to think while I was in his office, instead of getting out my list. Even so, after a year of therapy I was still having problems at work and I wasn't getting along with my sister, who was my only friend. Dr. Loring sent me to a psychiatrist for medication and I tried tricyclics, but the side effects were pretty bad. I gained weight, had a dry mouth, and my hands trembled so I stopped taking them.

Then Dr. Loring suggested I join his group. I did it to please him, but

I never felt any similarity to the others in group. Being in group made me feel weird and crazy—like "One Of The People Who Is Sick." That was my view of people who were in therapy. I was ashamed of needing therapy and I hated group. I wasn't able to think well enough then to see where I was headed. I didn't get the larger picture.

About three years into treatment, Dr. Loring moved. Talk about abandonment. The only thing that got me through it was we continued therapy by phone. That probably wouldn't have worked at first, but I knew him well enough by then that not seeing him was something like lying on the couch in analysis must be. The phone sessions were one of the most valuable parts of my therapy and we kept it up until I didn't need it anymore.

Depression has been an ongoing problem for me and I've read about the new treatments. When Zoloft came out, I decided to try it. The depression kept breaking through, though, and so I switched to Paxil a couple of years ago. Paxil works for me. I get it from my internist. I've never tried Prozac but my girlfriend did. You know the joke? "Listening to Prozac is hearing the sound of silence." You hear how great Prozac is, but a lot of people can't have orgasms when they're on it.

Things have changed since the Seventies. Because of the accident, I'll probably go to a chiropractor for the rest of my life. My managed care plan covers thirty chiropractic sessions a year, but only ten sessions for "treatment of a mental illness." I think that's pejorative. When I saw Dr. Loring, he charged $50 and my insurance covered most of it. If I needed to see him today, my insurance wouldn't pay for it unless he was on their approved provider list and then they'd only pay $20 a session. Dr. Loring always said he never turned anyone away if they couldn't pay. That's just the way he was.

Over the course of four-and-a-half years of therapy, I grew up. I went from being Dr. Loring's most difficult client—he said that!—to a person with a life worth living. I have my days just like anybody else, but now I know how to reach out for help and I can extend my hand to others, too. I've thanked Dr. Loring over and over for saving my life. He says I did all the work, but I couldn't have done it without him. I benefited tremendously—kicking and screaming.

Lynn reminds us of Henry Hammer (Chapter 4). They were both overly conscientious about their work and obligations, but anxious and depressed beneath the surface. Like Henry, Lynn could only value herself in terms of her performance and when she was physically unable to keep up, she plunged into depression. Like many young people who expect a quick fix, Lynn entered treatment unaware that it would take time to face and work through painful memories.

Group therapy didn't work for Lynn, but she tells us that in the years since, she has run support groups at her church. "There's a lot of power and wisdom in a group. I just wasn't ready to see it and use it fifteen years ago. Another thing I've learned is that depression was a gift. I would never have gone into therapy if I hadn't been depressed, and without therapy I'd never have grown psychologically."

Lynn received more from cognitive-behavioral therapy than she had anticipated. In the following case, a graphic artist also finds more in a Jungian analysis than he expected. He approached the endeavor as an intellectual pursuit, but found that transformation is what he really wanted.

Andrew Graham

Andrew Graham is a fifty-six-year-old graphic artist who lives in South Bend, Indiana. "I'd been fascinated with Jung from the mid-Sixties, the hippie era when Jung became a household word. In-depth soul searching, issues of mortality, and issues of the soul all came to the surface for me and I've been struggling with them ever since."

I began a Jungian analysis in 1982 just before my fortieth birthday. I was in analysis for about three years. I'd studied anthropology and psychology in college and I became intrigued with Jung's work. He looked at analysis as something you did in the second half of life, so, since I was there, I decided to do it.

I did not feel the need for help or transformation which seems to propel some people into analysis. I'd joined a Jungian study group where I learned that a Jungian analyst was moving to the area. Because of the availability and because I'd just inherited some money and could afford it, I decided to go ahead with an analysis. I come from a WASP background where no one ever went for psychotherapy. I believe my family viewed it with suspicion. Accordingly, when I asked to use my inheritance for analysis, I presented the idea to my family, and—this is important—to myself, as an educational need. In other words, if I was going to learn something I needed to know, it was okay; if I was going because something was amiss emotionally, or if it was for self-help, that was not okay. It took me a while in treatment to get past that and realize I had an unconscious need to be in some type of therapy and I had denied that need for years.

My analyst, Terry Packard, was perhaps forty-five. She was a social worker who had trained at the Jungian Institute in Zurich. Terry saw people in her home office. She was a rigid, formal woman who sat bolt upright and did not move around much during sessions. I echoed her rigidity and did not find it a comfortable atmosphere at all. It wasn't cold or hostile—just not laid back.

When I went for the evaluation, I was intimidated. I felt like I was back in college asking her to supervise my thesis! But we agreed to work together intensively, five days a week, face to face. Jungians, unlike Freudians, do not use the couch or sit in such a way that you can't see each other. We cut back to three days a week after a few months because Terry didn't feel we were making progress and I have to say I agreed with her. I found the work frustrating, and I think Terry found the five-day frequency strenuous.

What I remember best is the dream analysis. When we started out, she had me keep a dream journal, write down everything I could remember of my dreams every night. The more I wrote, the more it would bring up. I'd write five or ten pages a day. I still have thousands of pages in storage, and I still record my dreams. Terry would pick up on one piece of a dream and we would work on that. Her analytic interpretation was very intellectual. She would fit things into archetypal patterns. Those are overlying patterns—themes, ideas, concepts, or images—that transcend the personal and have meaning for a lot of people. For example, if I dreamed of a confrontation with an evil father figure, that figure could be personal, but it could also be common to many people. It could be an illustration of the patriarchal nature of society itself.

The experience of analysis turned out to be very different than I had expected. I got into analysis to study Jung's metaphysical theory. I had set my dream life and associations outside myself until the revelation came that I was not studying some body of metaphysics; I was studying myself. That was a shock. What I did in analysis got me into a very different place in life. I had a lot of adolescent narcissism left over of which I had not been aware. I saw myself as the center of the universe and I learned what part of the universe I actually was. The way it happened was that I put my emotional nature under a microscope through analysis. I would wake up in the morning and assess my mood and try to tie how I was feeling right then to what I had dreamed. I began to see that things were happening that I was not in control of. Things that were much bigger than me.

My whole life was altered by the analysis. It kicked me out of the introverted world I'd lived in and its impact was a very noticeable loss of innocence. That was one of the costs of the analysis—far greater and more important than the financial cost, which was about $18,000, and that was a discount from her regular fee because I was coming in so many days a week. I think a lot of analysts do that. But the point is, I learned that I had to grow up. I had to understand that if I wanted to experience anything in life, it was up to me to go out and get it. It would not just come to me.

Another impact of analysis on my life happened when Terry got very interested in yoga. She became body oriented. I started going to yoga classes at her suggestion and we were in the same class. I found that by becoming more in touch with my body and emotions, I could derail the intellectualizing process and get to the feeling level. That's when my life changed. That's transformation.

We planned for termination and for the last six months tapered off, meeting twice a week and then once a week. I didn't want to just stop abruptly. Terry left the door open, as the expression goes. She said I could always come back. I never went back for further sessions but we kept in touch for a couple of years.

Analysis with Terry was like this: She provided a framework and acted as the container in which transformation could take place. Jung talks about alchemy—putting two materials together to create a material worth far more than the individual materials. That's what happened in my analysis and that's why I was transformed.

Andrew had inherited enough money to afford to pay his analyst $40 a session. Now we will hear from two young musicians who could not afford standard analytical fees. Bond Meyer found a senior analyst in private practice who was willing to take him on as a pro bono patient. Andrea Weiss found an analyst-in-training at an institute that offered sliding scale fees based on income.

Bond Meyer

Bond Meyer is a forty-three-year-old first-chair symphony violinist. When he isn't traveling, home is Montreal. "I talked about the rise of AIDS in session. I'd been in treatment about a year at the beginning of the epidemic [1981], before AZT or any of the drugs we have now, and doctors couldn't provide anything but palliative measures. I watched friends young like me—I was 24— waste away, go blind, and die."

In 1980, I lived alone in an unguarded apartment building in a high crime area. One night on the way to rehearsal, I was mugged. Tied up and robbed. When the guys left, I struggled loose and went to rehearsal, but about a month later, I began to have anxiety attacks. I'd freak out inside.

A friend of mine knew a hypnotist who helped people with stage fright. I thought maybe he could help me, so I asked my friend for his name, but after we talked my friend said she thought there was more to it than anxiety and recommended I see her analyst.

Dr. Stone was sixtyish. She was in private practice and taught at an analytic institute. I'd had a great relationship with my mother, who died when I was fourteen. Because of her—not my father—I developed an ability to trust and I habitually transferred positively to older women, so Dr. Stone and I were a good fit.

I was very impressed at my first consultation. Dr. Stone was smart and incredibly empathetic. She recommended analysis or something close to it, intensive analytic psychotherapy, but I was living on loans and couldn't afford it. I asked her if I could get someone through the institute and she gave me three names, but warned me that an analyst-in-training might be more interested in studying me than helping me and when he finished training, I might be left stranded if he moved away or went into private practice and raised his rates.

I thought it over for a couple of months and called her again. I guess she'd thought it over, too, because she decided to take me for what I could afford, $75 a week. It was a Freudian analysis, on the couch, four sessions a week for six-and-a-half years.

When I ran low on money, Dr. Stone said, "Look, I understand there will be times when you won't be able to pay and I'll carry you." I kept track and it came to about a thousand dollars, but when I had the money and tried to give her a check, she wouldn't take it. She said it wasn't a loan.

I hadn't determined, when I saw Dr. Stone, whether or not I was gay and a large part of the analysis was devoted to that. I found it inconceivable that an upper-class Jewish woman would not have a vested interest in guiding me toward heterosexuality, but Dr. Stone was interested in what was best for me, not her.

It was very private, going to her office. There wasn't a common waiting room and you'd come in one door and go out a different one, so you never saw other patients. I was concerned about confidentiality, but she said over and over again, like a mantra, "Nothing you say to me will leave this room." I thought so highly of her I recommended her to my friends, but then I worried that if she took them, she'd hear things about me or I'd hear things about her. I was relieved when she said she wouldn't—that would be "muddying the water."

Dr. Stone was very good at what she did and had a busy practice. Maybe that's how she could afford to take on an essentially pro bono case like me in my scruffy jeans. She told me later she did it because she knew I was serious and would work. It's true that I wanted to resolve my problems and I had a fairly strong ego, but I had to do some heavy lifting in that analysis. I had not mourned the loss of my mother; I was estranged from my father because he did not want me to be a musician; there was the issue of my sexual identity; and I was lonely. I felt weighted down. "What can I do to feel better?" I'd ask. "You have to keep going back there—to childhood," she'd say, and all the pain and hurt would come pouring out. As we worked, my world lightened up. I started to feel better.

I took to free association. I kept a tape recorder by my bed and, living alone, I could wake up at 3:00 A.M. and tape my dreams. I still have four 90-minute cassettes. In the morning, I'd listen to the tape and take up where I'd left off in session.

I think of free association as being like spokes radiating out from a central point. To get to the center, you go down the spokes, deeper and deeper. For example, if I dreamed I was talking to a friend while driving to the theatre, my associations might start out, "This reminds me of a conversation yesterday with Greg." Then I might remember that my first car was a Chevy and the guy who sold it to me ripped me off, but I didn't try to connect or understand anything. I just let the words out. I could jump around in time, going back to things that happened twenty years ago, and after a while, I'd see the connections myself or she'd pick out a thread, like, "This goes back to the issue of trust," or "That sounds like your brother." Sometimes it was my brother, but she wasn't always right. I didn't buy it 100 percent but I didn't have to.

Sometimes I'd come in with a list of things to talk about and Dr. Stone would say I had an agenda. That would stop me cold and I'd lie there silent. I would hate those silences.

My solo debut at Carnegie Hall, a huge event in any musician's life, came about a year and a half into treatment. I asked Dr. Stone to come, but she wouldn't. She kept a professional distance. Instead, she arranged phone sessions all through the Christmas vacation before my performance. It was a big success due, in large part, to her support.

Dr. Stone almost always kept blank about herself. She only slipped up once and that was toward the end of analysis. My father had remarried and he and his new wife lived nearby. "You must know Harriet," I said, fishing. "Her friends like my father." Dr. Stone looked out the window. "Harriet's friends find your father a complete bore," she replied.

In 1987, Dr. Stone closed her office in the city but continued to see people at her home in Rye. We were able to continue by phone sessions, but sometimes I really needed to see her and I'd take the train up. The trip became part of the process. Talking to you, an understanding listener, is another way of getting in touch with the process again—which never ends.

Artists are usually good candidates for psychoanalysis because they live on the edge of their subjective unconscious. Sam Temple (Chapter 3) explains it this way: "Artists have to delve deep to create. When I'm painting, I go into a dream, but I'm able to tell myself when it's time to come up for air." One of the purposes of psychoanalysis is to help a patient become acquainted with the unconscious aspects of the self without interference from the analyst. Dr. Stone softened analytic technique by permitting phone contact—this is "bending the frame"—but she held the line in that she did not attend Bond's performance.

Our next musician was a child prodigy. She went into analysis to over-come self-defeating behavior. Like Grace Renard (Chapter 3) Andrea be-lieves *The Drama of the Gifted Child* was written for her.

Andrea Weiss

Andrea Weiss is also a forty-three-year-old first-chair symphony violinist. She lives in San Francisco. "In 1986, the space shuttle, Challenger, *blew up. I was home eating lunch and I saw it on TV. I knew I had to tell my analyst, but I didn't want him to know I had time to sit around and watch TV."*

One reason I went into analysis was to come to terms with having been an extraordinarily gifted child in a severely dysfunctional family. Have you read *The Drama of the Gifted Child*? That book was written for me. I'm the youngest of three children and the only girl. Both my broth-ers have Down's Syndrome.

My mother taught violin and started me when I was three. I was ac-cepted by the Royal Conservatory of Music in Toronto when I was four but they told my parents to wait till I was seven to enroll me. Growing up, I thought it was normal to practice, not play with other kids. I didn't have the luxury of playing with music, either. With two handicapped kids, my parents promoted me to the forefront so they could say, "Look, we did something right!" But my brothers were jealous and made fun of me and my parents didn't make them stop. To this day, I won't let anyone be ridiculed in my presence.

In 1985, just before I turned thirty, I went into a Freudian analysis, five days a week, on the couch, for six and a half years. In one of the big breaks that saved my life, I got the right analyst. Two things pushed me into analysis: I had married outside my religion—I'm Jewish, but religion played no part in my life at that time—and my family never accepted my husband. I thought the problems in that marriage were his fault, but after we divorced, I had a long string of unhappy relationships with men. I'd dump them or they'd dump me. The other reason—really, this was the more important one as far as I was concerned—was that I'd just screwed up in a major international competition I should have won. It had happened before and I was beginning to see a pattern. You play two pieces in competition and invariably, I'd play the first piece badly. One time, I heard the judges sigh. Then I'd play the second piece perfectly. It didn't make sense.

I was living off a grant and didn't have much money, so I went to an analytic institute and was assigned Dr. Rossides. He was an analyst-in-training, about forty, and he'd been a child psychiatrist. I was one of his first adult patients. My fee was $15 when I began—no insurance—and right away Dr. Rossides got permission to drop the fee to $10 because I couldn't afford $75 a week.

I had trouble free associating because when I entered analysis I had great difficulty expressing myself. It helped that Dr. Rossides didn't just sit there and say, "Um-hmm." He was acquainted with classical music and he'd ask me about the pieces I played. His interest made it easier for me to learn to converse. I got a voice through analysis.

I was unhappy if I wasn't perfect and since I was never perfect, I was always unhappy. Dr. Rossides let me know he wasn't perfect. He made a lot of mistakes. Once, he interpreted something at the end of a session and I had to sit on it until the next day when I stormed into his office berating him. "I'm sorry," he said. No big deal. I began to get a glimmer that it wasn't so terrible to make a mistake.

Losing in competition came directly out of my childhood. I thought—unconsciously—I should hold myself back to make my brothers feel better. I had to come to terms with the fact that I had major abilities I shied away from and that it was all right for me to win—to show how special I was. Because Dr. Rossides wasn't put off by my feelings of specialness, I became able to express—in session, at least—all the awful things you aren't supposed to say, like, "I am special in this weird, sick family." When I was a child, I could only imagine telling my brothers, "You are stupid and it's not my fault and I can't make you better and I am tired of feeling guilty because I'm not stupid." It was a great relief to tell Dr. Rossides things I'd loathed about myself: I liked to show off! I liked to compete and win!

Dr. Rossides could also deal with my manipulativeness regarding money. The strings my family attached to money affected me. While I was in analysis, I won a major competition and was accepted by a symphony orchestra. I began to have enough money to pay the rent and not worry so much if I needed rosin or a new set of strings. [Laughs.] Dr. Rossides promptly raised my fee to $35 and I burst into tears. "You don't love me anymore!" I sobbed, "Why are you raising my fee?" How quickly we forget. He'd offered to see me for nothing when I was broke and $35 a session wasn't that much in 1989, but I equated money and love.

You build analysis into your life and when you suddenly have five free hours, you notice it. The first time he went on vacation, I protested: "You'll go away forever! No one ever sticks by me." There were flowers in his office that day and while I knew nothing of his personal life, I presumed he was getting married or, if he was already married, his wife had just had a baby. Having a baby was a very big issue with me because of my brothers. Two years later, Dr. Rossides told me he'd been sharing that office and the flowers hadn't been for him. He added that he should have told me so at the time.

In analysis, I learned—and this came as a surprise—that character does not change. But you don't have to be your own victim. Analysis helped me spot behavior patterns I wanted to change—like screwing up in competition. I don't do that anymore! [Laughs.] But my hostility pattern is alive and well. The difference is, today I don't have to pretend I'm not angry. I don't have to be a saint.

After about six years, Dr. Rossides and I began to talk about termination. He thought I was ready and suggested we stop in June but when the time came, I was afraid I'd made a terrible mistake. He assured me I could always come back, so I "graduated"—by that, I mean a mutually agreed-upon termination took place. I understand I am one of the few people who has done that, but it was hard. There was no weaning. We went from five days a week to nothing and I felt the void. All that summer, I'd call and leave messages on his machine: "You bastard! I made a really big mistake. But don't call me back!" [Laughs.] I knew I was through. I just had to protest some.

I still miss him and I still call him, but less over time. I think I see him, and myself, more realistically than I did when I was thirty. Dr. Rossides had many positive attributes but some weaknesses, such as a tendency to speak as if he were an authority on things he knew very little about. He could be just plain wrong.

One of the reasons I'm interested in participating in your study is that I always kept my own analysis a secret, although I recommend it—and psychotherapy. But I don't know anyone else who's been analyzed and I'd like to know what other people have to say. How do their analyses compare to mine? Do they regard analysis as a philosophical endeavor? I think that if everyone were analyzed, there would be no more wars. People would fight with their brains instead of guns.

Andrea and Bond Meyer both saw analysts who were flexible about payment. Since Bond's analyst was in private practice, she could set her own fees, but Andrea's doctor was in training at an institute, so he would have had to go through some red tape to help her out. For Bond, termination included "winding down." That method seems a little more humane than going "from five days a week to nothing," as Andrea did, but that is the rule in a classical Freudian analysis. Yet, experience has shown that bending the frame—or breaking rules—can be helpful when patients need that sort of accommodation. A happy postscript: Andrea remarried and recently gave birth to a healthy daughter.

Our next patient, Laura Forte, also saw a candidate-in-training at an analytic institute. Laura had memories of sexual abuse but she was not sure that her memories were of real events. Her analysis went well but she, too, had a difficult termination.

Laura Forte

Laura Forte is a fifty-two-year-old college dean from Darien, Connecticut. "While I was in analysis, a whole lot of people were killed trying to rescue hostages at the U.S. Embassy in Tehran. Lying on the couch that day seemed slightly irrelevant. 'What am I doing this for?' I asked my analyst."

In 1987, my husband and I separated. Paul and I had been married twenty years and we had three children. He'd had many affairs but I never asked for a divorce and I was distraught when he did. After the divorce, I went to a psychiatrist who recommended twice a week sessions at something like $100 an hour. I couldn't afford that, so she suggested I contact one of the analytic institutes and see an analyst-in-training. I hadn't known trainees took patients.

I struggled with the idea of committing myself to an analysis. I was forty, worked full time, and I had two children still at home. Did I really have four or five hours a week to devote to analysis? For years? But I felt like I was having a nervous breakdown, so I went through the screening process and was accepted for treatment. I wanted a woman but was assigned a man—Dr. Reider. In the beginning, I was nervous and I didn't like him. I hated his furniture and the rug and I thought he looked about twelve. [Laughs.] I always thought he looked like a boy—too young to be really competent.

One of the problems I brought into analysis was that I had some fragmented memories of having been sexually abused by my father during my childhood. I defended against the feelings these memories aroused by intellectualization. "All I want to know," I told Dr. Reider, "is whether these things are true and verifiable." I wondered if he would interpret the memories as fantasies, but he didn't. If he had, I couldn't have worked with him. He allowed me to find out to the degree I could whether the memories were of real events and he helped me see that I could have the feelings the memories aroused—mistrust, fright, anger—without having to prove that sexual abuse had actually occurred. If that had been all I got from analysis, it would have been worth it. Dr. Reider did not judge me or my parents. That let me view analysis as a safe place to let stuff out. I couldn't see him when I was lying on the couch, but I felt his sympathy. Maybe it was his tone of voice.

My best friend's father molested me when I was ten. He did it several times and I didn't like it, but I remember thinking, "What he's doing is okay. It's like what my daddy does." The only reason I was afraid was that he was a policeman with a gun, but I finally told my mother and she called the police. There was a trial and I heard people saying what the man had done was terrible, so I reasoned that what my father did was terrible, too. That was confusing. My father's behavior provided me with close, physical touching I wanted desperately. I didn't get hugs and cuddling from my mother. She was depressed, distant, and cold. After the trial, I became estranged from my father and developed ambivalent feelings about him. I generalized those feelings to all men.

Dr. Reider never talked about himself but I noticed he wore a wedding ring. I would dream that he invited me to his house and introduced me to his family. In a nightmare, the house was all windows and I could see a burglar inside. I tried to get in to warn him, but I couldn't find the door. Dr. Reider asked me what I thought the danger was about—what feelings might I be having about him that I might think were dangerous? Certainly, I was jealous of his wife, but dangerous feelings about him? We had to keep working on feelings for a long time. This is the way it worked. First I learned that I had conflictual feelings. Then I learned the feelings came from childhood and, over the years of analysis, I examined how I acted them out—behaved—with other people by examining my feelings about Dr. Reider and my behavior toward him in the safe little world we established in analysis.

In another dream, I'm in church—I was raised Catholic but I'm not religious anymore—and a priest is on the altar. I run up the aisle and wrest the host away from him. I have to kill him to get it, and I use my fountain pen to stab him. Then I start doing the mass by myself, chanting "Clarice Le Spector! Clarice Le Spector!" My interpretation of the dream is that when I obtain the power—masculine power represented by the host—I become able to use the sacred words, which happen to be a woman's name, to lead the all-male congregation in the mass. The theme of that dream was that I was a destructive force that could kill men with knives or writing instruments and that I was interested in obtaining power. Dr. Reider connected the image of myself as a destructive force to my fear that if I spoke or wrote about my father, it would destroy him. About obtaining power, as a woman, it was hard for me to admit that I wanted to pit myself against others and win. I liked to win but I was somewhat covert about competing.

Dr. Reider always took off the whole month of August. It was horrible, especially the first year when I was feeling very needy. He told me there would be someone on call, but I didn't call his replacement. After that, we'd start preparing me for the summer "interruption" in March!

Discussing the fee is usually part of an analysis but I was shielded from that because of the institute's sliding scale. I started at $10 an hour and was only paying $15 five years later when Dr. Reider finished training and went into private practice. He raised his rates to $120 but offered me sessions at $45. Even so, that was three times what I'd been paying and I couldn't afford it so I had to stop. I think it was time and we discussed it, but I still think he should have left my fee low enough that I didn't have to terminate under pressure—especially when he was driving a brand new BMW!

I was enormously benefited by analysis. I finished my doctorate and wrote two books during analysis. I, who had been too shy to enter a room full of acquaintances before analysis, became able to mingle with strangers and speak up at meetings. I became a leader in my field. Analysis did not change my personality. I'm still shy, but I've learned to assert myself. I used to feel weighted down by the huge sack of garbage I carried around. Analysis freed me of that. I became able to regard myself with the same kind of nonjudgmental sympathy as Dr. Reider did, and when I learned to listen the way he did, I became a better mother and a better friend. These are some of the gifts of analysis, but Dr. Reider's greatest gift to me was helping me reconnect with my father before he died. That was healing for me.

I send Dr. Reider a Christmas card every year. He sends me one, too.

In Laura's case, the lowered fee provided by the analytic institute backfired when Dr. Reider went into private practice and raised his rates. Laura then got in touch with her anger toward men for taking advantage of her. In the 1980s, many women publicly disclosed instances of childhood sexual abuse. Laura's analyst helped her realize her feelings about her memories without having her dredge up and relive details of the events she was not sure had taken place. Some patients have been hypnotized or convinced by therapists to "recover" memories of abuse and confront their abusers. When such memories are later found to be untrue, reputations may have been irrevocably damaged and families are torn apart. "False memory syndrome" or "recovered memory syndrome" has been the subject of much controversy among mental health professionals, and has led to law suits against therapists.[3]

The case of Ross Chett, a political science professor at Brown University who spontaneously recovered a memory of sexual abuse during his childhood, caused the skeptical Harvard psychology Professor Daniel Schacter to amend the views he set forth in *Searching for Memory*. Dr. Schacter wrote that people can develop false recollections of traumatic events that never occurred. A jury believed Dr. Chett, however, and he won a $457,000 judgment against the perpetrator. What does this mean to Dr. Chett more than a quarter of a century later? "I'm glad I was vindicated," he says, "but I'm more glad to be moving on with my life and working on issues that are bigger than me."[4]

The next person we talked to, Valerie Vaughn, ended therapy feeling that her therapist used her. He kept her in treatment for years and she paid him an extraordinary amount of money.

Valerie Vaughn

Valerie Vaughn is a forty-three-year-old housewife from Cleveland, Ohio. "I had lost my connection to my church. My psychiatrist and I talked about my feelings about religion. He was a religious man, a church soloist. I started going to services to hear him sing and I began to reconnect with my faith."

The first time I sought treatment was when my mother was dying of cancer. No one in my family had ever been in therapy but I was having such a hard time my kids' pediatrician recommended a psychiatrist and I went a few times before Mom died. That was in 1987.

Jeff, my husband, was away on a business trip when she died. He's in international aviation and goes to Europe two and three weeks at a time. Our children, J. T.—Jeffrey Thomas Vaughn III—and the girls, Victoria and Vivienne, were five, two, and one. I lost two babies between J. T. and the girls, so I'd had five pregnancies in five years. I was thirty-one years old, I had barely mourned my lost babies, and here I was faced with mourning my mother's death.

I couldn't understand why, ten weeks after Mom died, I was still having such a hard time. A friend of mine urged me to go back to my first psychiatrist but when I called, his wife answered the phone and told me he'd had a heart attack and died. I couldn't believe it. He was so young. When I told my friend, Lisa, I broke down crying. She told me to call her psychiatrist, Paul Thomas. I hadn't even known she had a psychiatrist. My back was to the wall, so, fortunately or unfortunately, I made an appointment with Paul.

He practiced in his house on the same street Lisa lived on which made me feel weird. My sixth sense told me Paul was an arrogant man but I went in, tried to hold back my tears, and told him, "My mother died ten weeks ago and there must be something very wrong with me because I'm not fine and over it by now." All I wanted was to feel better.

Paul was fifteen years older than me. I know because he told me. He's a bright guy who went to an Ivy League college and teaches at a university. He said we should work twice a week because I felt so bad and I agreed. I wanted him to take care of me. No one else was. On the third visit, he put his fingertips together and said, "We are a good fit." There was something between us. A mutual attraction.

I was raised not to be wild. Not to sleep around. People said I was pretty, but not smart, and that's how I thought of myself. When I was with Paul, this just came out of my mouth: "I don't think I am very intelligent but I've always wanted to finish college." He encouraged me to go back to school and I did. I made such profound changes in myself. I owe that to therapy.

While I was seeing him, I began to write. I'd take my journals in and he'd read them. We discussed everything I wrote. Therapy got me in touch with my creative side. I've written two stories about my therapy and I'd like to get them published.

On the negative side, our relationship was not kept on a professional level. It became a friendship. Paul told me way too much about his personal life. I knew he'd been divorced and remarried. And he would call me when he was out of town. My husband hated his guts. "That's the wrong person for you," he said. It hurt my marriage. A therapist should be more of a blank slate—not have an office at home so you meet their wives and families.

I started to think I was in love with two men and it frightened me. After the first few months, I started trying to get away. I'd write to Paul and tell him I had to stop. He'd write to me and tell me to come back. I should have told him why I wanted to quit, but I didn't know how. He should have let me go. The therapist needs to take charge of ending treatment when the patient can't, but Paul wanted me around. He said we should increase our sessions to three days a week and I did it. I went along with it for eight years. The first four years, sessions were $110 for 45 minutes. The last four, they were $160. Blue Cross/Blue Shield paid for something like 80% of 50 sessions a year and my husband paid for all the rest of it. No wonder he hated Paul!

Paul's wife came between us. One day I was driving right behind her going to my session and it felt so weird that I turned down a different street so we wouldn't get there at the same time. I waited a few minutes and drove back to his house, but she was sitting in her car waiting for me. She had to hate my guts. When I got in Paul's office, I didn't take off my coat and sit down, I paced back and forth and told him I didn't think his wife wanted me to be there. "You want this session to be all yours," he said, "and it can't happen if my wife is guarding the house." She didn't do that again.

Then one day I was playing cards with my three best girlfriends. It was like group therapy and it came out that I was still in treatment three days a week after seven and a half years. "Val," they said, "something is not right here. You've got to talk to my guy." They all wanted me to go to their therapists! [Laughs.]

Therapy ended in a huge fight. Phone calls. Letters back and forth. It changes the good part of the relationship when it ends that way. I wanted Paul to give me back my journals and letters. It was a breakup and I didn't want him to have things from my heart. I wanted his notes on my sessions, too, but he claimed it wouldn't be good for me to read them. He sent that letter certified mail. It really hurt.

As much as I was hurt by Paul, I can't say I didn't get anything out of therapy. For one thing, I reconnected with my religion and I've become more spiritual—less worldly. I learned that I can write and that I am more than "just a pretty face." I finished college and decided to enter the mental health field, so I'm starting graduate school in the fall. My ideas about therapy come directly out of my own experience. I don't think people should stay in treatment forever. The goal of therapy should be to empower people to fly by themselves. When I wanted to quit, Paul should have let me try, and come back if I needed to, but he wanted me there for reasons of his own. What I learned in my own treatment is what not to do. It left me wondering, "Did he use me? Did he do it for the money? Did he love me?" I have to realize Paul is only a human being.

When treatment ends on a negative note, we seek reasons to prevent recurrences. While it is not unusual for female patients to fantasize about having love affairs with their male therapists (the same is true of male patients and female therapists), Valerie's situation was not handled appropriately. Paul should have helped her understand and work through her fantasies about him. When no light was shed on these feelings, they grew. Valerie's friends offered her a glimpse of reality, which helped her extricate herself.

Valerie and her friends seemed to know a great deal about each other's therapists. This can cause problems. Extraneous factors can slip into and complicate the transference. Therapists must remain alert to confusions that arise between the personal and the professional relationship and assure that therapeutic boundaries are maintained. Because Paul practiced in his home, Valerie's contact with his wife led to further complications, which also remained unexamined. Finally, since there were problems in Valerie's marriage, Paul might well have encouraged her to go with her husband to a marriage counselor.

The next therapeutic story stands in sharp contrast to Valerie Vaughn's. Martina Adams forged a powerful bond with her doctor of osteopathy in a little known and generally disdained type of mind/body experience known as Reichian therapy.

Wilhelm Reich (1897–1957) was born in Galicia, then part of the Austrian Empire. After serving in the Austrian army during World War I, he studied medicine at the University of Vienna. Freud invited Reich to join his inner circle but over time, Reich's practice and theoretical work became as unorthodox as his personal life, including rumored affairs with patients. After Reich was expelled from the International Psychoanalytic Society, he developed orgone therapy. Fleeing from Germany in 1933, he came to America where he was prosecuted for defying an injunction prohibiting the sale of the orgone box, which, he claimed, effectively treated cancer and impotence. In 1957, he was sentenced to prison, where he died. His downfall overshadowed the creative achievements of his early life.

Reich theorized that a primal element, orgone energy, permeated the universe and caused psychological disorders when it was incompletely released from the human body. He wrote that complete ridding of orgone could only be achieved by sexual climaxes strong enough to cause convulsions. Today's Reichian therapists attempt to unblock orgone energy through character analysis and by working directly on the musculature through breathing, massage, and body work. Reichians also work with transference and interpret resistance.

Martina Adams

Martina Adams is a forty-nine-year-old secretary from St. Paul who sought Reichian therapy in 1986. "While I couldn't talk, I could sing. I was in the choir at my church. But my experience in treatment was truly awesome. I learned that life is a path. I go through some horrendous times but my journey always leads to understanding. It's a spiritual experience."

When I was thirty-four, my voice became scratchy and I had symptoms of laryngitis. My husband [Larry] thought I should see a doctor and I wanted to find a medical reason and a pill that would cure me, so I went to an otolaryngologist who performed every possible test but couldn't find anything wrong. I wasn't surprised. I knew it wasn't just physical. I could step outside myself and observe the symptoms. They'd been around, on and off, for a long time. My old college roommate had remarked on my husky voice.

My condition worsened over the next year until I couldn't even answer the phone. My throat felt like a balloon stem squeezed so tight there was no room for the air to get through. The muscles in my chest and diaphragm were so tight I had to contract my stomach muscles to force air out of my chest and up through my throat to try to make a sound. The effort wore me out. People began to ask Larry if I had cancer. Believe it or not, I let this go on two or three years, hoping it would go away. Finally, for Larry and the children, I went to a medical research center. When one side of my vocal cords was anesthetized, I could speak. The diagnosis was spastic dysphonia. Speech therapy was recommended, but I knew I needed psychotherapy.

I had never been to a therapist and I wasn't sure what to do. I chose a woman near my home. She asked me to tell her why I needed therapy and I tried, but since I could only whisper, she couldn't hear me and kept asking me to repeat myself. The effort was exhausting and I left her office feeling worse. I didn't go back.

My father-in-law mentioned he'd heard of a man who might be able to help me, an osteopath. They know body structure and Dr. Schwartzman was a Reichian. He specialized in psychiatry and understood the mind/body connection, which made him perfect for spastic dysphonia.

At our first meeting, he took down my vital statistics and reason for coming. I had to whisper my answers. "The process you are embarking upon will help you recover your voice," he assured me. His manner and the authority of his degree and training allowed me to trust him, and his faith that the process would work increased my hope. He didn't present me with a formula, but explained that the work was like a path along which I'd discover what would lead me to health. The metaphor he used was "an onion with many layers." The path takes you from one layer of consciousness to a deeper layer, and you gain self-awareness along the way.

I was depressed when I went to Dr. Schwartzman. My oldest child was six and I realized my parenting of her was a repeat of how I'd been parented. I'd gone through childhood swallowing down my feelings, living in an atmosphere like a pressure cooker where high emotion—fury and hate—could only be expressed by parents. I wanted therapy to break the cycle.

Orgonomy involves tubes that are sensitive to energy passing over the body in the form of a breeze. Dr. Schwartzman used that with my father-in-law's friend, but he worked differently with me. At the second session, we went into a paneled, soundproofed, eight by ten foot room in the basement of his house. There was a couch, a chair with a credenza beside it, and a window.

Dr. Schwartzman asked me to disrobe except for my underpants and lie on the couch and breathe for him. He explained that my whole structure was very tight and he wanted to observe how the muscles of my chest, abdomen, neck, and face moved as I breathed and tried to talk. I must admit, down there in the basement with a total stranger, I was somewhat taken aback, but I did it—except for my bra. After about a year, he asked—seeming a little dismayed—if I thought he was looking at me any way but structurally. I felt a little vain and a little ridiculous because of course I wanted him to admire what he saw. Dr. Schwartzman was so honest. I could see I was safe with him, so I went ahead and took off my bra. I felt so good about the treatment I started recommending it to my friends, but their reaction was what you might expect. It does sound whacky. So although I believe in Reichian therapy, I stopped telling anyone the details.

During sessions, words were only used if I needed to change an appointment or something. Therapy was lying on my back on the couch breathing. It didn't include words. I was to inhale and exhale through my mouth, not just to oxygenate my body but to bring out emotion—sadness, unhappiness, rage—on the exhaled breath. Reichian therapists believe producing nonverbal sounds conveys affect more clearly than words. Breathing like that led me from my physical self to my emotions, like a rivulet leading to a lake. A whole range of sound and a whole range of emotion came out of operating at the gut level.

Breathing took about fifteen minutes of every session. As I breathed, I would sometimes cry at the deepest, most wrenching level, but there were other times when breathing did not reach my emotions. Then Dr. Schwartzman would tell me to use my feet and legs to kick and thrash and pound on the couch. Screaming and raging let out my fear and anxiety.

He gave me homework exercises. I was to drink a glass of water every morning before breakfast, put two fingers down my throat and gag it up, making retching sounds. This loosened my diaphragm, chest, and internal muscles. In his office, he'd give me a plastic basin and I'd sit cross-legged on the couch and gag and drool into it. These physical acts loosened my muscles, but still my voice did not return.

After eighteen months, I decided to quit. I told Dr. Schwartzman I didn't want to depend on him for the rest of my life. He said that was seeing therapy negatively and he thought I was running away because things were getting scary for me, but I was a free agent and he would not try to stop me.

Part of the reason I left was money. At the beginning, I was uninsured and he gave me a break. Instead of his normal fee of $100 a session, I paid $50 but that was still expensive since I was going twice a week. The real reason I left was that I felt I was paying the one person in the world who really could care about me and I didn't like feeling I had to pay to be cared about. I stopped for a month and got over feeling Dr. Schwartzman was only in it for the money. Then I went back and stayed until my treatment was complete. The second time, I had insurance, which paid half.

The breakthrough came one evening after about two-and-a-half years. I was sitting on the couch, gagging and drooling, and Dr. Schwartzman came over and gripped my larynx really hard. "What the hell is he doing?" I wondered. He almost choked me. When he loosened his grip, I gulped and swallowed and I was amazed. "My throat got bigger," I said. "The saliva has more places to go." Dr. Schwartzman had interrupted a nervous tic, a muscle spasm, and from that point on, my throat did open more but I did not become able to speak again overnight. The improvements were in tiny increments. It took five years.

When my muscles were really tight, Dr. Schwartzman might step up to the couch and push down on my chest, using both hands. I know it was a physical technique, but I always thought he had a healing touch and that's what made me better.

Therapy was not something I enjoyed. I dreaded the feelings that came up, but Dr. Schwartzman had told me that if I put in the effort and didn't run away, I would get well. I didn't want him to think I wasn't strong enough or committed enough. I expected therapy to take away my anxiety and it didn't, but I got the tools I needed to deal with my emotions, and I use them every day. My use of words had been stifled during my childhood because I'd learned to express myself in as few syllables as possible. At the age of thirty-nine, I was freed to fall in love with words. Language opened up for me like a flower. That's the most precious gift I received.

Dr. Schwartzman and I began in a parent-child relationship that evolved into a mature association. When I left, it was clear that I was ready. I am still in awe of his sensitivity. He was never one to blunder clumsily with someone's emotions. When I met him, I had feared becoming seventy, never finding my way, and ending life a total mess. I can truly say I met Dr. Schwartzman at a crossroads in my life and because of him, I changed. I never saw him after I finished therapy, but I write him now and then to let him know how I'm doing.

Since Martina Adams was unable to speak, she couldn't participate in traditional talk therapy, but her story speaks for itself. Martina was traumatized by her past experiences and could not form the words to express her intense feelings. As Dr. Schwartzman guided her along the path toward cure, he was careful to assure Martina that the resolution of her problems would come from her with only a little direction from him. He was not afraid to travel with Martina into her primitive, pre-verbal world, and he allowed her to move along at her own pace. Beyond trust and cooperation, the most important ingredient in this case seems to have been hope.

Since osteopaths deal with physically handicapping conditions, Dr. Schwartzman was accustomed to using his hands to manipulate constricted body parts. Martina's experience stands in sharp contrast to general psychiatry, psychoanalysis, and psychotherapy where touching is essentially forbidden except under the most limited circumstances. Occasionally, however, therapists will hug a patient, as in the next case.

Ian Spicer

Ian Spicer is a forty-six-year-old mechanic from Parowan, Utah. "In the Eighties, there was an inversion over a big city out west. The smog lasted for weeks and started making people sick. They had to wear face masks while bureaucrats at the EPA were dragging their feet on banning chlorofluorocarbons."

I am an only child. I went for counseling because I was an alcoholic but I have not had a drink in ten years now. I drank a lot before. Mom took tranquilizers when I was a kid, but I don't think she drank much—maybe a martini at dinner—until I moved out of the house. Then she became an alcoholic, but now she's in recovery. My father was a workaholic alcoholic commercial photographer who beat me, and both my grandfathers were alcoholics. I still have major trust issues with men.

My first counseling was in 1983 when I was thirty-one. [Note: At the time Ian was in treatment, psychiatric nurses in that state were not permitted to "diagnose and treat a mental illness." Since they were not eligible for licensure, they practiced as "counselors."] I saw a social worker for a few months but she moved away and had no one to refer me to, so I looked through the Yellow Pages and got lucky. I found Britt Finley and started serious counseling in the spring of 1984. I went once or twice a week, heavy-duty, for four years. After that, I'd go in for tune-ups. She charged $35 a session and kept it there all the way through. My insurance didn't cover psychiatric nurses.

> *Psychiatric nurses* are registered nurses with master's degrees. They work in hospitals, clinics, patients' homes, and private offices with individuals, couples, families, or groups. They must have a valid license from the state where they practice and are encouraged to consult a more experienced mental health practitioner periodically.

Britt was about ten years older than me. I credit her with saving my life with her patience and knowledge—or maybe she saved me from myself. I liked her right away, partly because she worked in this funky old house with a massage therapist, an acupuncturist, and a meditationist. The energy in that building felt very good to me.

I didn't just go for counseling because I was an alcoholic. There was something wrong with my life. I had all the right pieces but they weren't fitting together the way I wanted them to. I needed help to rearrange them. I'd had a string of dysfunctional relationships with women. I went for three years with a slightly older woman—a counselor, no less—but I became terrified being in a healthy place and ended the relationship. Then I met Laura, the one I really cared for, and she dumped me. Even though that relationship was as dysfunctional as most of the others, I couldn't get over losing her. I met other women and started to get serious about one—Ellen—but when we were planning on moving in together, an old girlfriend called to come back and I said okay, which was pretty adolescent, and Ellen left me. She told me I needed counseling.

When I went to Britt, I was a very judgmental person, especially of myself. Britt was very centered and nonjudgmental. She never looked down on me the way I did. She never came right out and said I needed a whole new set of friends either, but that's probably what she thought. The girl I was dating then drank and did recreational drugs, but Britt didn't condemn her. She said, "Diane is not a bad person but she is not good for you." And I would think Britt was right, but I don't like conflict so I didn't end the relationship. It ended by itself when I found Diane in bed with my best friend. That was tough on me and it's a good thing Britt was around. She was a person who would give you a hug if you asked and, believe me, I needed one.

We had goals in treatment: To find out why my life was like it was and what to do to make it whole. Britt diagnosed me as having post traumatic stress disorder with anxiety and adjustment problems. She wanted to learn all about me and my family because she thought the major issues I had came from my childhood. I was abused by both my parents. My father should be a poster father for battered children.

My parents divorced when I was thirteen and I stayed with Mom. Britt thought Mom sexually abused me but I never thought that. Yeah, Mom hit me and messed me up emotionally, but I don't think she did anything sexual. It would make me mad when Britt would say that. I don't think she ever changed her mind.

Once, I got frustrated by my lack of progress. I wanted all the layers of debris to be gone, I wanted a normal life, and I wanted it *now!* So Britt sent me to a psychiatrist. He gave me something like Xanax. I hate pills, but I kept it with me just in case and one day, I felt so depressed by my job I took one pill. Man, I felt like shit. I got eczema, diarrhea, you name it. I threw those pills away. And one session with the psychiatrist was plenty. It was way too intense. It made me realize Britt was helping me the way I needed.

Britt gave me literature, basic stuff, about the causes and effects of alcoholism. She said my drinking was self-medicating. I don't think she suggested AA and I never went, but we would have debates about the disease concept. In spite of everything I've read, I firmly do not believe alcoholism is a disease. It's a choice. I went to a few Adult Children of Alcoholics meetings but the people were like "Boo-hoo, poor me!" They'd already formed their own little cliques and I don't like cliques, so I quit. Another thing I did was journal for awhile. I bought a notebook called "Understanding Me." It had a place to write down people in my life that I would never forget. Britt's one of them.

I read books from her library and I bought a ton of self-help books. The most useful ones were *Way of the Peaceful Warrior* and *Co-Dependent No More*. Britt didn't tell me to do that. It was more of a true self-help type thing.

A lot of sessions were related to work. We tried to find ways for me to get out of the Postal Service, but I don't have many marketable skills. I never finished college. I love to work on cars, but I couldn't find a mechanic job so I was stuck being a letter carrier. I'm not blaming the job for making me an alcoholic, but it sure made things worse. My supervisors were incompetent and had their own personal problems. I strongly feel the horror of my job compounded my emotional problems. What made me hate it even more is every time I applied for small town postmaster jobs, I was told that I was second best. Since I was not a golfer and didn't hang out with the powers that be, I was being passed over. Britt encouraged me to file complaints with the Equal Employment Opportunity Commission. I won two and got a postmaster job near an

Indian reservation, but it was a boring eight-hour day with only three hours of work and the town was a racist backwater of conservative white people with no sensitivity for the Indians. I identified with the Indians' despair and hopelessness. It finally got so depressing I quit.

After that my wife and I moved out here and I had to stop therapy, but I was done. Britt had told me I'd know when I was done and she was right. There was nothing left to say. I was counseled out. I'd quit drinking and smoking and I'd gotten out of my dysfunctional relationships and gotten married. I'd read 4,000 self-help books and I'd confronted my parents as much as I could. I finished by winding down from twice a week to once a week and then once every other week.

When I was in counseling, I found that if I'd hang around with people who were in counseling, it was okay to admit it. With others, it was like, "Then you must be crazy." I wasn't crazy but I made some bad choices. One of the ways my life changed while I was with Britt is I attracted less dysfunctional people when I was less dysfunctional. My drinking buddies disappeared and I got a whole new set of friends.

Psychotherapy altered the course of my life completely. I went from a person I can hardly believe I was, drinking and immature, believing I was inadequate and having feelings of deep loneliness, to now. I have my flaws, but I am not a bad person and I like myself. I haven't been home in many years, but my father visited recently. It was the first time I'd seen him since 1988. Mom visited about a year ago. She's stopped drinking and become a born-again Christian. Abhors counseling. Says God can solve everything. But to my way of thinking, religion has done more harm than good. I've turned to meditation and spiritualism. My wife and I visited some remote sections of the desert recently. I can easily meditate in settings like that. The isolated Utah desert feels like a cathedral to me.

When Ian's therapist found out Ian liked to read, she loaned him books from her library. Self-help books proliferated in the 1980s and became, for some, a popular treatment alternative. Others, like Ian, used this literature to augment their personal therapy. Books for families and children of alcoholics were best sellers. Other books explained how to manage anxiety, depression, or marriage problems; still others taught how to survive divorce and find a new partner.

We talked to forty-five people, thirty-one women and fourteen men, who were in therapy during the 1980s. They were between twenty-five and thirty-nine years old when treatment began. Only Valerie Vaughn and Martina Adams were married and had children. Andrew Graham, Andrea Weiss, Laura Forte, and Ian Spicer were divorced. Father SJ, Lynn Ellison, and Bond Meyer, all of whom lost their mothers during childhood, never married.

From Chapter 1 on, we have heard that all practitioners talk, but Grace Renard (Chapter 3) describes treatment with Jenny as "a conversation, back and forth." To help his patient learn to converse, Dr. Rossides asked Andrea Weiss questions about music. Father SJ says Dr. Otto "was an active therapist who spoke at least half the time." He credits their conversations with deepening his comprehension.

Departures from generally accepted technique include therapy over the telephone and physical touch. Dr. Loring provided phone therapy for Lynn Ellison. Bond Meyer's senior analyst permitted him to call her during Christmas vacation. Some analysts and therapists touch clients and some do not. Mr. Emerson kissed Neisha Williams (Chapter 1) good-bye when she left treatment. She didn't like that, but Julia Mason (Chapter 4) appreciated it when Mary Kelly, her social worker, hugged her good-bye. In this chapter we hear about the beneficial use of physical touch in the treatment room. Ian Spicer's psychiatric nurse "would give you a hug if you asked." Martina Adams's Reichian doctor gripped her larynx and pressed down on her chest to interrupt the muscle spasms that prevented his patient's speech. "I know it was a physical technique," Martina says, "but I always thought he had a healing touch and that's what made me better."

Father SJ and Bond Meyer were in treatment until their analysts semi-retired and began seeing patients at home. When they stopped practicing altogether, Dr. Otto and Dr. Stone told their patients they were still available by phone. Lynn Ellison and Laura Forte keep in touch with their former therapists. Lynn calls Dr. Loring every year on his birthday. Laura and Dr. Reider exchange Christmas cards. Others, like Sam Temple (Chapter 3), choose not to keep in touch but have good memories.

When he couldn't afford to pay her, Bond Meyer's analyst charged him nothing. Andrea Weiss's doctor got her $15 sliding scale fee reduced to $10 when she was struggling financially. Laura Forte, also in analysis at an institute, paid $10 to $15. Insurance paid 80 percent of Father SJ's treatment which ran from $80 to $110 over eight years. Lynn Ellison's plan paid part of the $50 charge. When she was uninsured, Dr. Loring lowered his fee. Martina Adams's therapist charged her half his normal rate when she was not insured. She remarked that there are therapists who are not in it just for the money. But Valerie Vaughn, the only respondent in this group to rate her therapy an unqualified negative, discovered there are practitioners who appear to be in it for as much as they can get, be that love or money. Her fees ran from $110 to $160 over eight years while she was in therapy three days a week. Insurance provided coverage at 80 percent of fifty sessions a year. Her husband picked up the remainder.

Andrew Graham's Jungian analyst was a woman, as was Bond Meyer's analyst, and Ian Spicer's psychiatric nurse. Beginning in the mid-1970s, women constituted 75 percent of the health care industry work force. Seven percent of practicing physicians were women, gravitating toward pediatrics and psychiatry, and reporting an income of $27,000 compared to the $48,000 their male counterparts received.[5] During the 1980s, the average net income of all self-employed physicians rose from $94,000 to $120,000. At the top, surgeons and anesthesiologists earned $180,000. Psychiatrists averaged $97,000; family practitioners and pediatricians tied for last place at $85,000.[6]

Steven S. Sharfstein, M.D., writes, "Between 1954 and 1984, the mental health system and its financing were radically transformed. . . . The number of private mental health practitioners . . . increased greatly . . . psychiatrists by 200 percent, psychologists by 300 percent, social workers by 350 percent. The number of visits to mental health professionals quadrupled. . . . The cost of treatment for mental illness increased from 6 percent of total health expenditures in 1954 to 12 percent in 1984."[7]

Supply and demand increased, but stigma remained about the same. Like many who availed themselves of the therapeutic bounty, Father SJ found a socially acceptable reason for being in treatment: It was to help him with his work counseling young men going into the priesthood. He laughs when he admits it "was a screen for wanting to examine my own issues." Andrew Graham put off therapy until the second half of his life and even then worried that his WASP family viewed psychotherapy with suspicion.

Lynn Ellison liked individual treatment, but being in a psychotherapy group made her feel like "One Of The People Who Is Sick." Andrea Weiss recommended therapy to others but kept her own analysis a secret, while Valerie Vaughn and all her girlfriends were in treatment and discussed their therapists at card parties. Ian Spicer winds it up: "If I'd hang around with people who were in counseling, it was okay to admit it. With others, it was like, 'Then you must be crazy.' "

This chapter illuminates an array of psychiatric problems with treatment forms ranging from face-to-face analytic psychotherapy to cognitive-behavioral treatment by a pastoral counselor to classical Freudian analysis to analytical psychology (Jungian analysis) to Reichian treatment by an osteopath to counseling by a psychiatric nurse. Eight out of nine people, many of whom say they entered treatment because of dysfunctional relationships, formed good connections with their therapists and evaluate their practitioners and the therapeutic process positively. The centrality of the relationship is clear. It permits good practitioners to help patients get what they need.

6   The 1990s: What Does the Patient Need?

> What the patient needs is not a rational reworking of unconscious in-
> fantile fantasies; what the patient needs is a revitalization and expansion
> of his own capacity to generate experience that feels real, meaningful,
> and valuable.
>
> Stephen A. Mitchell

A GUIDE TO THE UNITED STATES OF THE 1990s

Population: 248,718,301

Average salary: $23,602 per year

Inflation: 5.4 percent

Unemployment: 5.6 percent (1990)
             4.7 percent (1997)

Social welfare: $617 billion

Births/1,000: 16.7

Marriages/1,000: 9.8

Divorces/1,000: 4.7

Deaths/1,000: 8.6

Average household size: 2.63

Women in labor force: 54.3 percent

Cost of living: Clothing: Ferragamo women's black patent pump, $230; Church's
             English shoes for men ("Kirk"), $125

Food: bread, 70 cents a loaf; coffee, $2.94 a pound; eggs, $1.00 a dozen; milk, 70 cents a quart; oranges, 56 cents a pound; round steak, $3.42 a pound

Housing: One-bedroom condominium, TriBeCa, NY, $184,000

Transportation: Jeep Cherokee, $22,652

Fun: roller blades, Beanie Babies, line dancing

Pulitzer Prizes: Biography: Sebastian de Grazia, *Machiavelli in Hell*

History: Stanley Karnow, *In Our Image: America's Empire in the Philippines*

Nonfiction: Dale Maharidge and Michael Williamson, *And Their Children After Them*

Sources: Robert Famighetti (ed.), *The World Almanac and Book of Facts, 1997* (Mahwah, NJ: World Almanac Books, 1997), pp. 325, 326, 381; Lois Gordon and Alan Gordon, *The Columbia Chronicles of American Life, 1910–1992* (New York: Columbia University Press, 1995), pp. 754, 758, 766; U.S. Bureau of the Census, *Historical Statistics of the United States, Colonial Times to 1970, Bicentennial Edition, Part I* (Washington, D.C., 1975), pp. 59, 74, 372, 398, 502; Front page headline, *The New York Times*, "U.S. Jobless Rate Declines to 4.7%," November 8, 1997; Advertisement in *The New York Times*, January 7, 1990, pp. A16, R6; January 17, 1990, p. A4; January 18, 1990, p. A3.

As our book goes to press, we are a year shy of completing this century's final decade. To show how far we have come, or not come, some comparisons of 1940 and 1990 figures follow, along with a summary of notable 1990s events.

When the Times Square ball proclaims midnight on December 31, 1999, the U.S. Bureau of the Census estimates that we will be a society of 275,000,000 souls, and counting. A mighty nation, we have at least progressed to the point where Barbara Bush, in her 1990 commencement address at Wellesley College, could say, to cheers and laughter, "Somewhere out there in this audience may even be someone who will one day follow in my footsteps and preside over the White House as the President's spouse, and I wish him well."[1]

In the summer of 1990, President Bush signed a bill raising taxes, despite his "read my lips" pledge. Iraq seized Kuwait, source of much of the world's oil, and threatened Saudi Arabia. Saddam Hussein defied United Nation's deadlines and sanctions for months, not believing Bush's promise to attack if he did not withdraw. U.N. forces—mainly American—smashed the Iraquis in January and February 1991, but stopped short of deposing Hussein. Bush's popularity surged to an unprecedented 90 percent.

At home another war, the much vaunted war on drugs, was being lost. The recession showed no sign of abating as 6,874,000 people were unemployed.[2] As the decade advanced, Clarence Thomas took his seat

Changes in Fifty Years

		1940	1990
Population		132 million	249 million
Americans living on farms		23.2 percent	1.8 percent
Male life expectancy		61 years	72 years
Female life expectancy		68 years	79 years
Births/1,000		19.4	16.7
Marriages/1,000		12.1	9.8
Divorces/1,000		2.0	4.7
Deaths/100,000:	Heart	485	289
	Cancer	120	202
	Tuberculosis	40	1
	AIDS	0	8.64*
	Car accident	26	19
	Homicide	6	10
	Suicide	14	12
Labor force: male to female		3 to 1	1.2 to 1
Bachelor's degrees:	Male	109,000	485,000
	Female	77,000	558,000
National debt		$43 billion	$3,233 billion

* U.S. Department of Health and Human Services Centers for Disease Control, *Monthly Vital Statistics Report* Vol. 41, No. 7, Supplement, "Advance Report of Final Mortality Statistics, 1990" (Atlanta, GA, January 7, 1993), p. 1.

on the Supreme Court, despite charges of sexual harassment by law professor Anita Hill. In Los Angeles, four white cops were acquitted of all but one charge for beating a black man, Rodney King; the ensuing riot took fifty-two lives. Political correctness, led largely by academics, took feminism and affirmative action to new levels, coupled with an assault on books by Eurocentric "DWMs"—Dead White Males—and a new emphasis on books by women and people of color.

In 1992, Governor William Jefferson Clinton was elected president with 43 percent of the popular vote. Bush had 38 percent, and Ross Perot 19 percent, perhaps costing Bush the election.[3] In 1993, Hillary Rodham Clinton's task force on health care reform imploded, Janet Reno became the first woman Attorney General, and Ruth Bader Ginsburg took Byron White's seat on the Supreme Court.

In 1994, a federal jury found two of the police officers who beat Rodney King guilty of depriving him of his civil rights; and Clinton announced his "don't ask, don't tell" policy for military gays and lesbians. The Whitewater investigation was launched when Attorney General Reno appointed an independent counsel. Mutating into hearings and other investigations, it may become a permanent function of government, notwithstanding the public's lack of interest. The opposite was true in the case of O. J. Simpson. Charged on June 17 with the murder of Nicole Simpson and Ronald Goldman, he was found not guilty on October 3, 1995, after a trial saturated with racial factors.

In 1995, after Democrats had held both houses of Congress for eight years, Republicans took control. They dominated the Senate, 53 to 47, and held the House, 235 to 197, with Senator Bob Dole as majority leader and Representative Newt Gingrich as Speaker. On April 19, a bomb demolished a federal building in Oklahoma City, killing 169 people. (Timothy McVeigh was later convicted.) In July, the United States resumed diplomatic relations with Vietnam, and in October, ten Muslim terrorists were found guilty of plotting to kill Egypt's President Mubarak and blowing up U.N. headquarters in New York.

President Clinton's State of the Union Address in January 1996 borrowed heavily from the conventional Republican lexicon: fight crime, balance the budget, family values, less government. Education and the environment were on Clinton's agenda, but the shift was clear and left Republicans with a small target to shoot at. As the campaign for the Republican nomination was launched in February, Pat Buchanan won in Louisiana by a two-thirds vote. Dole won in Iowa, and Texas Senator Phil Gramm dropped out, having spent $4 million of his own money, mainly on attack ads. In March, as Buchanan faded, Dole swept state after state and wrapped up the nomination.

In April, Theodore Kaczynski, a Harvard graduate and Michigan Ph.D. who had taught math at Berkeley, was charged with being the Unabomber. Dan Rostenkowski, former Chairman of the House Ways and Means Committee, pleaded guilty to two counts of mail fraud and was sentenced to seventeen months in prison.

May saw Dole resign from the Senate to devote himself full-time to his campaign. Both he and Clinton spoke up for welfare reform, including time limits and mandated work. In June, the Supreme Court held that confidentiality between doctors and patients extended as well to clinical social workers and other mental health professionals.[4] A pipe bomb exploded in July during the Olympic Games in Atlanta. The Congress passed a compromise welfare bill after Clinton vetoed two earlier attempts. Most of the votes against it were by Democrats, but Clinton signed it on August 22.

Dole, a "deficit hawk," surprised everyone by calling for a $548 billion tax cut, but he did not endorse the flat tax favored by Gramm and others. He selected Jack Kemp as his running mate at the Republican convention on August 15, an opulent gathering marked by General Colin Powell's pro-choice, pro-affirmative action speech.

The Democrats renominated Clinton and Gore, Clinton claiming credit for less crime, more jobs and lower deficits, inflation, and unemployment, but not for the primitive microscopic life form reportedly found on Mars. In the fullness of time, Dole ran an anemic campaign, and Clinton was reelected.

In the 1940s, every one of our respondents was in psychoanalysis. Of the five men and thirteen women[5] we heard from who were in treatment during the 1990s, only one was in psychoanalysis. During this decade, six people were in treatment with psychiatrists, four saw psychologists, seven saw social workers (two of these people were married and in couples counseling), and a couple saw a pastoral counselor. Two of the six psychiatrists were women; three of the four psychologists were women; and five of the six social workers were women. The only male social worker possessed a doctorate. The one pastoral counselor was a woman. One male psychologist and one female social worker were analysts in training.

We begin with a young woman who saw a female clinical social worker in analytic training at an institute.

Deborah Wolfe

Deborah Wolfe is a forty-three-year-old director of a regional theatre in Seattle, Washington. "I was in analysis from 1991 to 1993. 'Angels in America' won the Pulitzer Prize for Drama in 1993. Gays were out of the closet in full force—on talk shows, marching in the St. Patrick's Day Parade in New York. 'Don't ask, don't tell' was a joke."

The analysis I want to talk about is actually my second analysis. Things had changed considerably from 1975 when I was in college and went into analysis because I felt some uncertainty about whether or not I was gay. I was unsure which way to go and in the mid-Seventies, there was no one to talk to. My first analyst was a man old enough to be my grandfather. He was a training analyst with the Boston Psychoanalytic. The fee was $50 and my parents paid it. I went three days a week for my last two years of college, and analysis ended when I graduated and left the area. There were many differences between that analysis and my second one. Both times I was on the couch, but my first analyst was never a blank screen. He'd tell me where he was going on vacation, talk about his family, and so on.

My second analysis began when I was thirty-five. It was not motivated by a crisis. I was happy professionally, but I was dissatisfied with my personal life. I had many friends and I'd had a couple of romances, but no intimate relationship for a long time. I seemed to be choosing the wrong people. Another issue that cropped up around that time was my desire to have children. I wondered if I should have a child alone, but I began to ask myself if that would be fair to the child—and could I really do it alone? Questions like that made me decide to go back into analysis.

When you go to an institute, you're scrutinized carefully before you're accepted as a patient. They look for people with fairly strong egos. I was accepted right away, but a whole year passed before they found an analyst for me. The institute had a sliding scale fee for patients seeing analysts-in-training and my fee was $4 per session. That was all I could afford.

I was working twelve hour days at the theatre six or seven days a week, so no one said anything when I took a lunch hour, but it crossed my mind that when I left every day at the same time—I was in analysis four days a week—people might wonder why my lunch hours were so regimented. I ended up telling my immediate supervisor and it was clearly no big deal to her. The only other people I told were my parents, my two closest friends, and my lover—I met her during the year I was waiting to begin analysis.

My work habits were a subject of the analysis. I had always worked too hard. The fact that I could say to myself, "Yes, I can take an hour a day to devote to analysis," was a beginning which led to some other important changes in my life. I cut back on the weekend work.

I was assigned Claudia Rhodes. She was probably about fifty and was a social worker with a background treating children. I liked it that she had chosen to work with troubled children, and when I went to her office I liked it that the waiting room was filled with little kids. It seemed very humane. The fact that she was not a fully qualified analyst didn't matter to me at all.

In my first analysis, I remember being uncomfortable on that stupid couch [laughs], feeling self-conscious, and finding it hard to talk. The second time, I adjusted more quickly to the couch—and to analysis— probably because I was more mature. Still, I'd say it took about a year to get down to the business of analysis. The first year, I generally spent the time sputtering with annoyance about people at work. [Laughs.]

Claudia told me nothing about her personal life, but she was a very warm person I genuinely liked and admired. I thought she was intelligent and articulate. She helped me look at my situation from her perspective. That different point of view helped me resolve problems it would have taken me six months to work out alone.

We did a fair amount of dream work. Maybe six months into analysis, I dreamed that I was on the run, had to escape from something, and I went to a woman I know—sort of a friend—who had many cars. I asked her to sell me a junker of a car and I offered to pay her any amount of money, I was so desperate to get away.

Claudia seemed to feel that this dream related to her, although at the time I didn't associate the "sort of a friend" with her, but I could see the validity of the other point she made. Back then, I felt I was only entitled to a junk heap, not something really good.

I vividly remember another dream that took place after a year and a half in analysis. It was a turning point in the analysis and it allowed us to go on to deeper work. The dream begins in the analyst's house where I was in a session. In reality, Claudia's office was at the institute. I was never at her house. Anyway, I fall asleep and when I wake up, I go to say goodbye and find Claudia reading. She puts down her book and says, "I'm about to go work in my garden. Will you come and help me?" We go out and she shows me a patch of very rare flowers and asks me to do some delicate pruning while she digs up rocks. I start working away, trying to be careful, but I accidentally snip off a bud and I go show it to her. She says not to worry about it—that it probably wouldn't have bloomed anyway. Still, I was upset because it was apparent that the flower was about to bloom and I had destroyed it. I go back to my work, however, and when I look up, I see Claudia struggling to carry a heavy boulder. I think I should help her, but there's no way I could do that without touching her, and the thought of touching her makes me so uncomfortable I let her struggle with the boulder alone. That's where the dream ends.

The seed for that dream probably came from the fact that there were always fresh flowers in Claudia's office. I'm a gardener and I would sometimes comment that she must like to garden. She never said whether she did or not. In my interpretation of the dream, the first thing that seems important is the ruining of the delicate flower. I think that connects to how I saw myself then, as sabotaging myself by my own clumsiness. But in the dream, Claudia tells me it's okay. I take that to mean Claudia believes I have so many good, delicate, beautiful parts ready to bloom that losing one is not the end of the world. The significance of the boulder is that I let Claudia do the heavy lifting—the hard work of the analysis—alone because I am afraid of the feelings the possibility of closeness stirs up in me.

The structure of the analysis was such that I would free associate and then she would comment, but I always felt that I was the one doing the work and I was the one deciding the direction the work would take. In retrospect, I see the work as a joint endeavor, something I could not have done alone. Claudia would ask me questions or make an observation about something I had said—even long ago—and the fact that she remembered said to me that she was paying attention to me and noticed me. She was a gentle guide. Not a dictator. She helped me with understanding.

In addition to dreams, I would free associate about events in my everyday life. One winter night, I slipped on an icy sidewalk outside my apartment and fell into a deep puddle of water. I lay there waiting for someone to come out and help me until I realized that none of the people who lived there were likely to notice or care enough about me to come out and help. I was on my own. It gave me a profound feeling of isolation and loneliness.

In talking about it with Claudia, I remembered three incidents from my childhood. I recounted them in the order in which they came to mind. She suggested looking at them in chronological order. Doing that revealed a lot about how I developed as a child.

First, during kindergarten one day, the class was gathered around the teacher who was reading us a story. I desperately had to go to the bathroom, but I didn't know the protocol—should I just get up and leave or raise my hand and interrupt the story? Either seemed terribly embarrassing, so I just wet my pants and tried to make a quick escape when the story was over. I dashed into the coatroom and put on my snowsuit, but the teacher noticed the wet chair and realized what had happened. She put her hand down my snowsuit to see if I was wet. That was awful. Kids on the school bus teased me all the way home and I couldn't wait to get to my mother for comfort, but, unfortunately, my mother was in a bad mood that day and instead of being sympathetic, she was angry with me, which shocked me.

The second incident took place in first grade. There had been an ice storm and the bus let us off at the top of a hill across the street from our house. I slid halfway down the hill before I managed to stop myself by grabbing on to a bush. Frightened, I called out for help and eventually our housekeeper came to the door. She didn't like me. "Let go of the bush and come home," she called. I was afraid to let go and stood there—frozen. Finally, she got her coat and boots on and came to get me, clearly angry and unhappy about it. I was angry with her, too, but I didn't say anything. I knew it was her job to take care of me, and yet she was unwilling to help me when I was afraid and needed help.

The third incident was in second grade. I got to the bus stop early one morning before any other kids were there, and I needed to go to the bathroom. I didn't think I could wait till I got to school, and I didn't think I had time to get home and go before the bus came, so I decided to hide behind a bush and urinate on the ground. In the process, I got my underpants and socks wet. A new problem. I took them off and stuffed them in my bookbag, figuring that if I was careful, no one would know I didn't have any underpants on. I made it though a very tense day undetected and, at the end of the day, put on my then dry underpants and socks and went home. I never told anyone what happened.

When Claudia suggested looking at these incidents in chronological order, it became apparent how I had learned to cope with situations I found frightening—where I was in danger of losing control. In the earliest incident, I couldn't solve my problem very effectively. I didn't ask for help, nature took its course, and I ended up embarrassed. The adult to whom I thought I could turn for comfort, my mother, disappointed me. In the second incident, I had the sense to ask for an adult's help and eventually got it, but it was very unpleasant. I ended up feeling terrible for having asked for help. By the third time, I was all of seven or eight years old but I had learned to take care of myself, to struggle on my own, and to solve my problems without asking for help.

That pattern persisted into adulthood. When I was teaching at Princeton and using the shared office computer, I was in a senior enough position that I could have—should have—asked for a computer of my own, but I didn't. I guess I assumed the powers that be would see that I needed a computer and would get me one. I wouldn't have to ask. Looking at the incidents and recognizing how I had come to be that way was a helpful step toward breaking my old pattern and learning to solve my problems in a different way.

The end of that analysis came within three years because I was offered this job. I didn't seek it—they came after me—but it meant I had to terminate within three months, just when I felt analysis was becoming very deep and productive. The last two months were about leaving Claudia. It was hard for me and I could see it wasn't easy for her. We talked about whether I should complete analysis rather than take this job, but I had outgrown my old job and I needed to take the next step professionally. Still, I had ambivalent feelings about ending. I wondered if there was a way I could see Claudia when I was in town and sort of continue. [Laughs.] Claudia gave me several names and we both expected that I would continue analysis. We wrapped it up in a rush and said good-bye, and I never saw her again.

I wondered how the transition out of analysis into a new life in a strange city where I knew no one would be. The adjustment was surprisingly quick and comfortable, but I have to admit I missed Claudia for the first few months. It's hard to go from four days a week to zero. Even today when something happens I'll have the fleeting thought: "Oh, if only I could talk to Claudia." I know I could call her, but I never have. I know why. If you've read the Janet Malcolm book—I think it's called *The Impossible Profession*—it's about analysis—you'll remember that Dr. Green, the analyst, said that people who have had a good, thorough analysis will say it was useful but it's not something they think about every day, and that maybe the things that happened in their lives afterward would have happened anyway. That's how I want to be about my analysis. I was a little ashamed of myself when I missed Claudia. I told myself, "Get over it!"

I went to one of the analysts Claudia recommended and she was willing to take me on and reduce her fee somewhat, but not to a level that

I could afford. I have insurance with a "preferred provider" HMO. It pays for treatment by psychologists and social workers but not psychiatrists or analysts, so I'd have to pay the whole thing out of pocket. I guess the bottom line is I don't really want to go back into analysis, at least not right now.

I got several important things out of analysis in addition to those I've already mentioned. One is that I always thought if I did a good job, it would be recognized and I wouldn't have to push myself forward. That is not the way the world works, though, and I've become more comfortable promoting myself and being concerned about my needs as well as the needs of the organization. I still work hard, but I don't feel exhausted and torn apart by my job. I have a much more balanced life and I feel in control of it. None of these things were conscious goals I entered analysis with. They emerged over the course of treatment. I wanted professional satisfaction and a satisfying personal relationship and I've found both. The question of children is still not resolved but, at forty-three, it seems more and more unlikely that I will have children. That doesn't tear me apart anymore, either, partly because I've been able to enjoy some of the best aspects of being a parent in that I have a very loving relationship with my two young nieces. My life would probably have been easier if I had taken the more conventional route of marriage and children, but I don't think it would necessarily have been happier.

I'm interested in the study because it's helpful and interesting to reflect back, several years later, on what analysis meant to me. It ended so abruptly and, I felt, somewhat prematurely, that it had an unfinished feeling. Talking about it with you is a way of recapturing and completing the analytic experience.

Deborah describes her second analyst as a gentle guide, not a dictator. Claudia, unlike Deborah's first analyst and many of the 1940s analysts in Chapter 1, allowed Deborah to examine what her dreams meant to her. When patients participate in the interpretive process, the meaning of unconscious communications is more clearly understood and accepted. Christine Brown, in Chapter 2, resented the amount of time that takes, but allows that it led her to "self-derived understanding."

People found ways to afford the psychotherapy they needed in the 1990s. The types of therapy available now might surprise Dr. Freud, but maybe not. In the next case, psychotropic medications and guided imagery are used to help a young woman having panic attacks.

Theresa Smolka

Theresa Smolka owns Rockets Bar in Mobile, Alabama. She is forty-seven. "I started therapy in 1991. People who have been in psychotherapy need to speak

out so others going through the same thing can find out what to do. I recommend
a combination of therapy and self-help books.''

When I was thirty-nine, I started getting dizzy if I went outside. My
heart would pound, I couldn't catch my breath, and I'd feel like I was
going to pass out. I was afraid of heights and airplanes and small enclosed places like elevators. My palms sweat just remembering that time.
I couldn't stand being in groups of people, so I stopped going to parties.
My husband, Joe, would go by himself and he started spending all his
time working at the garage, he said. He only came home to sleep. Our
daughters were married or away at college, so no one was around to
notice I was housebound for the better part of two years.

My problems got a lot worse after I had to put my father in a V.A.
hospital. He was an alcoholic addicted to prescription drugs. His memory was gone and he couldn't take care of himself anymore. I was seven
when he had his first nervous breakdown, and I watched as he was
wheeled out to the ambulance laced up in a straitjacket. He looked terrified. Growing up, I never heard the word ''dysfunctional,'' but we
were. Dad would get drunk and beat my mother and all six of us kids,
and she'd get drunk and take it out on us but mostly me because I was
the oldest and closest to my dad. I thought I deserved the beatings. I
didn't have much self-respect.

I was fifteen when my parents got divorced. I stayed with Dad until
1964 when Joe got home from Vietnam. I dropped out of eleventh grade
to get married and start having kids. Sandy was born when I was seventeen, then Stacie, Steffie, and Suzie. Joe Jr. was stillborn when I was
twenty-one. I didn't want to try again and I had my tubes tied. Joe never
forgave me for not giving him a live son. He had a lot of girlfriends and
gave me chlamydia, but when I told our family doctor—who was treating me for the chlamydia—that I was depressed, he said I was just bored
and needed to get busy doing something with my life and to stop feeling
sorry for myself, but I just couldn't seem to get myself together. When
the panic attacks set in, I didn't want to go to a psychiatrist, but I was
afraid insanity was hereditary and if I didn't get help, I'd end up like
Dad.

I raced through the Yellow Pages, dialing psychiatrists' numbers and
hearing it would be six to eight weeks before I could get an appointment
without a doctor's referral. I kept looking, though, until I found someone
who could see me that day. I hadn't driven a car in two years but I drove
alone to Dr. Rajav's office thinking, ''I'm going to crash. I'm going to
die. I'm going to hit somebody.'' When I got there, I couldn't get on the
elevator, so I went to a pay phone and called her. She came down and
got on the elevator with me. She was young, an Indian, with all these
diplomas and certificates. I wondered about her life, but I never asked
her any personal questions. I didn't think it was my place.

I was in a hurry to finish because therapy was expensive: $110 an hour in 1991, and insurance only paid half. I took the rest out of the household money, hoping Joe wouldn't find out and make fun of me. Dr. Rajav told me I had classic panic disorder and my condition would be easily treated with prescription drugs. That scared me to death because of what had happened to Dad, but Dr. Rajav said the new medications were not addictive and would be effective right away, so I swallowed down the Xanax and Norpramin. She was right. The panic vanished. As soon as it was gone, I wanted to stop the medicine, but she had me stay on it for three months while I was going to her twice a week. Then she let me stop the medicine for a month while I saw her once a week just in case the symptoms came back.

Dr. Rajav said the same thing as my family doctor: I needed a more structured life. She started weaning me off her right away. When I'd go over the same old stuff, she would look out the window and seem bored. That was a good message to me. I went out and got a job and ended therapy, but when I think back on it, I can see I didn't give treatment my all. I held back painful episodes. All I did was answer surface questions, take my medicine, and be polite, but it was a start.

In June 1993, right after Stacie got married, Joe got one of his girl-friends pregnant and my father died. The panic attacks returned and when I wasn't hyperventilating, I was depressed. Everything looked gray and I felt about one centimeter big. I dialed Dr. Rajav's number but she had moved away, so I went to the Yellow Pages again and called every psychiatrist until I found one who could see me that day.

Dr. Su was an old Chinese man getting ready to retire. He ran a clinic where they didn't use medicine on anxiety. He explained the outpatient program was thirty days of organized activities, one-on-one sessions with him, and group therapy. I didn't want to be in a group, but I was so desperate I agreed. I went home and called my insurance company and learned, to my relief, that it covered the whole thirty days.

The program went like this: guest speakers in the morning, or maybe yoga, or a field trip to a museum. Then back to the clinic for lunch in a windowless room in the basement. That was for desensitization. I didn't have trouble with that, but people who panicked when they had to go into a tunnel had real problems going down into that room.

After lunch, we had group therapy with about eight people. I'm ashamed how little I contributed. I felt humiliated having to share my problems with people who had no solutions, only problems of their own, and I think I made it hard for the therapist. I think she tried to be careful when she had to drag my thoughts out of me. One woman my age had a terrible disease that had put her in a wheelchair. She was slowly losing every bit of her strength and was she furious! She didn't care what she said or to who or how loud she yelled. I probably got more out of listening to her and the others than anything else. I tried to put myself in her place and saw how much worse off I could have been. That woman moved me to change my views about the gift of life and good health. I was raised Catholic and I started thinking about the meaning of suffering in a person's life.

At the end of the day I had my individual time with Dr. Su. First, I looked to him for all the answers just like with Dr. Rajav, but as time passed, I realized the answers were inside me and I had to examine my roots to make sense of my life. I needed guidance to take it apart, put it out on the table, look it over, and throw out the garbage.

Another thing I got from therapy was to accept my feelings and not be frightened of them and to slow down and contemplate the results of my decisions. That's still hard. When I give myself time to think, I become indecisive and anxiety sets in. Maybe I have some sort of timing malfunction in my brain.

Dr. Su used guided imagery. I was supposed to focus on an event from my childhood and then we would go back over it right to the moment of suffering. My mother would hit me and say awful things that made me feel like it my fault. I didn't want to think about it and I would cry. Dr. Su would tell me to stay with the feeling and experience it to the maximum. It was agonizing, but I guess it was the right thing to do. The problem was that after thirty days, my insurance changed, and Dr. Su wasn't a provider on the new plan so I had to stop before I was really finished. I couldn't afford $150 an hour.

One of the final sessions was on how torn I was about whether to leave Joe. Dr. Su said that if I couldn't leave, I should accept things for how they were and learn to live with them. He told me, "Not everyone who is married is happy. Many people live together and make the best of their situations." I had never thought that other people might be as unhappy as I was. I realized I wasn't alone.

When I went to my doctors, I had a suspicion that if I went in deep and relived my childhood hardships and tried to change how I handled stuff, my system of knowing what was right for me might be lost forever and then how would I cope? But I'd spent years looking at myself from every angle I could find, and I ended up just spinning my wheels. It nearly drove me crazy. Dr. Su helped me a lot. That therapy was deeper than with Dr. Rajav, but the therapy with her made me strong enough to work with Dr. Su.

Psychotherapy hurt terribly while I was doing it, but I learned how to calm myself down and not let my emotions get the better of me. As a child, I learned never to cry or let loose, to be guarded and bottle up anger and resentment. As an adult, I learned not to be so hard on myself. I had to work hard to get rid of guilt I didn't deserve.

With both my doctors, it was always a clinical relationship. I just wanted them to get me over the panic attacks. They did their job, I paid them for it, and when the panic stopped, I wanted out. I never felt close to either one of them and I didn't miss them when I left. That's how I wanted it. I didn't want to become dependent and use psychiatrists as a crutch. What I learned is sometimes people need a push to get over the hill. That's what psychotherapy was for me. It gave me a push. I would go back for deeper work if I could afford it, but Dr. Rajav moved away and Dr. Su retired, so if I went back I'd have to start with someone new and right now I'm busy with my work and my children and grand-children. But maybe someday.

Guided imagery helped Theresa get in touch with hurtful memories from the past. An innovative technique developed by gestalt therapists to stimulate the imagination and memory, it has proven useful in both individual and group therapy. Some patients benefit from a combination of medication and psychotherapy, but patients like Theresa fear "pills." Other patients continue on antidepressants like Prozac for years and swear by their effectiveness, a fact cited as evidence that depression has biological roots.

Two popular approaches to therapy, cognitive-behavioral and psycho-dynamic (interpersonal) treatment, are combined in the next case. In a departure from the norm, the therapist also saw her patient's husband during the course of treatment.

Lauren Clark

Lauren Clark is a fifty-six-year-old secretary from White Plains, N.Y. "I re-member the Ruby Ridge Massacre where an FBI sniper shot and killed Vicky Weaver and the Weavers' teenaged son. He was just my son's age. That was in August 1992, and people began to talk about government conspiracies."

A friend of mine referred me to her therapist, Yvonne LeBlanc. She's a Ph.D. psychologist and I started with her in 1990 when I was forty-seven. I saw her three days a week for a couple of years and then two days and finally tapered off to once a week or so. Now I can go back if I need to—the door is open.

I am a totally different person in a totally different space because of psychotherapy. I recommend it—any time, any place, for anyone. That's why I'm interested in the study. If I can do anything to encourage anyone to do this, I will. I believe therapy works when you want it. If you don't, it won't.

Psychotherapy was exhausting for me. I would cry over my childhood, what my mother was like. I'd leave hard sessions with my teeth clenched, thinking, "I'm not coming back here!" It felt like a huge ball of string was in my head and I could see both ends, but I had to unravel it to make sense of it. It was time-consuming and it cost a lost of money—$85 a session—but I knew if I didn't stay with it, I'd never understand what was going on that made me feel crazy. For me, the intellectual grasp came first. That was the easy part. The emotional understanding, connecting the intellectual grasp to your gut, came later. While I was wading through it, sometimes I'd leave a session thinking, "Well, that was a waste." But nothing is a waste in therapy. It's all used at some point.

I entered therapy thinking I was losing my mind and needed to be put away. Defining moments in my life led up to this. I stayed in a bad marriage for twenty-three years. Bob wouldn't talk to me or socialize with me. Our sex life was terrible. When I tried to talk to him about what was on my mind, it was like talking to a brick wall. He'd say I was overreacting. Early in treatment, Bob came with me a couple of times, but he didn't stay. It let Yvonne get to know him, though. She said my feelings were valid whether or not my perception of reality was, but after she met Bob, she told me my perceptions were right on target. It was still hard for me to stop thinking that if I could just find the magic thing I should do differently, he would change.

Yvonne was a very low-key, low-pressure person, and she helped me learn to think things through. She told me to rent the movie *Gaslight*. In that movie, the husband is trying to drive his wife crazy. That's what Bob did. He tried to convince me that I was nuts. Yvonne helped me look at things from a different angle. I began to realize that I'd married a man similar to my mother. My mind was landscaped for such a man. Mother had been niggardly with affection and never encouraged me to develop my talents. She didn't give me what I needed to feel good about myself.

Yvonne could step back and take an objective look at how I could change things in my life. She would use a "What If" approach with me: What if I started doing the creative things I liked to do? What if I told Bob I wouldn't go to the money mover machine [ATM] for him? It was hard for me to contemplate changes like that. I'd think, "What if I did that and he left me?" Yvonne would try to help me see that I had options, but it was easier for me to fall into depression and not look at what was really going on. Sometimes I'd get furious with her when I'd get a view of reality I didn't like. Yvonne helped me see that the only person I could change was me.

After five years, I finally "got it." I told Yvonne I understood that I had developed a personality I used with Bob—my Stepford wife personality. You know that book about the Stepford wives? All the husbands kill their wives and turn them into these Barbie doll robots? The real me was the person my children and friends knew. I learned in therapy that there was nothing wrong with the real me and I was a valuable person, worthy of respect. When I told that to Yvonne, she started to cry. She was clapping her hands and tears were running down her cheeks. I was crying, too.

Yvonne always said, "Go with your strengths. Use your talents. Look back on your child part. Think about how your parents treated you and formed your attitudes." She impressed upon me that if you don't go back there—to childhood—you'll never learn to stop repeating your mistakes.

I finally divorced Bob. It's one of the hardest things I've ever done and I still have relapses, emotional setbacks when I wish Bob would change and we could get back together, but even as I'm relapsing, I can step outside myself and observe myself. That stops the emotional backsliding.

I keep in touch with Yvonne and she keeps in touch with me. Sometimes she'll call to see how I'm doing right when I'm thinking of her. I think we have sort of an ESP connection.

Lauren's therapist used cognitive-behavioral and psychodynamic (interpersonal) therapy to encourage Lauren to realistically assess the nature of her interactions with her narcissistic husband. She combined that with a "What If" (cognitive) approach to help Lauren change.

In the following case, a clinical social worker seeing a couple for marriage counseling asks his clients to invite their pastor to their sessions. Freud did not see couples, let alone three people, but he might be impressed if he read this case.

Suzie and John Smith

Suzie and John Smith, both forty-three, live in Burlington, Vermont. They saw a Christian psychotherapist for two years in the early 1990s for marriage counseling. "We were involved with an evangelical church that was destroying our marriage."

John begins: My wife and I were members of a church that had an authority structure and terminology one would have to understand to help us. Excessive involvement in the church threatened our marriage. There were expectations of members of that church; it was a world unto itself. We needed someone who could understand that world. We wanted to stay with our faith and work on our marriage.

There was a man on the radio who gave an hour-and-a-half program. Dr. Adams was a psychotherapist—a social worker with a Ph.D. He would address issues people were struggling with. It was Christmastime and we had Christmastime issues. Away from our families. No children. We live in an area where Christianity is not popular. If you are New

Age, Buddhist, or into witchcraft, though, you fit right in. [Suzie and John laugh.]

We started listening to Dr. Adams's program every week. He had twenty-five years' experience in individual and family therapy, had worked at a Salvation Army Church, and he published a column in "The War Cry." Here was a Salvationist who could understand evangelical-ism. When we went to him, he was probably in his mid-fifties and we were in our mid-thirties. He and his wife had no children at that time and neither did we.

Suzie: I'm a graphic artist. John and I had been married twelve years when we went to counseling. We're both originally from California and we moved here because of John's work. He is a consultant for a computer firm and teaches at the university. We didn't want children.

John: Well, you didn't want children.

Suzie: What? You didn't either!

John: At first, our church was very small. A melting pot for people who didn't fit in anywhere else. Then it got bigger and became a church for people who wanted to have children.

Suzie: We were at that church eight years. Then the pastor's wife, who had children, began to say things about my not having any. My mother had never wanted children but had me and my brother anyway. I de-cided a long time ago I would not do that and John had always agreed.

John: It had been mostly Suzie's choice not to have children. I used to bring pressure to bear, wanting children myself, but then I stopped and got busy getting tenure at the university and I was a deacon at our church, working my way up the hierarchy. My parents are both dead, but because of how my relationship with my father was, I have a ten-dency to want to follow authority figures.

Suzie: Then the pastor's wife told people in the church what I had told her in confidence. Ladies in the church began to gossip about me because I didn't want children. The church stressed that mothers must breast feed and children should be home-schooled. The message was: "The church is good. The world is bad." The other women stopped being friendly toward me because I was the only one who didn't want children. They didn't come over and talk. I felt shamed and ostracized—but it was still okay for me to deliver meals to shut-ins, teach Sunday School, and give showers for church members who were having babies.

John: I didn't realize how alienated Suzie felt. By 1989, I'd gotten tenure but the habit of working all the time stayed with me. I was teaching at the university, consulting for a business, and working hard for the church. Those are three very different institutions. I knew something was wrong but I had no time to figure out what.

Suzie: John was authoritarian.

John: Me? [Laughs.]

Suzie: We visited his sister in 1992. Just before that, when her marriage was almost breaking up, she and her husband had been to a counselor and it helped them. She begged John and me to get counseling. Before that trip, John and I were out raking leaves and I was angry that he was even alive. I would have liked to beat him over the head with the rake. But our church was very anti-counseling. Whole sermons were given on "Don't go buy self-help books." That would be a step out into the larger world. The church stressed that you should be able to get what you needed within its boundaries, so John and I secretly made an appointment with Dr. Adams. His office was in his house, about an hour from where we lived. We were very nervous going to the first appointment. We'd never had counseling before.

John: When we got there, Dr. Adams answered the door. He had a deep voice and was about a head taller than me. He had thick glasses—like Coke bottle bottoms—because he suffered amblyopia, and also he'd had polio, so he wore braces and special shoes. We learned later that because his wife loved to dance, he had learned to waltz—with those braces and shoes. So we looked at this guy and we both sort of thought, "*You're* going to help *us*?" [Suzie and John laugh.]

Dr. Adams's office was set up in a special way. It was a comfortable atmosphere, carefully lit—not too bright. The couches were big and fluffy. There were pictures and posters on the walls. One was of a rabbi and another was of Howdy Doody. Every session would start out the same way. He would go over and sit down in his Lazy Boy and flip his legs up. That signaled that the session could begin. At the first session, he asked about our backgrounds and then he asked us to describe the problem.

Suzie: I told him John believed things I no longer believed. His devotion to our pastor was so great I believed he was considering quitting his teaching and consulting work and entering the ministry full time. I also told Dr. Adams about wanting to kill John while we were out raking leaves.

John: We had three problems. One was the child issue. Another was Suzie's problems with her mother. And the third was the church, but at that time, I didn't see that as a problem. The way Dr. Adams constructed treatment was we each went one time individually. After that, all the sessions were together. We went once every two weeks for about nine months and then once a month for another year.

What made Dr. Adams good for me was that he's a tremendous listener. And he would not permit you to say negative things about yourself, like "I screwed up." He would ask a question, like "What was your Christmas like?" It seemed he knew the questions to ask to get us started on what we needed to talk about. Our Christmas had not been great.

Suzie: What made him right for me is that no matter how hard I cried or if I made bitter comments about others or ran my husband down, he would listen to me, he didn't hurry me, and he was never judgmental. He seemed very loving.

John: I could work with him because I trusted him. He belonged to an evangelical church and was clearly in the business to help people. He didn't seem to be in it for the money. What did it cost? I know exactly what it cost. $3,480 over the two years. Our insurance didn't cover it. We budgeted for it and paid for it ourselves. We could afford it.

Therapy was a learning process. It was not like, "You are in psychotherapy, you poor dears." It was like a class and, as an educator, that appealed to me. He would recommend books and most of them helped me—but not Bradshaw. What a turkey! I liked Alice Miller, though. And as we worked, Dr. Adams would ask us both, "Now tell me again, why are you still going to that church?"

Suzie: And I would say, "Because of my husband's position in the church."

John: Dr. Adams called the boundaries between me and Gregor, our pastor, "fuzzy." We had something like a soul tie. Gregor had a strong desire to dominate and I like authority figures, so I told Gregor everything, even when Suzie and I had sex. There were occasions of, the best I can describe it, psychic brutality. Once, something sort of snapped between us and he nearly hit me. He would look at me closely and say, "John, something is going on. What is it?" I told him about the problems Suzie and I were having and he said, "I don't care about John and Suzie. I only care about Gregor and John."

At first, Dr. Adams told us not to tell Gregor we were coming for treatment. Then, after about two months, he asked us to invite Gregor to come to counseling with us, and we did. During the first session with all three of us, Dr. Adams said, "Let's try to get consensus on what's going on. Let's take turns describing the problem." First Suzie did, then me, then Gregor, and Dr. Adams did a flow chart. Well, Gregor is from India. It must be culturally wrong over there to show emotions. He usually didn't but when I said, "My marriage is breaking up . . ."

Suzie: Gregor and John got into a shouting match! Then Dr. Adams calmed everyone down. "Okay, okay," he said. "I think we've gotten as far as we can tonight. We can't expect Gregor to pour out his heart the first time he's here."

John: I began to realize I was treating Gregor as a father figure. I also realized I could not have a relationship with him. I chose to end it slowly because of my work in the church. There were things I needed to finish. After that, we changed to a charismatic church.

Suzie: I talked about my mother. Dr. Adams pulled out the DSM [*The Diagnostic and Statistical Manual of Mental Disorders*] and showed me a page about borderline personality disorder. He asked me if the description reminded me of anybody. And I said, "My mother." Then Dr. Adams said, "Your mother is crazy." So I went to the library and read up on borderline personality disorder. All the things I read applied to her. My mother was hard to get along with and erratic. Dr. Adams encouraged me to bring in letters and photographs of my mother. When I talked about her, I'd start to babble. Dr. Adams would say, "What did she say?" and "How did you feel?" That would slow me down enough that I could think. I could begin to resolve my issues with my mother.

Then I started worrying that maybe borderline personality disorder was hereditary and I'd end up like my mother. Dr. Adams said, "You are not going to go crazy." He gave me an example from his own life. His father died of lung cancer because he smoked, but Dr. Adams said he could make a choice to live differently from his father—not to smoke. He helped me see I could also choose to live differently. I did not have to be 'crazy.'

John: There were two other books he recommended: John Gray's *Men are from Mars; Women are from Venus* and the Tannen book, *That's Not What I Meant*, about problems in communication. I did the same thing as Suzie about my father. Dr. Adams helped me understand the relationship I'd had with him and how that influenced my relationship with Gregor. When that was done, we discussed whether we could be turned loose. We came to agreement that we could, but he told us the door was always open.

We tried to thank him for the work but he said, "You guys did it all."

Suzie: [begins to cry] I wrote Dr. Adams a letter after we'd finished. I told him what the quality of his listening meant to me. And John and I sent some people to him. We'd been helped so much in lots of ways. One way is sort of funny—we were going to other people's parties and I wanted to dance. John would never dance, but Dr. Adams encouraged him to dance with me. And he did!

John: Well, I'd always been so self-conscious but I thought, if he can dance with those braces. . . . Anyway, I believe that more Christians would be interested in therapy by a Christian therapist if they knew what it was like. That's why, when I read your author's query, I wanted us to volunteer.

Suzie: I was interested for those reasons, too, but I also wanted to know how we were in comparison to other couples. Different? Average? What?

John: I thought the fact that we were Christians going to a Christian psychotherapist would make us sort of unique.

Marriage counseling is a twentieth-century development. Previously, couples in trouble called upon clergy and physicians. Today, there are many types of marriage counselors and their techniques vary widely. Dr.

Adams worked on irrational and unrealistic beliefs using a cognitive approach. He helped Suzie and John see how their responses to events and people reflect responses to people from their early lives (parents). Cognitive therapists also help clients see how they respond to their perception of an event rather than to the objective characteristics of a situation. This is what Lauren Clark did. A marriage counselor working cognitively might teach a couple techniques they can use to interrupt unwanted behavior. Dr. Adams would ask Suzie, "What did she say?" and "How did you feel?" when Suzie "started to babble," talking about her mother. He asked questions to help Suzie and John think through why they engaged in certain behaviors: "Now tell me again, why are you still going to that church?" He suggested current self-help books and did some educating, teaching Suzie about borderline personality disorder. Marriage counselors may also self-disclose, as when Dr. Adams told Suzie and John he had learned to waltz because his wife loved to dance. Inviting the pastor, Gregor, to participate was an innovative spin, which Dr. Adams handled well, possibly because he understood this couple's religious beliefs as well as their psychosocial issues.

The next two cases describe a woman who went into individual Inner Child work and a man who went into group Inner Child work for problems stemming from childhood abuse. Their church facilitated the therapeutic work.

Inner Child therapy is the work of John Bradshaw, who studied for the Roman Catholic priesthood and became a counselor, theologian, and public speaker. In his book, *Homecoming, Reclaiming and Championing Your Inner Child*, Bradshaw acknowledges a debt of gratitude to Carl Jung, whose work acquainted him with "the wonder child,"[6] and to others, including Erik Erikson, from whom he says he learned how the inner child develops and is wounded. He credits Virginia Satir for "mothering his own wounded little boy."[7]

To help people with unresolved grief resulting from childhood abandonment, abuse, and neglect, Bradshaw writes that in 1977 he began to use what he calls "a rather makeshift meditation" technique to relax his clients. He then encouraged them to remember back to an earlier age and contact their Inner Child at that age. His clients sometimes sobbed intensely and said things like, "My life has been transformed since I found my child." Bradshaw writes, "Three things are striking about inner child work: the speed with which people change when they do this work; the depth of that change; and the power and creativity that result when wounds from the past are healed."[8]

Shari McKee

Shari McKee, who lives in Des Moines, Iowa, is fifty-one. She has recently enrolled in college to become an Inner Child counselor. "I've always been interested in the study of religion and I'm in the lay ministry program at my church. Did you know there were originally nine deadly sins? The eighth was deception—like Clinton with the false image—and the ninth was fear. Fear was one of my problems. It came directly out of my childhood."

I saw your query in *The New York Times Book Review*. I'm a reader. Always have been. I read a lot of psychology and biographies. I'm interested in participating to help others because I felt like I wasn't living until I went through Inner Child counseling. That was in 1993 when I was forty-five. My mother was manic-depressive and she alienated my grandparents to the point that when my father died, we had no one to turn to. She put me in an orphanage and I stayed there eighteen months until she remarried. By then I'd developed thick walls. I liked people, but not too close.

What happened that got me interested in Inner Child counseling was that, during religious retreats some people were experiencing a great deal of past pain they were unable to deal with by themselves and got referred to a group of Inner Child counselors affiliated with our church. My therapist was a pastoral counselor with a master's degree in theology but a lot of the other counselors were clinical social workers. Another thing that happened was my husband's job changed and we moved, ending up in the same house I'd lived in as a child. Living in that house stirred up a lot of emotion and I started crying all the time. Then, at a retreat, a friend of mine started getting in touch with some major abuse that took place in her childhood and she needed to talk it out with someone so she'd come over to my house. Now, I have always been real good at avoiding things like that—getting in touch with my stuff. My personality is the type that uses happiness as a defense against pain, but my friend's story was so similar to my own that my feelings broke through. That's when I decided to try Inner Child work.

It's called Inner Child because you need to get the adult—the head and the intellect—in touch with the child—the spirit and the emotion— so that you can process your feelings. The counselors where I went were trained by the person I saw—Evelyn Sommers. She studied with Scott Peck, who wrote *The Road Less Traveled* and *People of the Lie*, and then she took Inner Child training. Evelyn was a few years older than I am. She was very compassionate, warm, nurturing, and accepting. I could say anything and she was not shocked. She validated my feelings. A traditional therapist would not sit down on the floor with you and hug you and let you cry on her shoulder, but Evelyn did.

I found that my best sessions were the ones where I came in without an agenda. Having an agenda fits right into my personality. I am a head person and like to avoid feelings, but sometimes I would come in with something I had realized about myself at work: I really don't like to wait on people. I was a cashier back then and I waited on people all day. Through Inner Child work, I learned that when there is a lot of emotion connected to something in my life, it's from the past. I began to ask myself, "What's going on here?"

The sessions with my counselor began with relaxation exercises, deep breathing in a calm atmosphere. When I was in that relaxed state, Evelyn would ask, "Where did you feel those emotions before?" Then a scene would pop up in my head from somewhere in my childhood. One was of my stepfather coming home. I was his favorite—the only girl—and I had to take his shoes and socks off. It was a sexual thing with him and very humiliating for me, but as a child I couldn't do anything but swallow down my resentment.

My counselor taught me how to use imaging. "There are his feet," she would say. "You're putting your hands on them." And I would mentally cut his feet up into little pieces. At first, the emotions—anger and rage—were hard for me to express. You have to have a lot of trust in your counselor before you can express strong emotions and I had to do a lot of grief work before I could get to that point but once I did, I could yell and scream. Evelyn had me pound on pillows to get the emotion out. She'd have me hang in there until I could not do one more punch or shed one more tear. It was physically exhausting and emotionally draining, but I was getting rid of garbage that had been hurting me for a long time.

I did Inner Child individually but you can do it in group. Group gets you to anger faster because when everyone else is expressing strong emotion, it's easier to join in. My sessions were scheduled for an hour, but sometimes we ran over. At the end, Evelyn would use imaging to help me get back to my adult self. "Okay," she would say. "Now see your adult self coming in. Lots of power. You're looking good!" And I would feel better. I gained insight: I had been the victim of delayed emotional reactions. For example, I loved my mother-in-law, but when she died, it was two years before I broke down and cried. The tool I received from Inner Child work is that I became aware of my emotions when they were happening so I could express them at the time—not years later. Then they don't stay inside poisoning you.

This is another example of how I've changed. I was going to meet my husband on a hike but I got lost and wandered for more than two hours trying to find my way out. I was bawling like a little kid—loud, too! The point is I was expressing the emotion while it was happening. When I finally found my way to my husband, it was over. Inner Child work cleared out a lot of junk so I can work in the present. I don't have to deal with old stuff.

This type of work is very quick and healing. I went once a week for nine months and it cost $45 a session. One reason it was so good for me is that a lot of psychotherapy stays in the head because we go for treatment as adults, while the damage occurs when we are children, a time when we are not in our heads. The emotion gets buried and I had to get back to the past to take care of it before I could claim my adult power. Now I can defend myself appropriately if someone hurts me. I can address the issue right then and not go into covert activities, like talking about the person behind his back or spitting in his coffee. [Laughs.] Defending myself like an adult gives me self-respect.

When I'd ask Evelyn when I'd be done, she'd say only I could know that: "You are your own healer." She was right. I knew when I was done because I didn't cry so much anymore and I felt in control. Things weren't coming up all the time that I couldn't handle. Evelyn agreed with me when I said I was done. If she'd said, "Oh, no, you're not," that would have taken away my autonomy. A person should always be allowed to leave and come back later if she wants to and I know I could, but now Evelyn and I are more on a friendship basis. We've had lunch together. It's nice. I am my own healer, but a friend of mine—she's also in Inner Child training—we do the process on each other. She's referred seventeen people to her counselor!

Evelyn never took any credit. She'd say, "I am here to elicit the emotions. You are the one who does the work." She validated my healing of myself. She and the other Inner Child counselors are not above the people they work with. They have all gone through the process and sometimes they share their stories with you. It's not like they take up the session with their own troubles, but my counselor shared some personal things with me. It helped me see how much we were alike—how much all people are alike. I wasn't the only one who'd had to struggle. Trainers have to look inside themselves and get healed so they don't push their stuff onto others, especially their clients. I learned who I was under my junk. My issues were rejection and loneliness and when I unlocked the emotions buried in the past and felt them, I was healed.

I am a very intuitive person and I chose the right husband. I've been blessed with a very happy marriage of almost thirty years, but when I went to my counselor and started to change, it was a little scary for my husband. The scale suddenly tipped in the whole other direction. He wasn't used to confrontation! Now our relationship is a lot healthier. He went for Inner Child work, too. Now we say what's on our minds instead of letting things fester and we've both started living.

I started college last year to get my degree in counseling. I want to do Inner Child work in the lay ministry program at my church.

This form of therapy, where the therapist takes a very active role in helping the person quickly get into emotionally laden material from the past, stands in sharp contrast to formal psychiatric tradition. We talked to Evelyn Sommers, who told us she had been to fifty-three mental health practitioners in her own search and finally found what she needed in group therapy. The similarity she felt to the other members was so great, she said, "I felt they had lived in my skin. It has been my experience that when clients are emotionally nurtured by their therapist, they remember, grieve, and heal." Evelyn asked Edward Roberts, a former member of her men's group, to describe that process.

Edward Roberts

Edward Roberts is a fifty-one-year-old choir director from Des Moines, Iowa. "I got interested in Inner Child counseling when I saw John Bradshaw's show on PBS. I read his book, Homecoming, Reclaiming and Championing Your Inner Child, *and I thought, 'That's what I need!' "*

I was a little worried joining Evelyn's men's group because the group had been meeting for some time, but she said, "Come on and join! The beginning is whenever you start." I found out she was right. There were three men in the group—a clergyman, a computer technician, and an electrician. Each member worked for forty-five minutes to an hour and it cost $37. Inner Child work is not like traditional psychotherapy—it's fast. I went once a week for less than a year and I was healed.

I guess I was a little uncomfortable for maybe the first ten minutes of my first group, but when you get the non-issues out of the way—like that Evelyn is a woman and we were all men—it became comfortable and I could work. Evelyn was very nurturing. She was not offended by street talk and could parrot it back to maintain the level of trust necessary. That let us know she had been there, done that.

The process went like this: After about ten to fifteen minutes where we would talk about anything "to let the dust settle," as Evelyn said, she'd ask, "Well, where is everybody today?" And we would talk about what was on our minds. Family. Work. Some of the things I talked about empowered others to talk about their stuff and some of what they said empowered me. After that, everyone would find a comfortable spot. There were sofas in the church basement arranged in a horseshoe shape. You could sit or lie down. And there were pillows to pound on.

Then Evelyn would begin a guided imagery back to some place in childhood. She would give an age, like age eight, and we'd try to see our Inner Child at that age. She would ask, "What does he look like?" Or, "What is he doing? Does he see you?" Then she'd have us go back farther—to age six, or age four—back to as young as we could.

I remember the first time I saw my Inner Child. He was about six. His back was to me and he was sitting on a log in the woods all alone. I can still see his little polo shirt. My Inner Child had a feeling of great loneliness. He wanted someone to come along and love him. Two or three sessions down the road, I could see myself in the womb. I could see the amniotic fluid and flesh forming on my arm. Evelyn volunteered to birth me—she said she was a good midwife—but I did not take her up on the offer.

Seeing my Inner Child led me to the feeling of needing, wanting to be loved. There was a terrible incident in my life when I was a freshman in high school. I had gone from a small, rural elementary school to a large, urban high school and I was short for my age. I smoked—trying to be macho—and I'd gone out to the quad for a cigarette with a friend. When the bell rang, me and my buddy were walking back inside when some kids grabbed me and threw me into the window well. They peed on me and spit on me until a teacher came out and they let me go. I couldn't do anything about it because I was afraid of them and even more than that, I was terrified by my fury. I could have done anything to those kids.

About six months into treatment, I could go into the window well with my Inner Child. I saw turmoil on his face and great anger. That was a pivotal experience. I know the kids who did that to me had their own Inner Child issues and as an adult, I could forgive them—but not back then. When I talked about that experience, I would cry and so would some of the other members. Evelyn then asked permission to sit near me. I had great fear and trust issues about having her or anyone near me when I felt like that, but she wanted to hold me and I let her. She would reflect on what I said and comfort me: "You did not deserve that. It is so painful. It is so mean."

I was amazed at some of the pain the others carried. Part of me was cheering another person on to get into painful issues. I wanted to talk to that person and help him, but you don't help a person by doing the work for him and you don't talk when someone is at the peak of experiencing in group. You watch and listen. Nurturing comments can occur when the person is coming down. You say things like, "When you said that, it triggered this in me," and you say what was triggered—an emotion, a memory—but you don't go fixing someone else. They do that themselves the same way you do your own fixing of yourself. Nobody discounts your emotions. No one can cry forever. No one can rage forever. You cry and rage until you are spent. When you leave you are not flying high, but you have done the feeling to its completion and it has lost its power over you. You regain your adult self at the end of the process.

From Inner Child work, you get a way of understanding your emotions and your relationships. Just because you've gone through this process, you're not immune from coming up against the same problems that have always thrown you. You'll still meet people who can push your buttons, but now you are an informed adult. I gained what I call "new equipment" to help when my Inner Child is wounded. I can now approach problems in living with strength, not fear. Evelyn told us we determined when we would "graduate," but that the door is open—we can return for a sanity check. I completely believe in the value of the process I went through, and I am in training to become an Inner Child counselor.

Inner Child therapy is short-term work. The next case illustrates extremely brief mainstream therapy.

Ted Kelsey

Ted Kelsey is a state trooper from Oklahoma City, Oklahoma. He is forty-one. "What happened that drove me into counseling was the bombing."

The bombing was on April 19, 1995. My life will never be the same, but neither will the lives of any of the other people who lost friends and relatives there.

I'd never been for counseling but I studied psychology in college and could realize I was suffering from stress—when I chose to think about it. I usually chose not to. My girlfriend is the one who wanted me to go, but I never told her I went. I didn't tell anybody. I made a quiet search and got an appointment with the best psychiatrist in the area but when I met him, I thought he was trying to impress me with who he was more than trying to help me solve my problems and lessen the burden. He prescribed Xanax. That's not an antidepressant or an amphetamine so it calms you down without the yo-yo effect.

Within two sessions, I could analyze what was going on. I put my own problems more in perspective by realizing I can't solve everyone's problems and that I needed to stop worrying about my work and take some time for myself.

That doctor wanted me to keep coming but I only went three times and it was expensive—$150 a session. I didn't claim it on my insurance, but I could have. I didn't want a claim going in, though. People would find out.

My advice to people who want to get out of treatment is to tell your doctor, "Doc, you're so damn good it's like a miracle. Double my bill!" Then run!

Almost all the 1990s patients we heard from, five men and thirteen women, paid for their treatment without the benefit of insurance coverage. Deborah Wolfe's analyst in training followed the traditional model of treatment. At $4 a session through a training institute with a sliding scale fee, Deborah could afford to stay in analysis for nearly three years. Lauren Clark paid $85 a session out of pocket and her eclectic treatment continued for five years. Suzie and John Smith also paid for marriage counseling, something on the order of $100 a session, completing their work in about two years. Shari McKee's pastoral counselor, an Inner Child therapist, used a combination of guided imagery, relaxation, and affective catharsis. Shari paid $45 a session and finished the work in nine months. Theresa Smolka paid "list price" for her therapy, up to $150 an hour out of pocket, but her insurance plan picked up her thirty-day treatment at an outpatient clinic. And Ted Kelsey, who saw a psychiatrist three times at $150 a session, tells us how to get out of treatment when your therapist wants you to stay in.

Over the decades, we have heard from people who are affiliated with religious institutions and those who are not. Some, like Bob Gordon in Chapter 2, have turned from religion to spiritualism. In Chapter 5, respondents like Philip Bohrer and Ian Spicer are among the disaffected. Philip says, "Christ was a great guy, but Christianity is a negative influence." Ian agrees: "By my way of thinking, religion has done more harm than good." He has turned to meditation and spiritualism. Valerie Vaughn (Chapter 5) rates her therapy an expensive failure but allows that, "I can't say I didn't get anything out of therapy. For one thing, I've become more spiritual." Martina Adams (Chapter 5) found her psychotherapy "a spiritual experience."

In Chapter 6, we have heard from a secular Jew in a classical Freudian analysis, a practicing Roman Catholic who saw a Chinese doctor who encouraged her to learn to make the best of her lot in life, a non-practicing Christian who believes in extrasensory perception, a Christian couple who switched from an evangelical to a charismatic church, and a man and a woman who saw an Inner Child counselor in the basement of their church.

All the people in this chapter were between thirty-five and forty-nine years old when they entered mainstream—or close to mainstream—therapies. Let us take a look at available alternative therapies.

7 Alternative Treatment Forms and the Move Toward Spiritualism

All too often, modern medical care already lacks the human touch, and its icily technocratic ethos has alienated many of the people it seeks to serve. That does much to explain why suspicion of medical expertise is growing, and why a good number of people are turning elsewhere for compassionate care.

Atul Gawande[1]

In most states, licensed mental health practitioners are required by law to obtain continuing education units (CEUs) in order to keep abreast of developments in the field. This has become an industry within the mental health profession. Practitioners receive a constant stream of notices describing workshops and seminars with special discounts for early registration and even more savings for group enrollments. Universities such as Harvard and Georgetown offer programs on mainstream treatment of depression, obsessive-compulsive disorder, eating disorders, and the like.

At the same time, classes in alternative therapies are booming. The Spring 1998 issue of *Pathways, A Mind-Body-Spirit Journal and Resource Guide*, a 178-page magazine in its twentieth year, describes hundreds of alternative treatment forms. The following offerings, culled from a stack of brochures, describe their reputed benefits.

AROMATHERAPY

According to a recent *Explorations* catalog, "Visions of the Past, Memories of the Future," aromatherapy is based on a biochemical response to the molecules released into the air when essential oils are diffused. Releasing aromas in controlled bursts provides levels perfect for therapy. The timed-release diffuser costs $89. A 55-minute video, *Aroma Therapy, the Therapeutic Effects of Essential Oils*, $24.95, shows how these oils can be used to alleviate emotional, spiritual, mental, and physical ailments safely and effectively. The video includes a sample session with an aromatherapy practitioner, practical demonstrations, and case studies. This therapy calms people by encouraging relaxation in a quiet environment while they inhale pleasant smelling vapors. It does not depend on verbal interaction with the aromatherapist or discussion of precipitating stressful factors, but is similar to meditation enhanced by floral scents.

AURAS

Auras are colored emanations that surround all of us and can be perceived by a medium. By noting variations in the aura's hues, the medium is able to describe the subject's personality, needs, and illnesses. A shriveling aura is thought to signal impending death. Auras that emanate from objects such as crystals or paintings, Rembrandts in particular, are said to have healing properties. This method of changing one's mental state does not necessarily involve interaction with a therapist and can be cost-free when the auras are found in public museums.

CHANNELING

Channeling, a form of mental mediumship, became popular in the United States and elsewhere as part of the New Age movement. It involves communication through automatic speech and automatic writing with various nonphysical beings, including angels, nature spirits, deities, demons, and spirits of the dead. Some channelers say they connect with a Higher Self.[2] *Random House Dictionary* defines "channeling" as "The practice of professedly entering a meditative or trancelike state in order to convey messages from a spiritual guide."

CRYSTALS

Crystals found increased popularity during the 1970s. Flyers in major newspapers include psychic directories: 800 numbers for psychic power lines and psychic seers. One taped message revealed the following information: All crystals have healing properties. They are amplifying devices that have the power to redirect and enhance energy, which is why a fortune teller uses a crystal ball. Clear quartz crystals enhance clarity of thinking and are excellent for healing because they align and center one's energy field. Amethysts have a high spiritual vibration, which enhances memory and helps prevent over-indulgence. Concentrating on an amethyst placed on the heart will produce a sense of warmth and well-being. Aquamarines help one receive answers from the higher realm, find one's true direction in life, lift the spirit, and allay depression. Rose quartz opens the love center, making one more loving and able to attract more love, and helps in overcoming negative childhood experiences and curing skin and kidney problems.

EYE MOVEMENT DESENSITIZATION AND REPROCESSING (EMDR)

EMDR was discovered by a graduate student in clinical psychology, Francine Shapiro, in 1987. She found that her distressing thoughts disappeared when she moved her eyes rapidly from side to side. Some find this behavioral-modification technique effective in treating post-traumatic stress disorder—an anxious response to serious trauma or assault, such as rape, or situations in which one witnesses loss of life or fears death, such as war, terrorist attack, or automobile accidents. The anxiety response is manifested in dreams or while awake: a car backfiring may cause a veteran to re-experience a combat incident. One respondent described the therapy as rapid and effective. After only four sessions at $75 an hour, she was cured. In EMDR, "The therapist asks the patient to call up an image of the distressing scene and describe it while watching the therapist's fingers as they are moved back and forth once every half second for five to fifteen seconds. The patient reports any changes in the image, description, or accompanying feelings and records his or her level of anxiety on a scale of zero to ten. For each distressing memory the procedure is repeated until the anxiety level falls to two." Mainstream critics of EMDR contend that, according to controlled studies, it is either ineffective or no more effective than standard treatments.[3]

FENG SHUI

Feng Shui is the study of locating, designing and arranging the environment, as well as the art of consistently being in the right place at the right time, according to a pamphlet from Singing Wind, the Healing Tao Center in Arlington, Virginia. A Feng Shui practitioner can assess a person's environment to harmonize energies of the workplace or home with that person's energy charge. Whether construction is of an office or a home, a Feng Shui practitioner can advise on optimal placement. Furnishings are also important. An antique may have a personal charge from its previous owner that conflicts with the present owner's energy. Feng Shui helps people deepen and strengthen personal, family, and professional relationships, build wealth, improve investment performance and cash flow, gain needed knowledge, enhance personal and professional stature, and replace struggle and effort with ease, balance, harmony, and grace. A personal, on-site evaluation is offered at $225 for two hours.

GUARDIAN ANGELS

A free five-hour seminar entitled "Guardian Angels and How to Contact Them" was offered in Rockville, Maryland, last year. Topics included: Your Purpose in Life and How to Find It, The Soul and the Physical Body, and Life after Death. The seminar was followed by a demonstration of how to read auras, which cost $4.

HEALING TOUCH

Healing Touch is promoted in a flyer from Healing Touch of the Greater Washington Area as a natural, safe, non-invasive and cost-effective way to harmonize and balance the human energy system to facilitate self-healing. It is said to be effective in managing stress and anxiety, decreasing blood pressure, and accelerating wound healing. A two-hour clinic is offered for $15. One of our respondents explained the dynamics of healing touch: Viewing a Rembrandt painting causes a whirlwind effect in the brain, which creates a super-increased energy flow down the neck, through the shoulders, and into the hands. Laying one's energy-filled hands on another person or oneself can effect physical or emotional healing.

PAST LIFE REGRESSION THERAPY (PLRT)

PLRT is a psychotherapeutic treatment form developed by Brian L. Weiss, M.D. It depends on hypnosis, a psychically induced sleeplike state in which the subject responds to the suggestions of the hypnotist/therapist. Dr. Weiss discovered this method in 1982 when, after a year of conventional psychotherapy, his patient, Catherine, who suffered fears, phobias, panic attacks, depression, and recurrent nightmares, did not improve. Dr. Weiss hypnotized her to uncover her repressed traumas. He asked her to remember back to her childhood and she did so, but the session did not produce improvement. Dr. Weiss hypnotized her again and asked her to remember back to the time when the symptoms arose. Catherine went back thousands of years into a previous life. After she and Dr. Weiss worked through a dozen of her past lives, she was cured. Dr. Weiss writes that he has regressed "hundreds of patients to past lives during their individual psychotherapy sessions. I have regressed many times that number in group workshops. . . . Perhaps even more important than the curing of physical and emotional symptoms is the knowledge that we do not die when our bodies do. We are immortal. We do survive physical death."[4]

PHILOSOPHER-PRACTITIONERS

Philosopher-practitioners believe that solutions to many personal, moral and ethical problems can be found not in psychotherapy or Prozac but deep within the 2,500-year-old body of philosophical discourse. A Philosopher Practitioners Association with several hundred members is lobbying for state-by-state certification that would qualify them for insurance reimbursement. The association's president, who charges $100 a session, asserts that "Psychiatry and psychology ultimately have failed people." *The New York Times* headline on the story: "I Bill, Therefore I Am."[5]

SOMATIC ENERGY THERAPIES (SET)

A flyer from The Somatic Energy Therapies Center in Arlington, Virginia, describes SET as a visionary birthing into form resulting from the soul's desire to co-create with the spirit. In a sixteen-hour, four-part workshop, The Shamanic Art of Healing, participants are guided and instructed in the inner journey of self-healing and serving others through shamanic journeying ($200). In a two-day, fourteen-hour workshop, Chakra Healing and Balancing, participants "learn through the use of muscle testing to erase negative patterns and limiting decisions within the chakra system [and] learn to anchor the energetic shifts of the body through Polarity Therapy" ($200).[6]

SPIRITUALISM

Spiritualism holds that the human personality continues to exist after death and can communicate with the living through a medium or psychic. Advocates argue that death merely means a change of energy wavelengths. Mediums say they are more closely attuned to psychic forces than the average person and can receive radiations, frequencies, or vibrations that cannot be sensed by ordinary people. Communication from the spirit world comes in the form of apparitions, clairvoyance, telepathy, trance speaking, and in physical phenomena—levitation, automatic writing, and the work of poltergeists. Mediums assert that spirits of dead people can contact the living through them. In 1998, *Talking to Heaven* by James Van Praagh zoomed to the top of the best-seller list. *The New York Times Book Review* capsule description reads: "A 'world-famous medium' discusses communication with the other side."[7]

THOUGHT FIELD THERAPY (TFT)

TFT is one part of a four-day conference on Creativity, Imagining and Healing ($329 for the conference). Specific disruptions to the body's energy system occur due to traumatic experiences. Participants are taught how to correct disruptions through "an energy therapy that catalyzes the intentional creation of transpersonal and positive life experiences."[8] The Power Therapies Integration Conference offers training in Emotional Freedom Techniques (EFT), "a synthesis of thought field therapy and a breakthrough in the ease of learning, using and teaching TFT." EFT can "reduce EMDR [Eye Movement Desensitization and Reprocessing] time by 50% or more." Yet another TFT is BSFF, Be Set Free Fast, a "new approach to the meridian-based 'tapping therapies'."[9] A two-day conference on TFT, EFT, BSFF, and more, is offered at $200 with early registration; $300 at the door.

This turn toward alternative treatment may be influenced by the approach of the millennium. In Chapter 20 of the Book of Revelations, it is written that an angel bound the devil in a bottomless pit for a thousand years but "after that he must be loosed for a little season."[10] *U.S. News and World Report* tells us, "Today, apocalyptic imagery is everywhere: in local churches where preachers expound on esoteric biblical texts; at corner bookstores, where the prophecies of Nostradamus, *The Bible Code*, and an array of American Indian and New Age books are hot sellers; and in theaters, where movies like *Contact* and *The Seventh Sign* draw viewers with their apocalyptic themes."[11]

In *The Road Less Traveled*, M. Scott Peck warns that "This interface between science and religion can be shaky, dangerous ground. We shall be dealing with extrasensory perception and 'psychic' or 'paranormal' phenomena as well as other varieties of the miraculous. It is essential that we keep our wits about us . . . that our critical faculties and capacity for skepticism not be blinded by the beauty of the spiritual realm."[12]

8   Mental Health: Six Decades of Treatment

Even the best therapists make bad decisions, misjudge or distort what is occurring in a session, or commit the cardinal sins of psychoanalytic lore—that is, to be seductive (promise more than you can deliver) or sadistic (deliver more than you promised). Yet in the pursuit of fame and fortune therapists tend to exaggerate what they can do and minimize what they cannot.

                                                        Jeffrey A. Kottler

Fifty years ago, psychiatric residents spent half their time studying Freud's work. The corresponding figure today is 2.5 percent.[1] The introduction of drugs such as Thorazine, coupled with the sadly mismanaged community outpatient program, cut the number of hospitalized mental patients by two-thirds during the 1960s.

When Prozac came on the market in December 1986, the trend from talking therapy to medication took another quantum leap. Today, Prozac is "the world's most widely prescribed brand antidepressant. It is also used to combat bulimia and obsessive-compulsive disorder (OCD). Vets prescribe it for hard-to-control dogs."[2] In 1995, in the United States alone, 18 million people used it. Depression afflicts 17.6 million Americans; 1 million are bulimic, and 3.8 million have OCD. Depression lowers productivity and increases absenteeism. Its economic cost to the nation in 1996 was estimated at $23.8 billion, not to mention the human suffering.[3]

Overarching all of this is the effort, both understandable and essential, to keep costs in check, but it has spawned harsh side effects. Some, such as a twenty-four-hour hospital stay for maternity cases, have evoked a counter-reaction, and health maintenance organizations (HMOs) beat a hasty retreat. Psychotherapy has taken a much harder hit. With symptoms that are not confirmable by laboratory tests, therapists are held on a short leash by insurers, and some patients undoubtedly seek less expensive alternative therapies, or are untreated.

Mental health benefits for almost 100 million people are now provided by managed care companies, according to James Sabin, Associate Director of Teaching Programs and Assistant Clinical Professor of Psychiatry at Harvard.[4] Like it or not, he says, that's the way it is and will be. Dr. Sabin predicts that by the year 2000 all mental health care will be under managed plans. These plans have different financial and clinical approaches and different moral perspectives on psychotherapy, which seeks to enhance the individual's thwarted potential.

It is likely that people with chronic illnesses such as schizophrenia will be permitted medication and ongoing psychotherapy, whereas people who are not mentally ill but are "diffusely unhappy" will have to pay for their own therapy or join support groups. What is "diffusely unhappy"? If a person's problems are ambiguously defined, it is difficult to make the case that psychotherapy is a medical necessity. Dr. Sabin says that therapists who practice under managed care must make a special effort to set clear, specific goals and accept that treatment must be planned and its progress evaluated.

By contrast, Alan A. Stone, Touroff-Glueck Professor of Law and Psychiatry at Harvard, writes that managed care is being sold to Americans in a blitzkrieg of ads from for-profit managed health care plans. Consolidating doctors, hospitals, and medical services into these plans, he says, allows entrepreneurs to lower standards of care by requiring doctors to spend less time with patients.[5] Dr. Stone asserts that many psychiatric hospitals are on the verge of bankruptcy, and that psychotherapists' earnings have declined because of HMOs' pressure to take short cuts. He says HMOs reward their employees and CEOs at the expense of people who need mental health care but points out that this is nothing new. Psychiatric patients have always been given short shrift and market reforms have restructured the health care industry to their further disadvantage.[6]

Our society has declared itself unequivocally in favor of quality health care, and just as unequivocally in favor of lower medical costs. The forces are mainly political and economic, as the struggles of HMOs, health care providers, and consumer groups reveal. We are far from resolving the issue, especially in the case of mental health.

With all of this, research continues. According to *U.S. News and World Report*, July 28, 1997, "psychiatrists at leading centers have found new clues about how genes govern behavior. For example, experience and learning may actually modify the chemistry of the brain, which had been considered immutable."[7] If confirmed, this finding would force a sea change, not only in psychotherapy, but in education and workplace training. Given the health care quandary of quality versus costs, perhaps we should look to science, not to solve, but to ameliorate the problem.

In the meantime, Alan Stone asks, "Where Will Psychoanalysis Survive?" He no longer asks his patients to lie on the couch and free associate; rather, he practices face to face psychotherapy working in the here and now to help people learn new problem-solving strategies and better ways to interact with the important people in their lives. "I still believe that a traditional psychoanalytic experience on the couch is the best way to explore the mysterious otherness of one's self. But I do not think psychoanalysis is an adequate form of treatment."[8]

Connie Claybrooke (Chapter 4) disagrees. She spent three-and-a-half years with a psychiatrist and concluded that "there were fissures and schisms within me that psychotherapy could not reach." She then undertook a six-and-a-half year psychoanalysis that, she estimates, cost over $100,000. Was it worth the time and effort? "It was worth every cent. Compared to analysis, psychotherapy is Wonder Bread. In analysis, you learn what real bread is."

On the other hand, Frederick Alexander (Chapter 1), now a practicing psychotherapist with twenty years' experience, said, "While I do not believe my own analysis could have been improved upon, I don't feel analysis is the only way to go." Christine Brown (Chapter 2) agrees. Analysis led her to some important "self-derived understanding" but "it takes too long." And Matthew Truax (Chapter 3) says that while psychoanalysis saved his life, "It is an absolutely lousy form of psychotherapy."

The fifty-two stories that make up this book were selected as the most representative and compelling of 200 interviews. In terms of people's response to treatment—was it helpful or not—here is what those 200 people had to say:

	Men	Women	Total
Positive Results	48	70	118
Mixed Results	21	52	73
Negative Results	4	5	9
Total	73	127	200

Individuals whose results were mixed generally had more than one course of therapy and described some positive and some negative reactions. By and large, they culminated in varying degrees of respect for their treatments. Neisha Williams (Chapter 1) reports a mixed response: negative to the lay analyst she describes as "a charlatan and a mind-scraper," and positive to her second therapist, a woman with "all the credentials one could wish." Ann Blake (Chapter 1) was also uncomfortable with her first analyst, whom her husband selected, but did better the second time around with an analyst she chose.

Joseph Hans (Chapter 2) suspects that the therapist he saw for nearly thirty years in individual and group psychotherapy tried to make the group into "his personal cult." Joseph's second therapist "saved my marriage by encouraging me to stay with it and not act out." While he must have spent more than $100,000 on his two therapies, he is satisfied with the results. "I believe psychotherapy made me the man I am and have been for some time. What else can you buy that's worth as much as a decent life?"

April Silver (Chapter 3) saw several therapists over more than twenty years. She characterizes some as "Talking Head New Age Flakes" and one as "an abusive charlatan." Why was her last therapist able to help her? "Because what she did was client-centered, not therapist-centered."

Martina Adams (Chapter 5) entered psychotherapy unable to speak. It is understandable that her first experience, with a therapist accustomed to talk therapy, failed. Martina improved in a subsequent Reichian treatment.

Among the individuals interviewed whose stories were not selected for inclusion were Victor Grumman and Benjamin Levy. Both men had negative experiences. Victor, whose mother was an analyst, was in therapy from age seven through much of his adult life. "I grew up believing analysis was a valid, scientific, objective method that could help with any problem. It was the religion where I lived. Well, a year or two after I ended with my fourth analyst, I realized psychoanalysis was really all bunk." Benjamin, whose father was an analyst, is another veteran of more than twenty years of analysis and psychotherapy. He feels his experience was harmful and a waste of money. Years after treatment, he tried to find one of his former analysts. "I wanted to punch him out, but the bastard had up and died on me."

Peter Johnson (Chapter 3) had a fetish he was desperate to be relieved of, but he felt coerced when his wife insisted that he enter treatment. People who are seduced or coerced into treatment are less likely to do well, and Peter rates his lengthy analysis a failure. "My behavior got under control but the fantasy never left. Today, I'm pissed off about all the money I spent and I want to damn the whole process."

Francine Donovan (Chapter 4) entered psychoanalysis as a depressed teenager with an eating disorder. During analysis, "I was hospitalized three times, began cutting myself with razor blades, hoarded prescription pills intending to kill myself, and abused drugs and alcohol." Francine's analyst told her she had a negative therapeutic reaction. After six years, Francine left analysis, depressed and with an eating disorder. She sums up the experience: "I think I overcame the analysis—isn't that something to have to say—through my own strength."

Lucy Katz, also in Chapter 4, is succinct: "I offer my story as a cautionary tale in the hope that no one else need subject himself or herself to such 'treatment'."

Mercifully, only a few patients encountered therapists who tried to impose interpretations on them and, when they balked, accused them of being in resistance. Laura Forte (Chapter 5), who entered analysis wondering if her memories of childhood sexual abuse were real, considers herself fortunate that her analyst-in-training collaborated with her, working in a way she could tolerate, and did not push her to explore her situation his way. She says her doctor helped her by letting her find out to the degree she could whether her memories were of real events, and helped her see that she could have the feelings the memories aroused without having to prove sexual abuse had occurred.

Even the best therapists suffer defeats, but in certain cases, the root cause may involve a breach of professional conduct: exploitation for financial gain, sexually provocative behavior, or outright sexual abuse as described by Kristin Palmer (Chapter 3). Patients need to be alert to therapists who are not available during a crisis, violate confidentiality, are hurtful or sadistic, or have serious problems of their own. Matthew Truax (Chapter 3) puts it well: "No one is without troubles but woe betide the patient whose problems are the same as his analyst's. . . . I am grateful that whatever troubles HB may have had, they didn't keep him from helping me with mine."

What makes a therapist effective? A pattern emerges throughout the course of this book: Effectiveness does not depend on theoretical orientation or a particular discipline (psychoanalyst, psychiatrist, psychologist, clinical social worker, or pastoral counselor) but on the therapist's character and style and that person's ability to create a trusting, honest, mutually respectful relationship.

Mary Ann Kelly (Chapter 2) says Dr. Kiernan "had what really fine therapists have—something that can't be learned in school—an innate understanding of human nature." Others comment on the centrality of the relationship. Hans Strupp, a Vanderbilt University psychologist, is quoted in *U.S. News and World Report*: "Psychotherapy is the systematic use of a human relationship for therapeutic purposes."[9] Frederick Alexander (Chapter 1) agrees: "I can't stress enough that it's the relationship which cures."

This oversimplifies an extremely complex process, but it is certain that if a sound relationship based on trust is not established, therapy will not be therapeutic. Andrea Weiss (Chapter 5) says it's sometimes a matter of luck: "In one of the big breaks that saved my life, I got the right analyst." Deborah Wolfe, the only 1990s respondent in psychoanalysis, could trust her analyst-in-training because she was "humane" and "a gentle guide. Not a dictator." Their relationship permitted "a joint endeavor, something I could not have done alone."

Of the 200 people interviewed, six men and fifteen women became psychotherapists after completing their treatment and volunteered their opinions as to what makes a good therapist. One was Brenda Shelton (Chapter 1): "A good therapist should be able to help people stop tripping over their own feet. A good therapist does not lay judgments. Above all, a therapist is a guide and as such, has to be real—not a blank slate. Blankness is confusing to a patient. Hiding behind blankness can be harmful."

The people we talked to valued warmth, genuineness, respect, acceptance, patience, a calm demeanor, a sense of humor, and openness to new ideas. They appreciated it when their therapists cared about them but maintained their objectivity. Sam Temple (Chapter 3): "Analysis should be a professional relationship built on the understanding that I am going to give you money to listen to me. . . . There is a lot of human caring, but don't make it into pals." Lisa Bea Weinberg (Chapter 2) feels the same. "I had friends; I needed a doctor."

Respondents like Bond Meyer (Chapter 5) found it hard to repeatedly go over painful material, but his analyst encouraged him "to keep going back there—to childhood." As he did, he found his world lightened up. Theresa Smolka (Chapter 6) saw a psychiatrist who used guided imagery. "[I'd] focus on an event from my childhood and then we would go back over it right to the moment of suffering. . . . I would cry [but he] would tell me to stay with the feeling and experience it to the maximum. It was agonizing, but . . . it was the right thing to do."

Edward Roberts (Chapter 6) supports Theresa's finding in his own experience. In Inner Child group psychotherapy, "You cry and rage until you are spent. When you leave, you are not flying high, but you have done the feeling to its completion and it has lost its power over you."

Sandra and Gavin Hilgardner (Chapter 4) belonged to a couples psychotherapy group. Sandra explains that experiencing a feeling to the maximum in a supportive setting leads to liberation. "When you are free of its hold on you, you no longer need to waste psychic energy suppressing [the feeling] and you have all that energy for other things." Gavin characterizes the group leader as "a screwed up dictator" and they both say the group was like a cult, but they note its positive aspects: "There was a lot of love and support in that group."

Patients are grateful for therapists who go out of their way to help in times of crisis. Steve Semmes (Chapter 2) had only begun analysis when he felt like killing his parents. "Melissa met with them once, without me, and the situation was defused." Forty years after treatment, he assesses Melissa: "She was a good person, always kind and gentle. My idea of a superb therapist." Yet another respondent called Melissa a bitch, a sharp reminder of the central role of the relationship.

Maggie Glass (Chapter 4) is grateful to her young psychiatrist. "Dr. Crispin came to see me [each time she was hospitalized] except when I was at Napa. I don't blame him—that was a 140-mile round-trip."

Several participants surfaced the question of professional detachment and boundaries. Caleb Keep (Chapter 2) says, "I never learned much about his personal life, but I didn't want to. We were there to talk about me!" Where professional boundaries were overstepped, patients wondered if they were being manipulated for their therapists' personal gains. Valerie Vaughn (Chapter 5) ponders her psychiatrist's behavior. "Did he use me? Did he do it for the money? Did he love me?"

And the tricky business of termination. Much has been written about why to do it, when to do it, how to do it. Peter Johnson (Chapter 3) hated being in treatment, but when he broached termination and his analyst quickly agreed, "I got the definite impression that he was glad to see me go." In another case, an analyst suggested termination after seven years. His patient was grief-stricken, even though he agreed that it was time. Andrea Weiss (Chapter 5), who graduated from analysis, worried that she should have continued and repeatedly telephoned Dr. Rossides after termination. She laughs about it now, but she called him a bastard at the time.

We also glimpsed analysts and therapists who simply could not engage their patients in the therapeutic process. Patients say unsuccessful therapists seem cold, rigid, insensitive, do not listen well, forget significant facts they should remember (such as that the patient is gay), or are arrogant and impressed with their own importance. Matthew Allbright (Chapter 1) interviewed an analyst "I simply could not tolerate. He talked a lot about himself, used the lingo, and seemed to want to impress me with the books he'd written."

As to rigidity, in *Hope and Dread in Psychoanalysis*, Stephen Mitchell tells us Sandor Ferenczi's view was that the human relationship between psychotherapist and patient was more important than the "frame"—the body of rules therapists are trained not to bend—that is, not to succumb to what the therapist perceives as a patient's wish for gratification. "It is apparent," Dr. Mitchell writes, "that one person's 'firmness' is another's rigidity."[10]

When psychotherapy is successful, it encourages people to feel the whole array of human emotions, sadness as well as contentment, pain as well as pleasure, to avoid the self-destructive behavior that got them in trouble in the first place, and to find responsible roles in their families and communities. Francine Donovan (Chapter 4) is now happy in a profession she loves and has reestablished close ties to her family. "After Confront [a drug and alcohol treatment center], I stopped starving myself and binging, and feelings began for me." Today, "to live like a normal person is unbelievably precious to me."

Each story in this book is unique. All describe aspects of the therapeutic process that have never before been so fully revealed to the public. Organizing the narratives into decades shows how attitudes toward psychotherapeutic treatment have evolved. Before Freud and the turn of the twentieth century, mentally ill people were often regarded as harboring evil spirits, or being possessed by the devil. They were marginalized and often abused.

Attitudes and trends in mental health have undergone a sea change during the last half of this century and fall into three time frames: In the 1940s and 1950s, there was excitement and hope for the new psychoanalytic "science." The 1960s and 1970s saw expansion of services for the mentally ill, coupled with massive deinstitutionalization—a wonderful idea that failed—and the discovery of psychotropic medications. By the 1980s and 1990s, psychoanalytic ideas had permeated and altered much of our culture through books, movies, plays, and the media.

Freud and his colleagues developed a radically new way of understanding the psyche. Some have called Freud's theories dogmatic or grandiose, especially the notion that analysis could cure almost any kind of mental illness, even some physical illnesses. Nonetheless, the core of Freud's ideas about the power of the unconscious and the effects of past experiences is broadly accepted. One problem is that it is difficult to design valid, reliable research instruments to measure the effectiveness of talk therapy. The economical and practical treatment methods of cognitive therapists can be better validated. Controversy continues.

It has been known for years that successful therapy depends upon the fit between client and therapist and the strength of their alliance. But this general understanding is not especially useful to people in need of therapeutic help. Listen carefully to the voices raised in this book, learn from their triumphs, their anguish, and their mistakes, and profit from the words of Karen Horney: "Fortunately analysis is not the only way to resolve inner conflicts. Life itself still remains a very effective therapist."[11]

Notes

INTRODUCTION

1. Abram Kardiner, *My Analysis with Freud, Reminiscences* (New York: W. W. Norton, 1977), p. 15.
2. Kardiner, *My Analysis with Freud, Reminiscences*, p. 16.
3. Kardiner, *My Analysis with Freud, Reminiscences*, p. 11.
4. Erik Erikson, *Childhood and Society* (New York: W. W. Norton, 1950), p. 16.
5. Jerome Bruner, *Acts of Meaning* (Boston: Harvard University Press, 1990), p. 118.

CHAPTER 1—THE 1940s

1. Ruth Cowan, "More Work for Mother," in R. Shenkman, *Legends, Lies and Cherished Myths of American History* (New York: Harper and Row, 1988), p. 161.
2. Victor Bondi (ed.), *American Decades, 1940–1949* (Detroit, MI: Gale Research Inc., 1995), p. 416.
3. Cecil Roth (ed.), *Encyclopedia Judaica*, Vol. 14 (Jerusalem, Israel: Keter Publishing House, 1973), p. 30.
4. This is the process called "winding down." It is a departure from the classical Freudian tradition in which patients terminate their analyses on the date the last analytic session is scheduled without going from five days a week to three days or possibly two days a week. Winding down has been compared to weaning.
5. Harold I. Kaplan and Benjamin J. Sadock (eds.), *Comprehensive Textbook of Psychiatry*, 4th Ed. (Baltimore: Williams and Wilkins, 1985), pp. 1403–1404.

6. Barbara A. Chernow and George A. Vallasi (eds.), *The Columbia Encyclopedia*, 5th Ed. (New York: Columbia University Press, 1993), p. 1270.

7. Kaplan and Sadock, *Comprehensive Textbook of Psychiatry*, p. 426.

8. Stuart Berg Flexner (ed.), *The Random House Dictionary of the English Language*, 2nd Ed. (New York: Random House, 1987), p. 1287.

CHAPTER 2—THE 1950s

1. James T. Patterson, *Grand Expectations* (New York: Random House, 1996), p. 167.

2. Victor S. Navasky, *Naming Names* (New York: Viking Press, 1950), p. 334.

3. Samuel Eliot Morison, *The Oxford History of the American People* (New York: Oxford University Press, 1965), p. 176.

4. Richard Layman (ed.), *American Decades, 1950–1959* (Detroit, MI: Gale Research Inc., 1994), p. 354.

5. "Postgrad" is The Postgraduate Center for Mental Health in New York City.

6. Robert Langs, *The Technique of Psychoanalytic Psychotherapy*, Vol. 1 (Northvale, NJ: Jason Aronson, 1989), pp. 33–35.

7. Joseph Weiss, *How Psychotherapy Works* (New York: Guilford Press, 1993), p. 23.

8. Weiss, *How Psychotherapy Works*, p. 24.

9. Lewis Wolberg, *The Technique of Psychotherapy* (New York: Grune and Stratton, 1954), p. 110.

10. The Supreme Court's ruling on abortion, *Roe v. Wade*, was in 1973.

11. Bruce L. Smith, "Winnicott and Self Psychology," in M. Gerard Fromm and Bruce Lazar Smith (eds.), *The Facilitating Environment, Clinical Applications of Winnicott's Theory* (Madison, CT: International Universities Press, 1989), pp. 58–60.

12. Karen Horney, *Neurosis and Human Growth* (New York: W. W. Norton, 1950), p. 17.

13. Horney, *Neurosis and Human Growth*, p. 17.

14. Layman, *American Decades, 1950–1959*, p. 353.

15. Layman, *American Decades, 1950–1959*, p. 342.

16. Layman, *American Decades, 1950–1959*, p. 342.

CHAPTER 3—THE 1960s

1. Census Bureau data reveal that 17,000 unmarried couples lived together in 1960 and 143,000, more than an eight-fold increase, lived together in 1970.

2. Stephen A. Mitchell and Margaret J. Black, *Freud and Beyond* (New York: Basic Books, 1995), pp. 139–141.

3. Dale W. Jacobs (ed.), *The World Book Encyclopedia*, Vol. 6 (Chicago: World Book, Inc., 1996), p. 239.

4. Paul S. Appelbaum, "What Are the Limits of Confidentiality in Mental Health Treatment?" *The Harvard Mental Health Letter* 11 (September, 1994): 8.

5. Dale W. Jacobs, *The World Book Encyclopedia*, Vol. 6, p. 239.

6. New York Jurisprudence 2d, Vol. 35, Sec. 3520 (Rochester, NY: Lawyers Cooperative Publishing, 1995).

7. Judith A. Rubin, "Art Therapy, What It Is and What It Is Not," *American Journal of Art Therapy* 21 (January 1982): 57, 58.

8. Thorazine, a potent neuroleptic, was marketed at the end of 1954 by Smith, Kline and French.

9. Edward Shorter, *A History of Psychiatry: From the Era of the Asylum to the Age of Prozac* (New York: John Wiley, 1997), p. 38.

10. U.S. Bureau of the Census, *Historical Statistics of the United States, Colonial Times to 1970, Bicentennial Edition, Part I* (Washington, D.C., 1975), p. 73.

CHAPTER 4—THE 1970s

1. Victor Bondi (ed.), *American Decades, 1970–1979* (Detroit, MI: Gale Research Inc., 1995), p. vii.

2. Bondi, *American Decades, 1970–1979*, p. 408.

3. Bondi, *American Decades, 1970–1979*, p. 408.

4. Bondi, *American Decades, 1970–1979*, pp. 410–411.

5. Bondi, *American Decades, 1970–1979*, p. 411.

CHAPTER 5—THE 1980s

1. Lois Gordon and Alan Gordon, *Columbia Chronicles of American Life, 1910–1992* (New York: Columbia University Press, 1995), p. 672.

2. Victor Bondi (ed.), *American Decades, 1980–1989* (Detroit, MI: Gale Research Inc., 1995), pp. 495–497.

3. Pam Belluck, " 'Memory' Therapy Leads to a Lawsuit and Big Settlement," *The New York Times*, November 6, 1997, p. A1.

4. Miriam Horn, "Recalling the Past, Embracing the Future," *U.S. News and World Report* 123 (August 4, 1997): 4.

5. Bondi, *American Decades, 1970–1979*, p. 418.

6. Bondi, *American Decades, 1980–1989*, p. 496.

7. Steven S. Sharfstein, "Economics and the Future of Mental Health Care," *The Harvard Mental Health Letter* 2 (September 1985): 4–5.

CHAPTER 6—THE 1990s

1. "Eye on the 90s," *U.S. News and World Report* 109 (December 31, 1990): 18.

2. Lois Gordon and Alan Gordon, *Columbia Chronicles of American Life, 1910–1992* (New York: Columbia University Press, 1995), p. 754.

3. Robert Famighetti (ed.), *The World Almanac and Book of Facts, 1997* (Mahwah, NJ: World Almanac Books, 1997), p. 509.

4. Famighetti, *The World Almanac and Book of Facts, 1997*, p. 39. (See also *Jaffee v. Redmond*, 6–13–96.)

5. Two of these people were married and saw their therapist in marriage counseling.

6. John Bradshaw, *Homecoming, Reclaiming and Championing Your Inner Child* (New York: Bantam Books, 1990), p. v.

7. Bradshaw, *Homecoming*, p. v.

8. Bradshaw, *Homecoming*, p. xi.

CHAPTER 7—ALTERNATIVE TREATMENT FORMS

1. Atul Gawande, "No Mistake," *The New Yorker*, March 30, 1998, p. 81.

2. *Facts on File*, Montgomery County, MD, Bethesda Regional Library.

3. James D. Herbert and Kim T. Mueser, "What Is EMDR?" *The Harvard Mental Health Letter* 12, No. 2 (August 1995): 8.

4. Brian L. Weiss, *Through Time Into Healing* (New York: Simon and Schuster, 1992), pp. 22–23.

5. Joe Sharkey, "I Bill, Therefore I Am—Philosophers Ponder a Therapy Gold Mine," *The New York Times*, March 8, 1998, Sec. 4, p. 1.

6. Lou Desabla (ed.), *Pathways* 20, No. 3 (Fall 1997): 18.

7. *The New York Times Book Review*, May 24, 1998, p. 18.

8. Anne A. Simpkinson (ed.), "Reconnect with the Joy of Creation," pamphlet for Common Boundary's 17th Annual Conference, November 6–9, 1997, p. 8.

9. Flyer from Advanced Therapeutics, Denver, CO, for a conference July 24–25, 1998.

10. The Holy Bible, King James Version, The Revelation of St. John the Divine, 20, Verse 3 (New York: Penguin Books), p. 224.

11. Jeffery L. Sheler, "Dark Prophesies," *U.S. News and World Report* 123 (December 15, 1997): 63.

12. M. Scott Peck, *The Road Less Traveled* (New York: Simon and Schuster, 1978), pp. 231–232.

CHAPTER 8—MENTAL HEALTH

1. Henry Allen, "A Capsule History of Psychiatry: In the Beginning There Was Freud . . . But Why Talk About It When a Little Pill Drives the Blues Away?" *The Washington Post*, May 7, 1997, p. D1.

2. Allen, "A Capsule History of Psychiatry," p. D1.

3. "Prozac at 10," *U.S. News and World Report* 121 (December 9, 1996): 17.

4. James E. Sabin, "Psychotherapy and Managed Care," *The Harvard Mental Health Letter* 11: pp. 4–7.

5. Alan A. Stone, "Psychotherapy and Managed Care: The Bigger Picture," *The Harvard Mental Health Letter* 11, No. 8 (February 1995): pp. 5–7.

6. Stone, "Psychotherapy and Managed Care," pp. 5–7.

7. *U.S. News and World Report* 123 (July 28, 1997): 102. This is a two-sentence prelude to a table, "Psychiatry," taken from Avery Comarow (ed.), *America's Best Hospitals* (John Wiley, 1996).

8. Alan A. Stone, "Where Will Psychoanalysis Survive?" *Harvard Magazine* (January–February 1997): 35–39.

9. Erica E. Goode with Betsy Wagner, "Does Psychotherapy Work?" *U.S. News and World Report* 114 (May 24, 1993): 59.

10. Stephen A. Mitchell, *Hope and Dread in Psychoanalysis* (New York: Basic Books, 1993), p. 194.

11. Emily Morison Beck (ed.), *Familiar Quotations of John Bartlett* (Boston: Little, Brown, 1968), p. 985.

Bibliography

American Psychiatric Association: *Diagnostic and Statistical Manual of Mental Disorders*, 4th ed. Washington, D.C.: American Psychiatric Association, 1994.

Beattie, Melody. *Codependent No More*. New York: Harper/Hazelden, 1987.

Bellah, Robert, Richard Madsen, William Sullivan, and Ann Swidler. *Habits of the Heart: Individualism and Commitment in American Life*. New York: Harper and Row, 1985.

Bowlby, John. *Attachment and Loss, Vol. I: Attachment*. New York: Basic Books, 1969.

———. *Attachment and Loss, Vol. II: Separation*. New York: Basic Books, 1973.

———. *Attachment and Loss, Vol. III: Loss*. New York: Basic Books, 1980.

———. *A Secure Base: Parent-Child Attachment and Healthy Human Development*. New York: Basic Books, 1988.

Bradshaw, John. *Homecoming, Reclaiming and Championing Your Inner Child*. New York: Bantam, 1990.

Bruno, Frank J. *The Family Mental Health Encyclopedia*. New York: John Wiley, 1991.

Casement, Patrick. *Learning from the Patient*. New York: Guilford, 1991.

Edwards, Joyce, and Jean B. Sanville (eds.). *Fostering Healing and Growth: A Psychoanalytic Social Work Approach*. Northvale, NJ: Jason Aronson, 1996.

Erikson, Erik. *Childhood and Society*. New York: W. W. Norton, 1963.

———. *Identity, Youth and Crisis*. New York: W. W. Norton, 1968.

———. *Life History and the Historical Moment*. New York: W. W. Norton, 1975.

Fairbairn, W. Ronald D. *Psychoanalytic Studies of the Personality*. New York: Routledge, 1992.

Foy, David (ed.). *Treating PTSD, Cognitive Behavioral Strategies*. New York: Guilford, 1992.

France, Ann. *Consuming Psychotherapy*. London: Free Association Books, 1988.

Franklin, Jon. *Molecules of the Mind*. New York: Atheneum, 1987.

Freeman, Lucy. *Fight Against Fear*. New York: Crown, 1951.

Freud, Sigmund. "Lines of Advance in Psycho-Analytic Theory," *Standard Edition* 17 (1919): 159.

Friedan, Betty. *The Feminine Mystique*. New York: Norton, 1983.

Fromm, Erich. *The Forgotten Language*. New York: Grove, 1957.

Gordon, Lois, and Alan Gordon. *The Columbia Chronicles of American Life, 1910– 1992*. New York: Columbia University Press, 1995.

Gray, John. *Men Are from Mars; Women Are from Venus*. New York: HarperCollins, 1992.

Griffith, H. Winter. *Complete Guide to Prescription and Nonprescription Drugs*. New York: The Body Press/Perigee, 1996.

Hallowell, Edward M. *Driven to Distraction*. New York: Pantheon, 1994.

Horney, Karen. *Neurosis and Human Growth*. New York: W. W. Norton, 1950.

———. *The Neurotic Personality of Our Time*. New York: Norton, 1937.

Janov, Arthur. *The Primal Scream*. New York: Putnam, 1970.

Kardiner, Abram. *My Analysis with Freud, Reminiscences*. New York: W. W. Norton, 1977.

Karp, David A. *Speaking of Sadness*. New York: Oxford University Press, 1996.

Kesey, Ken. *One Flew over the Cuckoo's Nest*. New York: Viking, 1962.

Kinsey, Alfred C., Wardell B. Pomeroy, and Clyde E. Martin. *Sexual Behavior in the Human Male*. Philadelphia: W. B. Saunders, 1948.

Kinsey, Alfred C., Wardell B. Pomeroy, Clyde E. Martin, and Paul H. Gebhard. *Sexual Behavior in the Human Female*. Philadelphia: W. B. Saunders, 1953.

Kohut, Heinz. *The Analysis of the Self*. Madison, CT: International Universities, 1971.

Kottler, Jeffrey. *The Imperfect Therapist*. San Francisco, CA: Jossey-Bass, 1990.

Lasch, Christopher. *The Culture of Narcissism: American Life in an Age of Diminishing Expectations*. New York: W. W. Norton, 1979.

Lewis, Hunter. *A Question of Values*. New York: Harper and Row, 1990.

Malcolm, Janet. *Psychoanalysis: The Impossible Profession*. Northvale, NJ: Jason Aronson, 1994.

Metalious, Grace. *Peyton Place*. New York: Messner, 1956.

Miller, Alice. *The Drama of the Gifted Child: The Search for the True Self*. New York: Basic Books, 1981.

Miller, Jean Baker. *The Healing Connection: How Women Form Relationships*. Boston: Beacon, 1997.

Millman, Dan. *The Way of the Peaceful Warrior*. Tiberon, CA: H. J. Kramer, 1980.

Mitchell, Stephen A. *Hope and Dread in Psychoanalysis*. New York: Basic Books, 1993.

Mitchell, Stephen A., and Margaret J. Black. *Freud and Beyond: A History of Modern Psychoanalytic Thought*. New York: Basic Books, 1995.

Peck, M. Scott. *Further Along the Road Less Traveled*. New York: Simon and Schuster, 1993.

———. *People of the Lie*. New York: Simon and Schuster, 1983.

———. *The Road Less Traveled*. New York: Simon and Schuster, 1978.

Piper, Mary. *The Shelter of Each Other: Rebuilding Our Families*. New York: Ballantine Books, 1996.

Poland, Warren. *Melting the Darkness*. Northvale, NJ: Jason Aronson, 1996.

Reik, Theodor. *Listening with the Third Ear*. New York: Farrar, Straus and Giroux, 1948.

Roth, Sheldon. *Psychotherapy: The Art of Wooing Nature*. Northvale, NJ: Jason Aronson, 1987.

Saari, Carolyn. *The Creation of Meaning in Clinical Social Work*. New York: Guilford Press, 1991.

Samuels, Andrew, Bani Shorter, and Fred Plaut. *A Critical Dictionary of Jungian Analysis*. New York: Routledge, 1996.

Schacter, Daniel. *Searching for Memory*. New York: Basic Books, 1996.

Segal, Hanna. *Introduction to the Work of Melanie Klein*. 2d ed. New York: Basic Books, 1974.

Shorter, Edward. *A History of Psychiatry: From the Era of the Asylum to the Age of Prozac*. New York: John Wiley, 1997.

Singer, June. *Boundaries of the Soul*. Northvale, NJ: Jason Aronson, 1994.

Starr, Paul. *The Social Transformation of American Medicine*. New York: Basic Books, 1982.

Statt, David. *Dictionary of Psychology*. New York: Barnes and Noble, 1981.

Stevens, Rosemary. *American Medicine and the Public Interest*. New Haven, CT: Yale University Press, 1971.

Storr, Anthony. *The Integrity of the Personality*. New York: Ballantine, 1960.

Sullivan, Harry Stack. *The Interpersonal Theory of Psychiatry*. New York: W. W. Norton, 1953.

Tannen, Deborah. *That's Not What I Meant*. New York: Ballantine Books, 1986.

Van Praagh, James. *Talking to Heaven*. New York: Dutton, 1997.

Vaughan, Susan. *The Talking Cure: The Science Behind Psychotherapy*. New York: Putnam, 1997.

Weiss, Brian. *Many Lives, Many Masters*. New York: Simon and Schuster, 1988.

———. *Through Time into Healing*. New York: Simon and Schuster, 1992.

Weiss, Joseph. *How Psychotherapy Works*. New York: Guilford, 1993.

Winnicott, Donald. *The Maturational Processes and the Facilitating Environment*. Madison, CT: International Universities, 1965.

Wolberg, Lewis. *The Technique of Psychotherapy*. New York: Grune and Stratton, 1951.

Index

About the Authors

DONNA D. COMAROW, a clinical social worker and board certified diplomate in her field, lectures on topics from attachment theory to creativity and psychosis, and is working on a book about how people resolve grief.

MARTHA W. CHESCHEIR, a former professor at Catholic University's School of Social Service and at Smith College, teaches advanced level clinicians at the Washington School of Psychiatry and maintains a private practice.